Experiencing Networked Urban Mobilities

Experiencing Networked Urban Mobilities looks at the different experiences of networked urban mobilities. While the focus in the first book is on conceptual and theory-driven perspective, this second volume emphasizes the empirical investigation of networked urban mobilities. This book is a resource for researchers interested in the field to gain easy access and overviews of different themes and approaches represented in the mobilities paradigm.

Malene Freudendal-Pedersen is Associate Professor in Sustainable Mobilities at Roskilde University, Denmark. She has an interdisciplinary background linking sociology, geography, urban planning, and science and technology studies which she has been using to investigate praxes of mobilities and their significance for (future) cities. She is the co-manager of the international Cosmobilities Network, and the co-founder and co-editor of the new journal *Applied Mobilities*. She is the author of the book *Mobility in Daily Life: Between Freedom and Unfreedom*.

Katrine Hartmann-Petersen is Associate Professor in Planning and Mobilities at Roskilde University, Denmark. She has a transdisciplinary background investigating the interconnectedness between modern everyday life, urban planning, and mobilities. She also has experience as a special advisor in municipality planning departments. She is a member of the Cosmobilities Network taskforce and book review editor of the new journal *Applied Mobilities*.

Emmy Laura Perez Fjalland holds a master's degree in Urban Planning Studies and Geography, and is currently a PhD student at Roskilde University, Denmark, and the Danish Architecture Centre. She studies how sharing and collaborative economic cooperations could be part of Danish urban governance and urban planning strategies. She is specifically interested in how different collaborative economic cooperations, communities, and organizations could help perform, develop, and run key municipal activities within environment and welfare. In the context of urban and mobilities studies, she pursues concepts such as co-creation, communities, commons, governance, platforms, and process designs.

Networked Urban Mobilities Series
Editors: Sven Kesselring
Nürtingen-Geislingen University
Malene Freudendal-Pedersen
Roskilde University

The Networked Urban Mobilities series resulted from the Cosmobilities Network of mobility research and the Taylor & Francis journal *Applied Mobilities*. This three-volume set, ideal for mobilities researchers and practitioners, explores a broad number of topics including planning, architecture, geography, and urban design.

Exploring Networked Urban Mobilities
Theories, Concepts, Ideas
Edited by Malene Freudendal-Pedersen and Sven Kesselring

Experiencing Networked Urban Mobilities
Practices, Flows, Methods
Edited by Malene Freudendal-Pedersen, Katrine Hartmann-Petersen and Emmy Laura Perez Fjalland

Envisioning Networked Urban Mobilities
Art, Performances, Impacts
Edited by Aslak Aamot Kjærulff, Sven Kesselring, Peter Peters and Kevin Hannam

"This set of vignettes is an important addition to transport scholarship. It invigorates often overlooked and ordinary aspects of moving and waiting and it provides innovative examples of ethnography and participant observation. Pulling together different disciplines in the social sciences, this volume is sure to enliven the expanding critical mobilities research agenda."

Jason Henderson, Professor, Geography and Environment,
San Francisco State University

Experiencing Networked Urban Mobilities
Practices, Flows, Methods

Edited by Malene Freudendal-Pedersen,
Katrine Hartmann-Petersen
and Emmy Laura Perez Fjalland

NEW YORK AND LONDON

First published 2018
by Routledge
711 Third Avenue, New York, NY 10017

and by Routledge
2 Park Square, Milton Park, Abingdon, Oxon, OX14 4RN

Routledge is an imprint of the Taylor & Francis Group, an informa business

© 2018 Taylor & Francis

The right of Malene Freudendal-Pedersen, Katrine Hartmann-Petersen and Emmy Laura Perez Fjalland to be identified as the authors of the editorial material, and of the authors for their individual chapters, has been asserted in accordance with sections 77 and 78 of the Copyright, Designs and Patents Act 1988.

All rights reserved. No part of this book may be reprinted or reproduced or utilised in any form or by any electronic, mechanical, or other means, now known or hereafter invented, including photocopying and recording, or in any information storage or retrieval system, without permission in writing from the publishers.

Trademark notice: Product or corporate names may be trademarks or registered trademarks, and are used only for identification and explanation without intent to infringe.

Library of Congress Cataloging-in-Publication Data
A catalog record for this book has been requested

ISBN: 978-1-138-71231-7 (hbk)
ISBN: 978-1-315-20025-5 (ebk)

Typeset in Sabon
by Apex CoVantage, LLC

To John

Contents

Notes on Contributors	xiii
Preface	xxiv

1 Networked Urban Mobilities: Practices, Flows, Methods 1
EMMY LAURA PEREZ FJALLAND, MALENE FREUDENDAL-PEDERSEN, AND KATRINE HARTMANN-PETERSEN

PART I
Moving and Pausing 11

2 'DING-DING-DONG': Shifting Atmospheres in Mobilities Design 13
SIMON WIND, DITTE BENDIX LANNG, AND OLE B. JENSEN

3 The Final Countdown: Ambiguities of Real Time Information Systems 'Directing' the Waiting Experience in Public Transport 19
ROBIN KELLERMANN

4 Bus Stops Matter: An Ethnography of the Experience of Physical Activity and the Bus Stop Design 27
ANNE VICTORIA

5 Solid Urban Mobilities: Buses, Rhythms, and Communities 32
KATRINE HARTMANN-PETERSEN

6 On Social Cracks in Train Commuting 38
HANNE LOUISE JENSEN

x *Contents*

7 *Road Radio*: Taking Mobilities Research on the Road
and Into the Air   43
ASLAK AAMOT KJÆRULFF AND KAARE SVEJSTRUP

8 Managing Mobilities in the Working Context   48
SARAH NIES, KATRIN ROLLER, AND GERLINDE VOGL

9 Tracing Trans-Atlantic Romani Im/Mobilities: Doing
Ethnography in a Hyper-Mobile Field   52
ESTEBAN C. ACUÑA

PART II
Communities and Collaborations   57

10 The Little Mermaid Is a Portal: Digital Mobility
and Transformations   59
LILYANA PETROVA

11 Viscosities and Meshwork: Assembling Dynamic Pathways
of Mobilities   64
LAUREN WAGNER

12 Parked Students, Surfing Workers, and Working in Third
Places With Mobile Technology   68
MICHEL DESPRÉS

13 Urban Borderlands of Mobility: Ethnographic Fieldwork
Amongst Unconventional Elderly City People   73
JON DAG RASMUSSEN

14 Understanding Everyday Mobilities Through the Lens
of Disruption   78
KAROLINA DOUGHTY AND LESLEY MURRAY

15 Experiences of Mobile Belonging   83
MIA ARP FALLOV AND ANJA JØRGENSEN

16 The Spaces, Mobilities, and Soundings of Coding   88
SUNG-YUEH PERNG

17 Mobility, Media, and the Experiences of Airbnb's
Aesthetic Regime   94
PAULA BIALSKI

Contents xi

PART III
Modes and Emotions

99

18 Senses Matter: A Sensory Ethnography of Urban Cycling
PETER COX

101

19 Feeling Community: Emotional Geographies on Cycling
Infrastructure
NJOGU MORGAN

106

20 Urban Velomobility and the Spatial Problems of Cycling
TILL KOGLIN

112

21 The Role of the Driver-Car Assemblage in the Practices
of Long-Distance Aeromobility
JULIE CIDELL

119

22 U.Move 2.0: The Spatial and Virtual Mobility
of Young People
DIRK WITTOWSKY AND MARCEL HUNECKE

123

23 Inhabiting Infrastructures: The Case of Cycling
in Copenhagen
JONAS LARSEN AND OSKAR FUNK

129

24 Comparing and Learning From Each Other for a Better
Cycling Future
HENK LENTING

135

25 The Velomobilities Turn
TIM JONES

139

PART IV
Sites and Strategies

145

26 Governing Everyday Mobilities: Policymaking
and Its Realities
CHELSEA TSCHOERNER

147

27 Planning for Sustainable Mobilities: Creating New Futures
or Doing What Is Possible?
NINA MOESBY BENNETSEN AND JULIE OVERGAARD MAGELUND

152

xii *Contents*

28 Let People Move! The New Planning Paradigm
of 'Shared Spaces'   158
ENZA LISSANDRELLO

29 Travels, Typing, and Tales   163
EMMY LAURA PEREZ FJALLAND

30 Are Emerging Mobility Practices Changing Our Urban
Spaces? A Close Look at the Italian Case   170
BRUNA VENDEMMIA

31 (In)Consequential Planning Practices: The Political Pitfall
of Mobility Policymaking in Lisbon's Metropolitan Area   175
JOÃO MOURATO, SOFIA SANTOS, DANIELA FERREIRA,
AND RENATO MIGUEL CARMO

32 Motility Meets Viscosity in Rural to Urban Flows   180
CATHERINE DOHERTY

33 Routes and Roots: Studying Place Relations
in Multilocal Lifeworlds   185
ROBERT NADLER

Index   189

Contributors

Esteban C. Acuña is a doctoral candidate at the University of Freiburg, Germany, and a member of the research group Cultures of Mobility in Europe (COME). In 2011 he earned his MA in Cultural Anthropology and Developmental Sociology at Leiden University, the Netherlands. His latest work concentrates on the deconstruction of binary categories in the study of human movements, the intersections of mobilities and race, mobilities as strategies and tactics of resilience and resistance, and testimony and biographical narratives in ethnographic work. He recently co-edited the volume *Education for Remembrance of the Roma Genocide: Scholarship, Commemoration and the Role of Youth* (2015), the fruit of emerging relations between his academic work and non-formal education.

Nina Moesby Bennetsen holds an MSc in Urban Planning Studies and Geography, and a BSc in Social Sciences from Roskilde University, Denmark. Currently she is employed as project leader in the Department of Environment at the Municipality of Gladsaxe, Denmark, where her primary focus is co-creation and transformation of urban spaces in climate adaption projects and promotion of sustainable modes of mobilities. She is driven by the relationship between climate change and social sciences and her primary research interests are cracks for sustainable mobilities, notions of mobilities in everyday life, in the planning system, and in society, Internet-based platforms for mobilities, co-creation, and communities.

Paula Bialski is a postdoctoral researcher at Leuphana University's Digital Cultures Research Lab (DCRL), Germany, and a freelance journalist as well. Her past work ethnographically studied Couchsurfing.org and online hitchhiking websites in order to map out digitally mediated mobile interaction. Her findings have been published in her book *Becoming Intimately Mobile* (Frankfurt: Peter Lang, 2012), where she described the effects of mobility and new media use on intimacy, trust, and strangerhood. Her current topics include digital infrastructures, programmer worlds, anonymity, the sharing economy, and digitally mediated sociality. She spent the summer of 2015 conducting fieldwork in Silicon Valley, xiv *Contributors*

studying the social and technical conditions of how forms of anonymity are practiced today, and is currently conducting an organizational ethnography of a corporate tech company in Berlin.

Renato Miguel Carmo is a research fellow at CIES-IUL and Assistant Professor at the University Institute of Lisbon, Portugal. He holds a PhD in Sociology from the Institute of Social Sciences. His research has been orientated towards the subject of social and spatial inequalities. Issues such as social exclusion, territorial marginalization, spatial mobilities, and social capital have been at the core of his individual and collective research projects. Recent publications include 'The Persistence of Class Inequality,' *Sociological Research Online* (2015); 'Social Capital and Socio-demographic Changes,' *Sociologia Ruralis* (2014); and the edited book *Translocal Ruralism: Mobility and Connectivity in European Rural Spaces* (2012).

Julie Cidell is Associate Professor of Geography and GIS at the University of Illinois at Urbana-Champaign, USA. She is a native of the Chicago area with a PhD in Geography from the University of Minnesota, USA. Her areas of research include mobilities, urban infrastructure, sustainability, and local governments. She studies how local governments and individual actors matter in struggles over large-scale infrastructure and policy development and the corresponding urban environments that are produced, including airports, railroads, and logistics hubs as well as green buildings and urban sustainability policies.

Peter Cox is Lecturer in the Department of Social and Political Science, University of Chester, UK. He holds a PhD in Philosophy from Chester College in Liverpool. In 2014–2015 he was awarded a Leverhulme International Academic Fellowship to work at the Rachel Carson Center for Environment and Society in Munich, where he focused on developing mobile research methods to better understand how people interact in public spaces of mobility. He serves as a member of the advisory board of Scientists for Cycling for the European Cyclists' Federation, connecting research with policymakers and practitioners. He was a founding member of the Cycling and Society Research Group and co-edited *Cycling and Society* (2007). He is the author of *Moving People: Sustainable Transport Development* (2010), and editor of *Cycling Cultures* (2015) and *Cycling: A Sociology of Vélo-Mobilities*, to be published by Routledge.

Michel Després is a PhD student in the Montréal University School of Urbanism and Landscape Architecture, Canada. He has been member of the Interdisciplinary Research Group on Suburbs since 2008, and worked as a research assistant on numerous research projects. One example is a collaborative urban design project reuniting urban planners and members of various public organizations around design solutions to alleviate social inequalities in housing and climate change effects in various neighborhoods, and to facilitate mobility in three Québec sectors. His

PhD focuses on the mobility strategies of various profiles of aging individuals in Montréal metropolitan areas and how they are configured and adapted depending on the way these aging individuals experience the built environment in their daily mobility.

Catherine Doherty is Professor of Pedagogy and Social Justice in the School of Education at the University of Glasgow, UK. She works in the sociology of education, with research interests around the educational choices, concerns, and strategies of mobile populations, and the associated issues for curriculum design and pedagogy. She has published research on international students in higher education, and internationalized curriculum in secondary schools. Her recent book with colleagues, *Family Mobility: Reconciling Career Opportunities and Educational Strategy*, was published in Routledge's Changing Mobilities series. Her current research addresses the educational strategies of transnational families, and questions of multivalent citizenships in curriculum.

Karolina Doughty is Lecturer in Cultural Geography at Wageningen University & Research in the Netherlands. Her research explores everyday mobile lives through the use of ethnography and creative research methods. She is particularly interested in the intersections between mobilities, wellbeing, and enactments of public social space (both urban and 'green'). Her work draws on more-than-representational approaches and the interdisciplinary field of sensory studies to examine mobile practices through a focus on embodiment, emotion, affect, and the senses. Over the last few years she has examined the role of sound in encounters with urban public space and others within it. She co-edited and contributed to a special issue on 'Emotional and Affective Geographies of Sound' for the journal *Emotion, Space and Society*, published in 2016.

Mia Arp Fallov is Associate Professor of Social Integration and Social Policy Strategies at the Department of Sociology and Social Work, Aalborg University, Denmark. She has worked for many years researching neighborhood regeneration, local community work, and social policies targeting local areas. Her main publications include 'Capacities of Participation and Local Inclusion—A Double-Edged Sword,' in Aila-Leena Matthies and Lars Uggerhøj (Eds.), *Participation, Marginalization and Welfare Services: Concepts, Policies and Practices Across European Countries* (2014); 'Mobile Forms of Belonging,' *Mobilities* (2013); 'Community Capacity Building as the Route to Inclusion in Neighbourhood Regeneration,' *International Journal of Urban and Regional Research* (2010).

Daniela Ferreira is a Dipl Human Geography and MPhil Spatial Planning and Urbanism at the Institute of Geography and Spatial Planning of the University of Lisbon (IGOT-UL), Portugal, who has been conducting studies in the field of consumption and retail, spatial planning, commercial urbanism, public policies, and socially creative spaces. She was a core xvi *Contributors*

researcher of *Localways—Ways of Local Sustainability: Mobility, Social Capital and Inequality* (2013–2015), an FCT (Foundation for Science and Technology—Portugal) funded project.

Emmy Laura Perez Fjalland holds a master's degree in Urban Planning Studies and Geography, and is currently a PhD student at Roskilde University, Denmark, and the Danish Architecture Centre. She studies how sharing and collaborative economic cooperations could be part of Danish urban governance and urban planning strategies. She is specifically interested in how different collaborative economic cooperations, communities, and organizations could help perform, develop, and run key municipal activities within environment and welfare. In the context of urban and mobilities studies, she pursues concepts such as co-creation, communities, commons, governance, platforms, and process designs.

Malene Freudendal-Pedersen is Associate Professor in Sustainable Mobilities at Roskilde University, Denmark. She has an interdisciplinary background linking sociology, geography, urban planning, and science and technology studies which she has been using to investigate praxes of mobilities and their significance for (future) cities. She is the co-manager of the international Cosmobilities Network, and the co-founder and co-editor of the new journal *Applied Mobilities* (Taylor & Francis). She is the author of the book *Mobility in Daily Life: Between Freedom and Unfreedom.*

Oskar Funk is currently working as a project manager in the City of Copenhagen, Denmark, with a specific focus on children and cycling. He has previously worked as a research assistant at Roskilde University focusing on velomobility and urban planning, covering both issues of physical planning as well as everyday practice and cycling culture.

Katrine Hartmann-Petersen is Associate Professor in Planning and Mobilities at Roskilde University, Denmark. She has a transdisciplinary background investigating the interconnectedness between modern everyday life, urban planning, and mobilities. She also has experience as a special advisor in municipality planning departments. She is a member of the Cosmobilities Network taskforce and book review editor of the new journal *Applied Mobilities* (Taylor & Francis).

Marcel Hunecke is Professor for General Psychology and Organizational and Environmental Psychology at the University of Applied Science in Dortmund, Germany, and a senior researcher in the Workgroup for Environmental Psychology and Cognition at Ruhr-Universität Bochum, where he earned his PhD and Habilitation in Psychology. He has led more than 20 inter- and transdisciplinary research projects in environmental and sustainability science. He is the Vice Dean of the Faculty of Applied Social Sciences and the head of the master program Social

Sustainability and Demographic Change at the University of Applied Science in Dortmund.

Hanne Louise Jensen is Assistant Professor of Spatial Sociology at Aalborg University, Denmark. Her research focuses on various spatio-temporal organizations of social life, experience of and production of places and mobilities, as well as qualitative methods, mainly mobile methods and mapping. Within these fields her publications include 'The Life and Influence of the 1925th Chicagomap,' *Geoforum Perspectives* (2016), and 'Emotions on the Move: Mobile Emotions Among Train Commuters in the South East of Denmark,' *Emotion, Space and Society* (2012). Currently she is engaged in developing her teaching on various uses of nature in the late modern society and is co-editing a book on ethnographies.

Ole B. Jensen is Professor of Urban Theory at the Department of Architecture, Design and Media Technology, Aalborg University, Denmark. He holds a PhD in Planning, and a Dr. Techn in Mobilities. He is deputy director, co-founder, and board member at the Center for Mobilities and Urban Studies (C-MUS), director of the research cluster in Mobility and Tracking Technology (MoTT), PhD program coordinator at the Media, Architecture and Design Doctoral Program, and editorial board member on the journal *Applied Mobilities*. He is the co-author of *Making European Space: Mobility, Power and Territorial Identity* (2004), author of *Staging Mobilities* (2013) and *Designing Mobilities* (2014), the editor of the four-volume collection *Mobilities* (Routledge, 2015), and co-author of *Urban Mobilities Design: Urban Designs for Mobile Situations* (Routledge, forthcoming).

Tim Jones is Reader in Urban Mobility with the Faculty of Technology Design and Environment at Oxford Brookes University, UK. His interest is understanding how urban environments can be (re)configured to support and promote healthy and sustainable urban mobility, and in particular, how certain types of mobility are given meaning within certain geographical, social, and cultural contexts. He has experience implementing novel mixed-method approaches to try to reveal the physical, social, and cultural factors that influence everyday travel decisions and how this affects journey practice and experience.

Anja Jørgensen is Associate Professor of Sociology at the Department of Sociology and Social Work, Aalborg University, Denmark. She is head of the research group SocMap and is co-organizing the MSc in City, Housing and Settlement Patterns, Aalborg University in Copenhagen. In her career she has worked with a wide range of questions and themes within Urban Sociology that are related to mobility, place-based belonging, local social interaction, neighborliness, and local communities. Her main publications include 'The Sense of Belonging in the New Zones

xviii *Contributors*

in Transition,' *Current Sociology* (2010); 'The Life and Influence of the 1925th Chicagomap,' *Geoforum Perspectives* (2016); 'Mobile Forms of Belonging,' *Mobilities* (2013); and *When the Neighbourhood Discovers Itself* (Aalborg Universitetsforlag, 2006).

Robin Kellermann is DFG Associate Fellow and a PhD student in the International Graduate Research Program 'The World in the City: Metropolitanism and Globalization from the 19th Century to the Present' at the Center for Metropolitan Studies, TU Berlin, Germany. He is researching the historical evolution of waiting in public transportation by retracing the coevolution of physical environments and social practices in airports and train stations. He is an appointed member of the Executive Committee of the International Association for the History of Transport, Traffic and Mobility (T2M) and book review editor of the *Journal of Transport History* (JTH) as well as the T2M newsletter editor.

Aslak Aamot Kjærulff holds a PhD in Mobilities and Action Research from Roskilde University, Denmark, and currently organizes a transdisciplinary research organization called Diakron. The core trajectory of his practice is to trace how concepts and ideas travel across cultures and disciplines. Most of the research he takes part in is carried out in ways that engage several disciplinary and organizational backgrounds at once. This involves exploratory methodological designs, where problem formulations, research processes, and artistic productions are invented collaboratively. Ultimately this means engaging with and contributing to several types of organizations and public spaces.

Till Koglin holds a PhD in Transport Planning and a bachelor's and master's degree in Human Geography. He is currently working as Assistant Senior Lecturer at Lund University, Sweden. His research mainly deals with mobility, transport, and urban planning with a strong focus on the marginalization of cycling in urban space. Within his research he combines critical theory with transport and mobility in order to shed light on injustice issues within transport planning and transport systems. He also works on public transport issues in connection to urban and transport planning. Moreover, he has worked on issues related to road safety, urban planning, pedestrian planning, and sustainable cities.

Ditte Bendix Lanng is Assistant Professor in Urban Design and Mobilities at the Department of Architecture, Design and Media Technology, Aalborg University, Denmark. She holds a PhD in Urban Design and Mobilities. Her research interests are within Urban Design and Mobilities Design examined through cross-disciplinary theory, and design experiments as modes of sociocultural enquiry, ethnography, and as a collective enterprise with planning and architectural practice. She merges relational approaches with Urban Design, and develops Urban Design's and Mobilities Design's theoretical and methodological stream of materialities as networked and active hybrids. She is the co-author of *Urban Mobilities Design: Urban Designs for Mobile Situations* (Routledge, forthcoming).

Jonas Larsen is Professor at Roskilde University, Denmark, in Mobilities and Urban Studies and he is part of the MOSPUS research group. He has published widely in the fields of mobilities, tourism, and photography. More recently, he has been involved in research projects on urban cycling and running.

Henk Lenting studied Traffic Planning/Mobilities at the NHL Hogeschool, the Netherlands, between 2010 and 2014. During this program, he specialized in traffic psychology with a particular interest in research and traffic policies related to cycling. He did research at the leading Dutch knowledge center for cycling, CROW Fietsberaad, as well as the Dutch Cycling Council. He investigates possibilities for making cycling safer, better, and more pleasant. He is most interested in finding ways to improve cycling systems by applying knowledge from a variety of fields to the subject. By working like this, he looks for creative, new, and yet well-founded solutions to the problems faced when trying to get more cyclists or caused by the shortcomings of a system faced with increasing numbers of cyclists.

Enza Lissandrello is Associate Professor in the Department of Development and Planning at Aalborg University, Denmark. As an interdisciplinary social scientist, her research interests range widely but all have been concerned with sustainable urban and spatial transitions and governance of innovation in public planning, reflexive sociology and mobility studies, and on power, discourses, and performativity in planning politics and infrastructural projects.

Julie Overgaard Magelund holds a BSc in social science and an MSc in Urban Planning Studies and Geography from Roskilde University, Denmark. She is currently a PhD student in the joint PhD program 'Sustainable Mobility in the Metropolitan Region of Munich' at TU Munich and Nürtingen-Geislingen University (DE), funded by the Hans Böckler Stiftung. She is studying cooperative housing in Munich and Copenhagen in order to investigate how mobility cultures could be changed through housing. Her research interests revolve around the mutual impact between mobilities and everyday life practices as well as how societal changes and individuals influence each other.

Njogu Morgan is a PhD candidate in the School of Architecture and Planning at the University of the Witwatersrand, South Africa. His research explores changes in societal acceptance of everyday bicycle use from a historical comparative perspective. By focusing specifically on bicycle usage and attitudes to cycling in Amsterdam, Beijing, Chicago, and Johannesburg, he seeks to understand the cultural dimensions of urban xx *Contributors*

sustainability. He also has a master's degree in Public and Development Management from the University of the Witwatersrand and a BA in Political Science and International Studies from Northwestern University, Chicago, USA. He blogs on the global urban cycling agenda and its relationship with politics and social change (http://cyclefriendlycities.org/).

João Mourato is a research fellow at the Institute for Social Sciences of the University of Lisbon ICS-ULisboa, Portugal. He holds a PhD in Town Planning (2011) from the Bartlett School of Planning, University College London, UK. His research delves in the evolution of planning as a public policy in Portugal, with a particular focus on the dynamics of institutional adaptation and policy learning processes in the face of a shifting policy environment. He recently edited, with E. Gualini and M. Allegra, the book *Conflict in the City: Contested Urban Spaces and Local Democracy* (Jovis, 2015).

Lesley Murray is Principal Lecturer in Social Science at the University of Brighton, UK. Her research centers around urban mobilities and she has previously worked as a transport researcher for the London Research Centre and the Greater London Authority, before moving to Transport for London. She is a transdisciplinary researcher whose interests center on the social and cultural aspects of mobilities. Her research includes collaborations with artists, architects, and creative writers. She has published extensively in the field of mobilities and has co-edited several books including *Mobile Methodologies* (2010); *Researching Mobilities: Transdisciplinary Encounters* (2014); and *Intergenerational Mobilities* (forthcoming).

Robert Nadler is a geographer and researcher at the research group Urban Development and Mobility at ILS—Research Institute for Regional and Urban Development in Dortmund, Germany. He holds a PhD in Urban and Local European Studies from the University of Milano-Bicocca, Italy. He has completed several research projects on creative industries, regional development, migration theories, multilocality, and economic geography in Central and Eastern Europe. He was the project coordinator of the EU project 'Re-Turn: Regions Benefitting from Returning Migrants' (www.re-migrants. eu) and coordinates a research project on civic engagement of returning migrants and their impact on urban development (www.ort-schafft.eu).

Sarah Nies is a research fellow at the Institute for Social Science Research (ISF München) and the Ludwig-Maximilians-University in Munich, Germany. She holds a PhD from the Friedrich-Schiller University, Jena, Germany. Her research interests include sociology of work, theory of capitalism, and sociology of macroeconomic thinking. Studying current developments of work organization and discovering the implications of mobility within the sphere of work, she recently got more and more interested in combining sociology of work with mobilities research.

Contributors xxi

Sung-Yueh Perng is a postdoctoral researcher on the ERC-funded Programmable City project at Maynooth University, Ireland, after receiving his PhD in Sociology from Lancaster University, UK. He is the co-editor of *Code and the City* (Routledge) with Rob Kitchin. Drawing upon mobilities studies, science and technology studies, and human and cultural geography, his current research examines emerging digital living and data-driven urbanism, focusing on how civic hacking practices can meaningfully adapt programming skills for communities' purposes and how personal data obtained through wearable computing and quantified-self projects can lead to unintended changes in social interactions, memory, and state security.

Lilyana Petrova is a Franco-Bulgarian artist and researcher working on the intersection of art and communication. Currently she is a full-time lecturer in France and is working on a PhD at the University of Grenoble and the University of Savoie Mont-Blanc as a member of the inter-laboratory research group for Image, Communication and Digital Arts (GSICA). Her doctoral work focuses on the subject of 'Digital Practices in Mobile Situation: Visual and Interdisciplinary Approach of the Immersion.' It investigates the concept of *parcours* (path creating) as a hypermedia and immersive experience of mobile phone users and in particular the users of the alternate reality game *Ingress*, amongst other mobile applications.

Jon Dag Rasmussen is a PhD student at the Department of Sociology and Social Work at Aalborg University, Denmark. He is based in Copenhagen, Denmark, and is currently in the process of finishing his PhD dissertation. He is preoccupied with long-term ethnographic explorations of the urban world and has been engaged in projects on this subject, most recently aimed towards the everyday lives of marginalized elderly people. Alongside the ethnographic interest he is intrigued by seeking out potentials in different odd and experimental encounters between science, philosophy, art, and poetry, and based on this enthusiasm he works with ways of bringing a more explicit artistic wonderment into the academic practice, its language and writing genres.

Katrin Roller is a sociologist and is working on her PhD, funded by the Hans-Böckler-Stiftung, at the Technische Universität München, Germany. Her topic is 'Mobility at Work—Mobility as Work?' where she analyzes the role of recognition and reciprocity in the field of business travel. Her research interests include (mobile) work, mobility, questions of social inequality, gender research, and qualitative methods.

Sofia Santos holds a PhD in Sociology, University Institute of Lisbon, Portugal (2016), and an MSc in Geography, Faculty of Letters of the University of Lisbon. She has published research in the field of regional and local development, public policies, spatial planning, identity and territory, xxii *Contributors*

geographic mobility, and sociology of the territory. Her doctoral research focused on the practices and representations of mobility. The goal is to increase understanding on the relations between daily mobility, social inequalities, and discourses of place identity and social differentiation in the Lisbon Metropolitan Area (LMA).

Kaare Svejstrup holds an MA in Philosophy and Journalism and currently hosts a live morning radio show on the Danish national talk radio station *Radio24syv*. His academic work in relation to audio and radio has focused on the transition of noise as an aesthetic concept in modern music and the semiotic role of 'real sound,' music, and montage in science radio.

Chelsea Tschoerner is a scientific researcher and lecturer at Nürtingen-Geislingen University of Applied Sciences and a PhD candidate at the Chair of Environmental Governance at Albert Ludwig University of Freiburg in Germany. She has a background in anthropology as well as political sciences, sociology, economics, and empirical research methods. In her PhD project she studied local policymaking in the transport and mobility sector in Munich, Germany. Her research approach draws strongly upon critical policy studies, the mobilities turn, and governance theory and approaches, and she is especially interested in developing knowledge on and methods for studying mobilities dimensions in policymaking, particularly in the fields of transport and mobility management.

Bruna Vendemmia is an architect and urban designer and holds a PhD in Territorial Management and Design at Politecnico di Milano, Italy. In 2007 she started the European Postgraduate Master in Urbanism. She is the co-founder of 2d4, an architectural and urban design office based in Naples. She has been awarded first prize for several international design competitions such as Europan 11 and the requalification of Acerra (Naples) historical center, and designing flexible urban spaces, adaptable to contemporary urban practices. She conceived and realized 'NoStraNa,' an urban regeneration experiment for the historical center of Naples. Her research interest focuses on spatial transformations engendered by contemporary changes in mobility practices.

Anne Victoria earned her MA in cultural anthropology from the University of Tennessee, Knoxville, USA, with the thesis, *An Ethno-Historical Account of the African American Community in Downtown Knoxville, Tennessee, Before and After Urban Renewal* (2015). She is the Service Delivery Specialist for Knoxville Area Transit and combines traditional and artful modes of engaging the public and policymakers with the value of public transportation. Her research interests include urban public transportation, multimodal transport users, mobility and functional health, gender analysis, urban renewal, landscape memories, and racialization. Her previous publication is *Bus Stop Matters: Exploring the Gendered Perspective of Functional Health* (2014).

Gerlinde Vogl is a sociologist, and holds a PhD from the Technische Universität München, Germany. Her current and other various research projects are on work, mobility, and technology. Important publications include *'Travelling Where the Opponents Are': Business Travel and the Social Impacts of New Mobilities Regimes* (2010); *Betriebliche Mobilitätsregime—Die sozialen Kosten mobiler Arbeit* (2010); and *Mobile Arbeit* (Bund Verlag, 2013).

Lauren Wagner is Assistant Professor in Globalisation and Development at Maastricht University, the Netherlands. Her research focuses on issues of diaspora and belonging through microanalysis of everyday encounters, based both in linguistic recorded data as well as in ethnomethodological participation in materialist atmospheres. As an interdisciplinary mobilities researcher, she participates in geography, anthropology, sociology, and sociolinguistic discussions. She is currently publishing work on face-to-face negotiations of diasporic belonging in Morocco, through public space interactions and in the viscous flows of leisure consumption. She is currently working on two books, co-authoring *Moroccan Dreams* and authoring *Becoming Diasporic*.

Simon Wind is Assistant Professor with a special focus on mobile ethnographies and digital technologies at the Department of Architecture, Design and Media Technology, Aalborg University, Denmark. He holds a BA in Architecture & Design, an MA in Urban Design, and a PhD in Urban Mobilities Studies. His research interest lies in the intersection of urban design, mobilities studies, and (smart) technologies. What should our urban infrastructural spaces be in the future? How can we investigate the mobile experience? How can we make the city and its mobility smarter? He is furthermore a board member of the Center for Mobilities and Urban Studies (C-MUS).

Dirk Wittowsky is head of the research group Daily Mobility and Transportation Systems at the ILS—Research Institute for Regional and Urban Development, Germany. He holds a PhD from the Institute for Transport Studies, University of Karlsruhe, Germany, and has more than 17 years' practical as well as research experience in the field of transportation. He has been manager for the project Congestion Free Hessen 2015 and senior analyst for traffic demand and modeling for the DB Long Distance. He researches mobility behavior of different social groups, demand and traffic modeling, and the development of sustainable and innovative transportation systems. Additionally he examines barriers and conflicts in the transport sector during the energy transition and the effects between ICT and mobility behavior.

Preface

'Networked Urban Mobilities': This was the title for the conference and art exhibition that the Cosmobilities Network organized from the 5th to the 7th of November 2014 in Copenhagen. It was a big scientific event and the reason for it was the tenth anniversary of the international research network. The conference was jointly organized by a team from Aalborg University and Roskilde University.

About 160 participants came to Aalborg University's campus in Copenhagen and in this three-volume set many of them are presenting their work and ideas. The book you hold in your hand is the second volume and presents a wide range of contributions which have the ambition to illustrate the strength of and variety in subjects and empirical broadness within the mobilities paradigm. Its subtitle indicates this in a pithy way: 'Practices, Flows, Methods'. Volume one is edited by Malene Freudendal-Pedersen and Sven Kesselring and it compiles theoretical debates, conceptual considerations, and new ideas and perspectives which are prominent within the new mobilities paradigm. Volume three is edited by Aslak Aamot Kjærulff, Sven Kesselring, Peter Peters, and Kevin Hannam. It collects contributions from the conference on 'Art, Performances, Impacts', as the subtitle tells. By so doing it propels a topic which has been a significant element of the work within the Cosmobilities Network since the 2008 conference on mobility and art in Munich: to demonstrate the analytical power of art and social science.

The Conference in Copenhagen was a special event and a milestone for the network in many ways.

Firstly, the Cosmobilities Network celebrated its birthday. Ten years before a small crowd of people came together in Munich for a workshop on 'Mobility and the Cosmopolitan Perspective.' At this time no one considered this the birth of a long-lasting collaboration and research network. The name Cosmobilities was mostly a running gag on how to shorten cosmopolitan mobilities during these days. At some point John Urry laughingly said, 'This name calls for a network!' And more than a decade later, the Cosmobilities Network plays a substantial role within the mobilities turn in social science and beyond. At the tenth anniversary conference we were celebrating Cosmobilities as an academic space, a place for encounters and a synonym for cutting-edge research and scientific innovation. A huge number of individual scholars and research institutions worldwide have generated a new interdisciplinary literature and a new thinking on the social transformations of the modern mobile world, its risks and opportunities. The 'new mobilities paradigm' has influenced work and thoughts of academic scholars as well as practitioners in public authorities, industry, and civil society.

Secondly, what we luckily didn't know at this time, it was the last Cosmobilities conference where two very important academic personalities and thinkers, who both played an important role in the 2004 workshop and the beginning of the network, were still with us.

German sociologist Ulrich Beck was invited to the 2004 workshop and in the aftermath he fostered the founding process of the Cosmobilities Network. In the 2014 Conference catalogue he wrote a welcome note to the participants stating that Cosmobilities "has become a reflexive place and space for re-thinking the basic principles of modernity and for the future of modern societies."

John Urry's role since 2004 and up until a very sad day in March 2016 cannot be overestimated. In many ways he was and still is the 'spiritus rector' and the mentor of the network and of many, many mobilities scholars. Without his unique personality and his brilliant mind the network would not be what it is today. And this is said without any exaggeration. For the 2014 conference catalogue he wrote:

> Throughout the last decade Cosmobilities has provided a really brilliant space that has nurtured the emerging mobilities paradigm. As a horizontal network of many senior and junior colleagues you have done a great job in bringing together scholars from many different fields and theoretical approaches as well as research traditions. You have been bridging the gap between academia and practitioners, too. And hopefully Cosmobilities will long continue.

The book series *Networked Urban Mobilities* is dedicated to these two thinkers. Both of their words we consider as the assignment and the mission of the Cosmobilities Network. We hope that the book in your hand and all three volumes together will give an overview of the depth, the diversity, and analytical sharpness of the new mobilities paradigm and the potentials of the scholars of the network. Beyond this we wish you an exciting and illuminating reading experience.

We would be glad if this book aroused some interest in our work, and maybe we will see you at one of the next Cosmobilities conferences.

Malene Freudendal-Pedersen, Sven Kesselring
Copenhagen, September 2016

1 Networked Urban Mobilities
Practices, Flows, Methods

Emmy Laura Perez Fjalland, Malene Freudendal-Pedersen, and Katrine Hartmann-Petersen

An understanding of cities can no longer be attained purely through focusing on specific sites when cities today are networked through diverse mobilities systems. Cities are increasingly produced and reproduced through flows and fixities, particularly over the last decade (Hannam, Sheller, and Urry 2006; Freudendal-Pedersen, Hannam, and Kesselring 2016; Ritzer 2010). These mobilities entail the large-scale movements of people, goods, capital, and information, as well as more local processes of daily transportation, communication, and consumption (Urry 2000; Sheller 2014). Diverse complex settings of social, technological, geographical, cultural, and digital networks of mobility are today defining how cities develop and are comprehended (Urry 2007; Graham and Marvin 2001). Thus analyzing and discussing these networked mobilities becomes essential in framing modern social life and urban cultures.

Ten years ago, Mimi Sheller and John Urry (2006) deliberated on how powerful the discourse on mobilities had become within the twenty-first century. They suggested a set of questions, theories, and methodologies that could help grasp the global connectivity affected by mobility, fluidity, and liquidity. Since then the mobilities research field has been steadily growing and researchers from sociology, anthropology, geography, communication, political science, ethnography, and other disciplines within social science and humanities are today researching these and many more aspects of a mobile world (Sheller 2014; Cresswell and Merriman 2011; Canzler, Kaufmann, and Kesselring 2008; Freudendal-Pedersen, Hannam, and Kesselring 2016; Hannam, Sheller, and Urry 2006). Research and disciplines are interconnected, overlapped, and related, but what signifies mobilities research is that it differs in "scope, foci, and methodologies" (Sheller 2014, 789). Mobilities research brings together "social concerns of sociology . . ., spatial concerns of geography . . ., and cultural concerns of anthropology and communication . . ., while inflecting each with a relational ontology of the co-constitution of subjects, spaces, and meanings" (Sheller 2014, 791).

Urban lives, cultures and economies are significantly challenged by different mobilities (Ritzer 2010; Urry 2011). Time-space compression, the fast-moving digitization of modern life, and the ongoing flux between

2 *Emmy Laura Perez Fjalland et al.*

individualized and communal life impact all spheres of the urban. Working, tourism, pausing, moving, communicating, nursing, dwelling, playing, and so forth are somehow connected and related to the global scale (Beck 2016). Related through actually moving—virtually or physically—in connection with work or leisure time, through the global economy affecting housing prices, through the news media juxtaposing global events with local issues, through increasingly cosmopolitan social (digital) networks, through the logistics behind our everyday consumption like food, beverages, music, etc. Thus the future of networked urban mobilities is a key topic for the risk society.

Practices, Flows, Methods

The Networked Urban Mobilities conference in 2014 was the best attended conference in the Cosmobilities Network's history to date. The variety of disciplines, methodologies, and scopes displayed the vast range of the mobilities paradigm. In this book, the aim is to underline this broad academic scope and these multiple approaches and to demonstrate their strength and import within mobilities research. Through a focus on practices, flows, and methods—both in mobilities research and while conducting such research—this book offers a broad introduction to researching mobilities. The different chapters involve, merge, and overlap with different disciplines and practices, assembling new kinds of disciplinary hybrids, thereby stressing the importance of new ways of thinking about our social networked urban realms and realities. Together the articles outline the use of creative, experimental, and explorative approaches to pose new questions, undergo new studies, and reach new understandings. They combine movements of people, objects, and information in all of their complex relational dynamics to deal with the realities of the mobile risk society (Kesselring 2008).

Through its inter-/trans-/post-disciplinary studies, mobilities research calls for multiple methods that can address the complexity of scales, speeds, and in-betweens, and capture present, and sometimes even intervene in, processes of mobilities (Büscher, Urry, and Witchger 2010). In 'The New Mobilities Paradigm,' Sheller and Urry (2006) called for 'mobile methods' that could 'measure' the changing nature of time, space, and motion, and capture these dynamic mobile processes. Büscher, Urry, and Witchger (2010, 2) advanced this agenda by arguing that "the mobilities turn folds analysis into the empirical in ways that open up different ways of understanding the relationship between theory, observation, and engagement." The practices within mobilities are multitudinous and are, in many ways, constituted by an effort to cope with the complexity and reflexivity enforced on urban lives. These practices are always, in one way or the other, determined by the flows (be it moving, pausing, or dwelling) that mobilities penetrates the networked city with. This also means that methods within mobilities research are wide reaching, from the micro-mobilities to macro-mobilities, and they also bridge these scales (Adey et al. 2013; Freudendal-Pedersen, Hannam, and Kesselring 2016; Hannam, Sheller, and Urry 2006).

Reflecting on Experiences With Mobilities Research Practice

In order to underline the multitude of approaches within mobilities research, the authors were asked to engage in a reflexive writing process addressing the implications of the methodological choices made when seeking to identify the dynamics and interdependencies of networked urban flows and practices of mobilities. To a wide extent, the authors subscribe—though not explicitly—to an abductive approach:

> In abduction, an (often surprising) single case is interpreted from a hypothetic overarching pattern by new observations (new cases). . . . During the process, the empirical area of application is successively developed, and the theory (the proposed overarching pattern) is also adjusted and refined.
>
> (Alvesson and Sköldberg 2000, 4)

By focusing on underlying patterns, on understanding, and on explanatory models (in the widest sense), the authors relate their specific cases and their theoretical inspiration to their perception of mobilities in reflexive modernization.

Since the 1990s, qualitative researchers in particular have been addressing their own research practice as one that involves *writing* based on the acknowledgement that there is no 'natural' writing, no 'natural' representation of results, but that the writing is a method of inquiry in itself (Denzin 2001; Brinkmann 2009). Sociologist Norman Denzin defines this as the narrative turn (Denzin 2001) in line with the communicative (Healey 1993) and argumentative turn (Fischer and Forester 1993; Fischer and Gottweis 2012) within planning theory. This is based on an acknowledgement that language constitutes, shapes, and sometimes determines our perceptions of reality. Language and communication are considered as active processes, which socially construct meaning and reality. Grounded in the works of philosophers such as Wittgenstein, Austin, Derrida, and Habermas, this approach puts emphasis on the social processes of defining problems and critique, on identifying solutions, and on finding consensus (Sandercock 1999; Sandercock 2003; Freudendal-Pedersen 2009; Flyvbjerg 1998; Denzin 2001).

New Format—New Understanding?

This book illustrates the wide range of approaches to methods, practices, and flows of urban mobilities. One of the very important qualities from working within the mobilities paradigm—going to conferences, workshops, or other events where mobilities research is presented—is the opportunity to

4 *Emmy Laura Perez Fjalland et al.*

learn about very different empirical fields connected through the same theoretical reference. This book wishes to convey this in written form by empha-
sizing and strengthening diversities and un-aligned perspectives through a
different writing format. In order to create this experience, we developed
dogmas—guidelines—for the writing style as well as specific questions for
reflection that each writer answers (in quite different ways).

The dogmas requested short chapters written in an essay style with a
particular emphasis on the empirical perspectives of the research, including personal reflections on the significance of their research for Networked
Urban Mobilities. The following questions were distributed to the authors
to reflect upon in writing:

- What does your mobilities research bring to the field, and how is it
  related to the networks of urban mobilities?
- What are your methodological reflections on your work?
- How has the mobilities turn influenced and inspired your work?
- What (if any) are your critical reflections on your own work?

Through this undertaking an opportunity arises to learn about multiple
approaches and perspectives within the international mobilities research
scene. The book consists of chapters that function as 'appetizers,' encouraging the readers to learn more about mobilities research, further develop their
own research, or discover new areas for further investigation.

Outline of the Volume

How to assemble these different chapters—embracing the differences in perspectives and empirical outset—has not been an easy task. Many headlines
and divisions were composed and then abandoned when the constant negotiation of the meaning and significance of words muddied the intention of
the headline. *Moving and Pausing, Communities and Collaboration, Modes
and Emotions, Sites and Strategies* are thus not determining signifiers of the
research presented, but to a higher degree a picture of an eternally moving
research field guided by the reader's interpretations of the text in question.
The following sections of the book need to be understood in this context.

Moving and Pausing

How you spend your time while on the move is the common theme of this
section. On the basis of auto-ethnographic everyday train commuting studies, Simon Wind, Ditte Bendix Lanng, and Ole B. Jensen are advancing the
notion of mobilities design. Identifying shifting atmospheres, they highlight
the affective performance of mundane mobilities artifacts and spaces in
specific alliances with networked socio-material bodies. Robin Kellermann
investigates how passengers' waiting experiences have changed in the light

of digitalization and the information age, related to real time information systems (RTIS). He focuses on 'pausing' as an overlooked element within mobilities, a valuable element for passengers enabled by real-time information. This relates to Anne Victoria's research on the design of the bus stop strongly contributing to the experience of active transportation. Through an outset in walking and health, she focuses on the armatures and their relation to movement. The bus is also central for Katrine Hartmann-Petersen discussing the meanings and values of pausing for a moment while being on the bus. She identifies the bus as a moving anchor in people's everyday life and argues that passengers' stories contribute to knowledge on networks, rhythms, and variations in urban life. These values are, according to Hanne Louise Jensen, also present when commuting by train. She explores how mobile friendships develop among commuters who are socially diverse and live relatively segregated lives. These social possibilities of networked urban mobilities illuminate how trains can become an important place for forming various types of social relations. Aslak Aamot Kjærulff and Kaare Svejstrup also discuss networks on the move through a *Road Radio* experiment, investigating how to document research and research processes in a different format. Their methodological experiment seeks to understand how travel and flow change over time and between lives and contexts. Sarah Nies, Katrin Roller, and Gerlinde Vogl's research engages in work and private life practices under increasingly mobile conditions and identifies mobility patterns of highly qualified business travelers who commute weekly. They argue that the dissolution and (re)drawing of boundaries between work and private life cannot be adequately understood without considering perceptions of space, time, and physical movement. This is also a focal point when Esteban C. Acuña explores the mobile/immobile lives of Romani groups, families, and individuals. He addresses the challenges arising within the Romanis, but also, as a researcher, those he finds while exploring daily life's translocal connections and mobile practices across and beyond the Atlantic.

Communities and Collaborations

Networked mobilities connect communities through all sorts of local, global, virtual, digital, and material collaborations. This section shows examples of interconnectedness at different scales.

Lilyana Petrova explores how digital mobility has influenced our way of experiencing movement within the city and the related transformations taking place in this process. Defining a Parkour Method, she uses the alternate reality game called *Ingress* to walk us through a Little Mermaid's metamorphosis. Lauren Wagner investigates how working from an assumption of humans-as-mobile configures viscosity and meshwork as useful theoretical dynamics for approaching networked urban mobilities. Through observations on diasporic circulations, she explores how summer vacations in a diasporic homeland are part of practices of 'being diasporic.' Michel Després

6   *Emmy Laura Perez Fjalland et al.*

presents the terms 'parked students' and 'surfing workers' to show the variety of time strategies and lifestyles within students and workers of Québec City. He discusses how mobile technologies create 'third places' for studying and working as skills-based and generational, but also as a matter of social context. Based on ethnographic fieldwork, Jon Dag Rasmussen explores the entangled social lives of elderly people on the fringes of society. His research reveals the existence of a non-transparent world of micro-mobility among marginal elderly city dwellers and emphasizes the ability to move as significant in these communities. Karolina Doughty and Lesley Murray suggests that the individualized approaches to mobility-dominating policy debates need to be challenged by seeking to understand mobilities as interdependent and culturally embedded. They elaborate upon this through a focus on situated everyday mobilities, disruptive events, and their impacts on mobility decision-making. In line with this, Mia Arp Fallov and Anja Jørgensen question the idea of mobility as an antithesis to local belonging. They argue that they constitute each other in complex and networked interconnections in everyday life and, through a focus on the link between fluidity and solidity, a more accurate picture of modern everyday life evolves. Sung-Yueh Perng uses the process of software writing to show how software and data processing capabilities have become pervasively embedded in urban sociotechnical systems. Through 'code-alongs' Perng investigates the transforming of everyday experiences into sequences of code by observing the social and sonic activities of coding. Through a focus on virtual platforms evolving into communities Paula Bialski discusses the way home-stays, hospitality networks, and short-term rental websites can foster uncanny experiences. The digital platform Airbnb can be seen as a mobilization constituting our mobility, informing our experience, and promising a place-to-come.

Modes and Emotions

Different modes of mobility encourage different emotions. But emotions are also influenced by urban design, life stage, cultures, and norms. In this section, authors discuss different ways of approaching and analyzing senses and impressions related to specific modes—but also related to the connectedness *between* modes. Peter Cox stresses that urban design makes cycle commuters respond emotionally and pre-rationally and that the city shapes how commuters cycle—space shapes feelings and feelings change actions. In line with this, Njogu Morgan draws upon an auto-ethnographic approach while exploring how emergent emotions while cycling can create a sense of community. He argues that emotions generated on street-level moments of assembly may weave feelings of mutuality. Mutuality among strangers on bicycles is shaping future practice when cycling in the city. Till Koglin identifies 'meetings' across modes creating conflicts conceptualized as space wars in motion. By combining quantitative and qualitative methodologies, he finds that motorized traffic has more space and power in public space, making cycling stressful and conflicting. Julie Cidell discusses aero- and automobility as a hybrid system in the case of long-distance travel. She argues that long-distance aeromobilities often require consideration of the automobile as connecter between sites. Thus global air transportation systems need to be understood as being interconnected with local places and experiences of mobilities. Through a multi-method survey approach, Dirk Wittowsky and Marcel Hunecke examine the influence of ICT on activity patterns and daily mobility modes among young people. They discuss the consequences of mode choices due to the increasingly precise real-time data and information available in the city. Jonas Larsen and Oskar Funk investigate the 'strong regime' of distinctive, legitimate everyday practices of cycling in Copenhagen. They argue that cycling practices are always staged 'from above' and there is always something 'more-than-designed' to people's practical engagement with the world. Henk Lenting uses a comparative perspective to enable better understandings of cycling as social practice and the attitudes towards those practices. He argues that by using comparisons, do's and don'ts for encouraging cycling in different countries can be identified and used to improve urban cycling as a vision. And finally, in the closing chapter of this section, Tim Jones lays out the story of how research on cycling changed through its interaction with the mobilities turn. Especially in relations to urban planning and design, critical mobilities thinking offers new ways for cycling research to understand, communicate, and potentially shape the world of movement.

Sites and Strategies

Combining strategies of mobilities planning at multiple levels with impressions and implications of specific sites is the focus of this section of the book. It highlights how planners implement concepts and policies aiming at developing visionary urban futures and how intentions and realizations are not always aligned. With an outset in the case of Munich, Chelsea Tschoerner analyzes understandings and meanings in socio-temporal spaces. She argues that multiple interconnected policies and mobilities realities in policymaking exists, and stresses that alternative discourses construct 'visions of mobilities futures.' Nina Moesby Bennetsen and Julie Overgaard Magelund also discuss visionary futures, but with a focus on the implementation among planners creating Super Cycle Highways across municipalities in Greater Copenhagen. They show how future mobilities planning to a wide extent becomes the 'art of the possible.' The way planners perceive and create alternative urban mobilities strategies are also addressed in Enza Lissandrello's discussion of shared space as the 'meetingness' of mobility patterns. She highlights how shared space as a planning paradigm transforms status, structure, and social order within urban mobilities. Emmy Laura Perez Fjalland emphasizes the power of stories as method and representation in strategic, political, and civil processes of rationalization. Based on

8 Emmy Laura Perez Fjalland et al.

ethnographic work, she discusses how storytelling contributes to strategic planning as a nuancing tool for negotiations in complex networked urban contexts. On the other hand, Bruna Vendemmia uses visualizations to put focus on the spatial implications in everyday life among highly mobile people. She constructs synthetic maps of activities, places, and intensities based on statistic transport data. By using this as a supplement to analyses, the spatial dynamics created by mobilities becomes visible. João Mourato, Sofia Santos, Daniela Ferreira, and Renato Carmo explore mobilities inequalities in Lisbon's metropolitan territorial governance, addressing the political pitfalls of mobility policymaking. They identify crises that lead to internal power imbalances—for example unsuitable design, and institutional path dependencies, etc. Catherine Doherty suggests the concept of institutional viscosity to handle the rate, absence, or ease of mobility. This entails a dual focus on both agency and structure providing more comprehensive analyses of empirical mobilities studies. Finally, Robert Nadler introduces the notion of 'plug&play places' as a heuristic concept that enables an understanding of place relations in a mobile world. Through 25 biographical interviews with highly mobile and multilocal creative knowledge workers, place relations in multilocal lifeworlds help to grasp new forms of flexible rootedness.

All together the contributions to this book offer an exciting and diverse insight into networked urban mobilities, how our cities are shaped and molded by the mobilities of people, objects, and ideas. The approaches and the different fields of research highlight the interdisciplinarity of the mobilities turn and as such it is also an invitation to learn from other approaches when moving on or into the mobilities turn.

References

Adey, Peter, David Bissell, Kevin Hannam, Peter Merriman and Mimi Sheller. 2013. *The Routledge Handbook of Mobilities*, edited by Peter Adey, David Bissell, Kevin Hannam, Peter Merriman and Mimi Sheller. London: Routledge.

Alvesson, Mats and Kaj Sköldberg. 2000. *Reflexive Methodology: New Vistas for Qualitative Research*. London: Sage.

Beck, Ulrich. 2016. *The Metamorphosis of the World*. Cambridge: Polity Press.

Brinkmann, Svend. 2009. "Literatur as Qualitative Inquiry: The Novelist as Researcher." *Qualitative Inquiry* 15 (8): 1376–1394.

Büscher, Monika, John Urry and Katian Witchger. 2010. *Mobile Methods*. London: Routledge.

Canzler, Weert, Vincent Kaufmann and Sven Kesselring. 2008. *Tracing Mobilities—Towards a Cosmopolitan Perspective*, edited by Weert Canzler, Vincent Kaufmann and Sven Kesselring. Aldershot: Ashgate.

Cresswell, Tim and Peter Merriman. 2011. *Geographies of Mobilities: Practices, Spaces, Subjects*. Farnham: Ashgate.

Denzin, Norman. 2001. "The Reflexsive Interview and a Performative Social Science." *Qualitative Research* 1 (1): 23–46.

Fischer, Frank and John Forester. 1993. *The Argumentative Turn in Policy Analysis and Planning*, edited by Frank Fischer and John Forester. Durham: Duke University Press Books.

Fischer, Frank and Herbert Gottweis. 2012. "The Argumentative Turn Revistited." In *The Argumentative Turn Revisited*, edited by Frank Fischer and Herbert Gottweis, 1–27. Durham: Duke University Press.

Flyvbjerg, Bent. 1998. *Rationality and Power: Democracy in Practice* (1st ed.). London and Chicago: University of Chicago Press.

Freudendal-Pedersen, Malene. 2009. *Mobility in Daily Life: Between Freedom and Unfreedom*. Vol. 2012. Farnham: Ashgate Publishing, Ltd.

Freudendal-Pedersen, Malene, Kevin Hannam and Sven Kesselring. 2016. "Applied Mobilities, Transitions and Opportunities." *Applied Mobilities* 1 (1): 1–9.

Graham, Steve and Simon Marvin. 2001. *Splintering Urbanism: Networked Infrastructures, Technological Mobilities and the Urban Condition*. London: Routledge.

Hannam, Kevin, Mimi Sheller and John Urry. 2006. "Editorial : Mobilities, Immobilities and Moorings." *Mobilities* 1 (1): 1–22.

Healey, Patsy. 1993. "Planning Through Debate: The Communicative Turn in Planning Theory." In *The Argumentative Turn in Policy Analysis and Planning*, edited by Frank Fischer and John Forester, 233–253. London: Duke University Press.

Kesselring, Sven. 2008. "The Mobile Risk Society." In *Tracing Mobilities*, edited by Weert Canzler, Vincent Kaufmann and Sven Kesselring, 77–102. Aldershot and Burlington: Ashgate.

Ritzer, George. 2010. *Globalization: A Basic Text*. Oxford: Wiley-Blackwell.

Sandercock, Leonie. 1999. "Expanding the 'Language' of Planning: A Meditation on Planning Education for the Twenty-First Century." *European Planning Studies* 7 (5): 545–548.

Sandercock, Leonie. 2003. "Out of the Closet: The Importance of Stories and Storytelling in Planning Practice." *Planning Theory Practice* 4 (1): 11–28.

Sheller, Mimi. 2014. "The New Mobilities Paradigm for a Live Sociology." *Current Sociology* 62 (6): 789–811.

Sheller, Mimi and John Urry. 2006. "The New Mobilities Paradigm." *Environment and Planning A* 38 (2): 207–226.

Urry, John. 2000. *Sociology Beyond Societies: Mobilities for the Twenty-First Century* (International Library of Sociology). London: Routledge.

Urry, John. 2007. *Mobilities*. Cambridge: Polity Press.

Urry, John. 2011. *Climate Change and Society*. Cambridge: Polity Press.

Part I
Moving and Pausing

2 'DING-DING-DONG'

Shifting Atmospheres in Mobilities Design

Simon Wind, Ditte Bendix Lanng, and Ole B. Jensen

Hobro Train Station, 12 September, 2014

It's early and I'm the first at the platform (Figure 2.1). The morning fog that the sun hasn't yet managed to burn away shrouds the surroundings. This endows the air with a certain feel, at the same time hot and cold, damp. When screwing up my eyes I can see tiny, almost invisible, droplets of moisture slowly bathing the platform's large concrete surfaces. The platform, sharply delineated by tracks on either side, is a composite surface, a patchwork of asphalt, concrete, tiles, dirt, and rubble, showing signs of the wear and tear of daily journeys as well as ongoing repairs and upgrades. In the center are two glazed waiting sheds and around them commercial boards, info screens, light poles, and benches populate the platform. I choose to stand underneath the extended roofing of the waiting shed trying to dodge the falling mist that dampens everything. The deserted platform, its somewhat derelict surfaces, and the misty fog encapsulate the platform in an eerie, almost unreal, ambience. The arrival of more people, especially a group of children, breaks this spell and returns me to my everyday routine of waiting for the train.

This small vignette originates from a series of auto-ethnographic everyday train commuting studies performed by the first author during the fall of 2014. The auto-ethnographic mode of inquiry is particularly powerful for engaging with the notion of atmospheres as it personally commits and attunes the researcher to the researched in multiple registers. Despite of this, the vignette illustrates that capturing and conveying atmospheric encounters in a satisfying manner is still an arduous task. We know atmospheres exist because they affectively move us, yet they are not prone to description, nor can we fully account for how they come about. Surely, the shape and feel of atmospheres is not reducible to its parts, but emerges from the complex networking of "the human bodies, discursive bodies, non-human bodies, and all other bodies that make up everyday [mobile] situations" (Anderson 2009, 80). At a place, such as the train station, atmospheres form and deform in volatile and fluid networks of travelers (in multiple modalities),

14 *Simon Wind et al.*

Figure 2.1 12 September 2014, Hobro Station, early morning
Source: Simon Wind.

trains, station sheds, newspapers, bags, tickets, mobile phones, daydreams, and many more human and non-human bodies.

We wish to advance the notion of *mobilities design*, an approach to urban design infused with theoretical and empirical insights from mobilities studies (Jensen and Lanng 2017; Jensen, Lanng, and Wind 2016). Mobilities design concerns a conceptual mobilization of fixed solidities—the designed physical environment and its architectural artifacts such as the platform, sheds, asphalt, and benches—in their specific alliances with multiple ongoing mobilities flows (Lanng 2015). Mobilities design engages in making physical spaces and architectures by invigorating 'active' artifacts (Yaneva 2009; Fallan 2008) and networked in multiple 'mobile situations' (Jensen 2013). Through this approach we get to know ubiquitous mobilities artifacts and spaces in the midst of ongoing mobilities, embedded in lived lives, and in cultural, political, and social formations. Atmospheres are key to this work, since mobilities artifacts and sites are often affectively charged, and since this charge is coproducing the specific 'active agencies' of these materialities. Atmospheres generate action, and they engender propensities and embodied dispositions that are capable of affectively priming us (Bissell 2010; Thibaud 2011). In the context of trains, Löfgren writes, "The intense and almost overpowering materiality of trains and stations shapes both modes of motion and moods of feeling" (2008, 333). However, as we also know from the emotive experiences with atmospheres we inhabit in everyday journeys, atmospheres are never fully stabile and permanent but they are themselves continuously on the move.

In the academic literature on atmospheres, there is a general consensus of understanding atmospheres as constantly in formation and deformation, either coming into focus, gaining strength, or fading away, falling apart (Anderson 2009). Indeed, Albertsen (2013, 230) evokes the concept of 'meta-atmospheres' denoting that what chiefly characterizes an atmosphere is its shifts. Böhme (1993) states that even minor changes might incite the processes of formation and deformation. Sometimes this happens abruptly and instantaneously, and at other times it happens gradually. Returning to the auto-ethnographic account of waiting for the train, we will try to explicate this shifting nature of atmospheres.

The Event of DING-DING-DONG

The loudspeakers at the station suddenly burst into life: "DING-DING-DONG!" This sound stops everything: The children's chatter drops, people take out their ear pods and look up into the air as if someone would peek out from the fog and speak to them. Within the next few seconds, not more than two at the most, thoughts are racing through my head: Is MY train late?, how late?, will I make it to work? However, it's not only my mind which is at work, my body is also priming itself, bracing for impact, slightly raised heartbeat, my ear directed towards the speaker to hear better, my face probably shows involuntary signs of worry, raised eye-brows and wrinkles in the forehead. At this very moment the platform is charged with an intense suspense—everybody at the station is affected by it, there is no escape, even the service worker collecting garbage has stopped and is glancing around. "The incoming train to Aalborg will be a few minutes delayed . . . (repeat) . . .,"

16   *Simon Wind et al.*

a man's voice announces twice. A collective sigh goes through the platform. It is unclear whether it is a sigh of relief or annoyance.

Arrival of the Train

A few minutes later the tracks start to hum. This signals the arrival of the train. People around me look up from their phones and newspapers; the group of children is called to attention by their teachers stating the train is coming. Everything is coming to life now, movements spread across the people at the station, the background hum of waiting is shifting, as people are starting to huddle together facing towards the tracks. At first slowly, picking up their things, securing phones in pockets, checking their bags, some run to sign in at the travel card reader. Concurrently the train's white headlights start to burn through the fog and the high-pitched singing of the tracks gradually drowns in the deep hum of the train's diesel engines and the shrieking and metal grinding sound of the breaks kicking in. I move within the crowd, squeezing past a couple of people trying to negotiate a better position. In collective movements we follow the train doors until they finally come to a halt. The children are clearly excited of getting on board the train, and we, the regular commuters, are anxious to get in before them. As the doors open with a hydraulic hiss followed by a metal clonk sound, the tension that has been gradually building at the platform is released.

The first event demonstrates an abrupt stirring of the atmosphere as the DING-DING-DONG sound in the announcement system cuts through the chatter on the platform. Everybody familiar with travel on the Danish Railways recognizes this sound and its ominous premonition of future events. This sound alone instantaneously and aggressively shifts the atmosphere, which is evident by the forceful affective impact it has on people at the platform.

The event of the arriving train, on the other hand, is an example of the slow gradual transition of the atmosphere. Whereas the DING-DING-DONG was unexpected, although easily recognizable, the arrival of the train is a sure-fire event. The arriving train, with its sensorial spectacle of sounds, lights, symbols, and movements, effectively stirs up the affective landscape of the platform. Surely, the arrival of a train has somewhat lost its magnificence and grandeur of old times, but still when the train arrives one cannot avoid being affected by its size, mass, its forceful and controlled deceleration brutally changing the platform space and pushing aside several other bodies significant for the atmosphere which was felt just before. Boredom, suspense, anticipation with anxiety, relief, and excitement is replaced. Indeed, as we are gathering in front of the train doors, "the atmosphere on the platform shifts from the lull of waiting, to a more competitive and aggressive mode" (O'Dell 2009, 90).

The arrival of the train is predictable, it is the event that all people of the station is waiting for to occur, and hence, the atmosphere is always changing towards this event, like a pulse or a rhythm, intensifying as the time grows near, people entering at the platform, the humming of the tracks, the lights, the train moving in the distance to the opening of the doors. All these bodies contribute to the accumulation of affective intensity in the atmosphere of "nervous energy" (Löfgren 2008, 338) as it circulates at the station. Hence, this mundane train station is not a neatly aligned social space, rather it is a site of "multiple overlapping journeys" (Bissell 2010, 275) in which the constant flows of mobile bodies of commuters, children, workers, bikes, cars, buses, trains and so on, physically and socially disturb the mobile situation and any attempt to coagulate atmospheres.

Concluding Remarks

Mobilities design works to extend form-giving capacities beyond inert matter. We find that to design a physical environment like a train platform is to engage in a processual, composite network; it is form-giving and an organization of volatile and affectively charged materials. Shifting atmospheres, as those on the platform in Hobro, highlight the affective performance of mundane mobilities artifacts and spaces in specific alliances with networked socio-material bodies. Thus, they demonstrate the urgency to revive and renegotiate these spaces beyond minimum functional standards and beyond the privileging of vision in much design.

We have in this chapter sought to explore these ephemeral phenomena through auto-ethnography. This methodical infrastructure has through active and embodied participation allowed us to gain a glimpse of an affective realm and its emotive efficacy that emerges in the socio-material mobile situation. Surely, it is not possible to fully grasp these shifting atmospheres through an auto-ethnographic inquiry alone, and hence other methods might too prove effective or provide other perspectives. Our contribution in this chapter is thus an evocative call for methodological experimentation and inquiry into shifting atmospheres that aims at cultivating novel insight and foresight into the ways in which artifacts and spaces take part in staging affective embodied mobile ways of life.

References

Albertsen, Niels. 2013. "Atmosfærernes by: Fænomenologi i bystudiet." In *Fænomenologi—teorier og metoder*, edited by Bjørn Schiermer, 215–241. Copenhagen: Hans Reitzel.

Anderson, Ben. 2009. "Affective Atmospheres." *Emotion, Space and Society* 2 (2): 77–81. Elsevier.

Bissell, David. 2010. "Passenger Mobilities: Affective Atmospheres and the Sociality of Public Transport." *Environment and Planning* D 28: 270–289.

Böhme, Gernot. 1993. "Atmosphere as the Fundamental Concept of a New Aesthetics." *Thesis Eleven* 36 (1): 113–126.

18 *Simon Wind et al.*

Fallan, Kjetil. 2008. "Architecture in Action: Traveling with Actor-Network Theory in the Land of Architectural Research." *Architectural Theory Review* 31 (1): 80–96.

Jensen, Ole B. 2013. *Staging Mobilities*. London and New York: Routledge.

Jensen, Ole B. and Ditte B. Lanng. 2017. *Mobilities Design: Urban designs for Mobile Situations*. Abingdon: Routledge.

Jensen, Ole B., Ditte B. Lanng and Simon Wind. 2016. "Mobilities Design—Towards a Research Agenda for Applied Mobilities Research." *Applied Mobilities* 1 (1): 26–42.

Lanng, Ditte B. 2015. "Gesturing Entangled Journeys: Mobilities Design in Aalborg East, Denmark." PhD thesis, Aalborg University.

Löfgren, Orvar. 2008. "Motion and Emotion: Learning to be a Railway Traveller." *Mobilities* 3 (3): 331–351.

O'Dell, Tom. 2009. "My Soul for a Seat: Commuting and the Routines of Mobility." In *Time, Consumption and Everyday Life: Practice, Materiality and Culture*, edited by Elizabeth Shove, Frank Trentmann and Richard Wilk, 85–98. Oxford: Berg.

Thibaud, Jean. 2011. "The Sensory Fabric of Urban Ambiances." *Senses and Society* 6 (2): 203–215.

Yaneva, Albena. 2009. "Making the Social Hold: Towards an Actor-Network Theory of Design." *Design and Culture* 1 (3): 273–288.

3 The Final Countdown

Ambiguities of Real Time Information Systems 'Directing' the Waiting Experience in Public Transport

Robin Kellermann

Waiting truly belongs to the greatly overlooked practices of everyday life. Among the many fields enforcing waiting times, transportation and mobility certainly account for the most prominent generators. Unlike hardly any other domain, transportation systems permanently induce spatial, temporal, and organizational constraints that cause passengers to be stilled temporarily in situations of waiting *for* transportation or *while* moving.

Despite the phenomenon's centrality for the transit experience, explicit research on waiting in the transport and mobility context for the longest time remained a surprisingly unchallenged and trivialized subject. Concealed by a predominant attention for *moving* or *active* subjects, waiting phenomena have rather been treated implicitly in terms of a tacit enemy, regarded as an imperative to be defeated by all means. As a result, we still know remarkably little about the evolution of passengers' in-transit experiences such as waiting in pre-trip situations at stops or stations, particularly regarding the ambiguous ways in which digitalization and information technologies actively change such experiences. Thus, despite a recently growing strand of pioneering studies triggered by the 'mobility turn,' waiting, as Harold Schweizer summarizes, remains a "temporal region hardly mapped and badly documented" (Schweizer 2008, 1).

This chapter questions how passengers' waiting experiences in public transportation have changed in the light of digitalization and the information age. Referring exemplarily to the deployment of real time information systems (RTIS) at stops and stations, I argue for a historically novel quality of the waiting experience induced by such systems with the result of 'taming' the wait, but at the same time creating a number of ambiguities and negative rebound effects. More precisely, I argue that we are witnessing the phenomenon's informational transformation towards what may be termed 'directed waiting,' illustrating an increase of supplementary technologies facilitating the wait *for* public transportation and providing a literal sense of today's urban mobilities' genuinely networked characteristic.

Approaching the novelty as well as the ambiguities of 'directed waiting,' in a first step a brief literature review on empirical studies targeting passengers' perceptual responses to RTIS will provide a basic understanding of the

20 *Robin Kellermann*

phenomenon's psychological and cognitive magnitude. Reflecting on those empirical findings, in a second step I will follow a hypothetical approach by providing four speculative assessments regarding ambiguous side effects prompted by the arrival of new information technologies in public transport waiting environments.

Engaging with passengers in the state of waiting derives from two motivations. First, thematic attention to moments of stoppage or immobility is believed to be an inevitable approach in following a relational and holistic understanding of mobilities (Sheller and Urry 2006). Second, the identification of the role technologies play in presently changing the transit experience and generating benefiting (or limiting) perceptual qualities is believed to form a needful approach in order to understand the ways in which urban mobilities are experienced presently.

The views presented here are part of a broader research project aiming to understand the historical evolution of transport-induced waiting experiences in different transport modes since the mid-nineteenth century with analytical focus on the transformative coevolution of physical environments and social practices of waiting. Consequently, this chapter also aims to encourage mobility scholars to focus thematically on formerly overlooked aspects of everyday life mobility that might appear mundane or trivial but form a fundamental aspect of the mobility experience.

Waiting Phenomena as Objects of Research

Since the 1970s, social psychology was spearheading the analysis of people in either enforced or voluntary states of queuing and waiting. Therein, waiting formations were examined as paradigmatic expressions for the social organization of access, as results of social inequalities (Schwartz 1975) as well as for comprising qualities of 'embryonic social systems' (Mann 1969). As a main outcome, time distribution in service reception was found to be strongly asymmetric (Schwartz 1974), facilitating the acceleration of specific groups for the price of decelerating others. More important, to wait, especially *before* receiving a service, was most often considered a tedious waste of time (Dubé, Schmitt, and Leclerc 1989), and, from psychological perspectives, was consistently supposed to be a source for affective responses such as stress, anger, and uncertainty (Osuna 1985; Taylor 1994).

However, beyond numerous verifications of waiting's preponderant negative connotation, interim pausing of flow was also considered to play a complementary organizational role for the provision of transport. Whereas waiting for a bus on the personal level might often appear a routine charged with negative attributions, on a more abstract level it has been claimed a functional necessity and a required precondition for the organization of mobility and speed. In this sense, any kind of motion depends relationally upon spatial fixities and the organizational need of pre-structuring passengers, resulting in physical 'moorings' (Urry 2003), and, as I would complement, temporal 'moorings' in which passengers appear to be exposed (and tied) to other temporalities.

In recent years remarkable pioneering studies have revealed the social, experiential, and bodily complexities of waiting (Bissell 2007; Bissell and Fuller 2011; Vannini 2011; Vozyanov 2014), thus challenging the dominant narrative of *mobile* and *active* mobilities as the more desirable relations to the world (Bissell 2007). Hence, though waiting has been traditionally treated as the "neglected Achilles heel of modernity" (ibid., 277), we are witnessing growing awareness that moments of relative immobility, stasis, or friction (Cresswell 2014) not only represent mobility's inseparable twin, but form complex corporeal phenomena and active processes. As a result, the current research continuously emphasizes conceptualizing waiting as *congenital* and *inherent* to movement (Adey 2006; Cresswell 2012). Against this backdrop, I focus now on how information technologies actually changed the waiting experience by using the example of RTIS at public transport facilities.

Real Time Information Systems (RTIS) and the Rise of 'Directed Waiting'

RTIS are telematic-based public transport information systems that may include both predictions about arrival and departure times, estimated waiting time, and information about the nature and causes of disruption (Figure 3.1). Several studies have explored their effects on the customer and RTIS implementation has been claimed to have overwhelmingly positive effects for both passengers and providers (Infopolis2 1998; BMBF 2002; Sekara and Karlsson 1997; Dziekan and Kottenhoff 2007; Chow, Block-Schachter, and Hickey 2014). Subsuming these findings, the evolution of stops and stations forming dynamic informational spaces can be claimed to have drastically reshaped and mediated the waiting experience. From a long-term perspective, RTIS's beneficial implications of increased certainty, situational control, and processual knowledge can be considered a seminal moment in the history of passenger experiences, which in fact has seen reasonable levels of available information by the provision of timetables but has seen a rather constantly low level of *real time* information. Since affective responses to and assessments of waiting are strongly dependent on frequent information, RTIS, as well as passengers' mobile devices, presently fill informational gaps which previously couldn't be filled adequately by psychologically limited or even insufficient capabilities of 'static' media such as conventional paper timetables. Instead, RTIS can compensate for the absence of loudspeaker announcements in the majority of smaller waiting environments. As a consequence, today the waiting passenger might still find similar environments but he is well *informed* and—more unbound from uncertainties—is supposed to be liberated to do other things while waiting. Passengers receive assistance, regain control, and are not left alone any

22 *Robin Kellermann*

Figure 3.1 'Directed waiting'—real time information system at a Berlin bus stop
Source: Robin Kellermann.

longer, thus facilitating an atmosphere of 'directed waiting' in which waiting times have been tamed and orchestrated, and might even become a friendlier part of the journey.

Speculations and Ambiguities of 'Directed Waiting'

Despite a quantifiable increase in certainty and general trust in the system, the rise of 'directed waiting' may also imply ambiguous side effects that may relativize the celebratory promises of information and communication technologies in the realm of public transport facilities. Here are four critical speculations:

1) Reinforcing the Otherness of Waiting

When time is displayed on screens it is also the time value that is displayed, and more precisely for the case of stops and stations, the value of time *lost*. Thereby, a prevailing perception of waiting as a waste of time—sustained implicitly by RTIS deployment—might reinforce the otherness of waiting as the 'stepchild of mobility,' which by far is too narrow and simplistic. Despite customers' appreciation of RTIS, such technologies might entail the effects of confirming and complicating an already questionable temporal culture of Western societies—centered on time efficiency, speed, and linearity—and might foster growing opposition towards its temporal niches instead of incorporating different temporalities more innovatively. RTIS implementation in transport environments—driven by unilateral 'productivist' perceptions of waiting as an incriminatory obligation—may abet and sustain traditional modernist notions of "quiescing time, in effect to silence it" (Bissell 2007, 278), and thus miss the actual relevance of recognizing the heterogeneous natures of waiting as a 'meaningful experience' (Gasparini 1995).

2) Increased Time Sensibility and New Dependencies

Despite RTIS's evident effect of reducing perceived wait times, the 'informational turn' in *directing* the wait might—in the long run—increase passengers' time sensibility due to amplified centrality, visibility, and thus tangibility of time regimes which are materializing in such systems. In this vein, RTIS and the rise of 'directed waiting' for some may reappraise waiting time as a 'temporal friend,' while for others it may become another field of increased time presence, implicit time pressure, and system contingency, especially in cases where the indicated arrival time doesn't correspond to the operational reality and leaves passengers with feelings of deception. Dziekan and Kottenhoff (2007) pointed out the probability that after a while people may grow accustomed to the new actual and perceived time savings with the consequence that "it becomes more difficult to meet their needs and expectations" in the near future. Hence, the continuous fight for minutes and seconds might turn out to be "a losing battle for the public transport industry" (ibid., 499) and opens the question of when transport operators will have reached the 'marginal utility' of fighting waiting time. Additionally, sinking trust in the correctness of displayed waiting times can easily lead to psychological rebound effects that increase or become the actual source of evoking negative affective responses to the service provision.

3) Dislocating the Wait and Diffusion in Activities

Instead of just going to the stop, passengers spent considerable amounts of time for loading apps, typing, searching, etc., in order to not have to wait at the actual point of departure. Hence, pre-trip planning via Internet for the aim of reducing actual waiting time at stops or stations might turn out to be a zero-sum game in the light of the actual time spent organizing the journey. What is believed to increase travel efficiency might rather be considered a mere relocation of waiting into other environments or its translation into other activities.

24   *Robin Kellermann*

4) Lack of (Creative) Interstices

Within the technological race for time and travel efficiency we might diminish our invaluable ability to employ temporary discontinuities for the creative power of 'doing nothing' (Ehn and Löfgren 2010). According to social psychologist George Herbert Mead, discontinuities are indispensable for experiencing our reality. "Without this break within continuity," he argued, "continuity would be inexperienceable" (Mead 1929, 239). In this respect, we might be on the verge of forfeiting the ability to be patient as an important virtue of a person's cultural equipment (Gasparini 1995). Instead, RTIS technology may generate a new imperative for activities other than waiting (e.g. shopping) and might reduce opportunities for the socio-psychological needs of self-reflection or mere contemplation.

Concluding Remarks

This article critically addressed the connection between information technologies and passengers' in-transit experiences through recognizing an 'informational turn' in waiting experiences induced by real time information systems (RTIS) at stops and stations. Arguing for a historically novel quality of such 'directed waiting' experiences generated by the increase of supplementary technologies facilitating the wait, systems like RTIS—informing passengers about live departure and arrival times—have been widely appreciated by passengers for reducing perceived wait time and mediating positive psychological effects. Real time information—if reliable (!) and in complementary addition to personalized services on, for example, smart phones—reduces uncertainty and liberates the passenger to do other things while waiting, thus 'taming' the wait seminally.

However, on the other side, the rise of 'directed waiting' entails ambiguous side and negative rebound effects. Through extensive implementation of RTIS we might miss conceptualizing the temporal region of waiting beyond prevailing considerations of a 'stepchild of mobility' or a dreadful period. Instead, RTIS's final countdown logic might in the long run—once more increase overall time sensibility, dislocate waiting into other areas, or even diminish the psychologically and culturally necessitated ability to wait uninformed and creatively (Figure 3.2). Despite a modernist vision of eliminating the temporal region of waiting, it will yet remain mobility's twin and will remain an anthropological constant. It is thus up for debate when we will have reached the 'marginal utility' of fighting waiting time and—seen through the lens of the temporal region of waiting—it might thus be up for debate to think about time use differently.

Moreover, this chapter has called for focusing thematically on the forgotten aspects of everyday life, illustrated by the sociotechnical and psychological peculiarities of the waiting passenger. Stipulated by the mobility turn's impulse for assertive considerations of experiences, usage, and mobility

Figure 3.2 RTIS's final countdown logic
Source: Robin Kellermann.

practices, waiting is believed to be a fruitful approach, both for an empirical understanding of networked urban mobilities as well as for the theoretical exploration of the dialectics of movement and immobility.

References

Adey, Peter. 2006. "If Mobility Is Everything Then It Is Nothing: Towards a Relational Politics of (Im)mobilities." *Mobilities* 1 (1): 75–94.
Bissell, David. 2007. "Animating Suspension: Waiting for Mobilities." *Mobilities* 2 (2): 277–298.
Bissell, David and Gilian Fuller. 2011. *Stillness in a Mobile World*. Milton Park: Routledge.
BMBF. 2002. *Mobility in Conurbations—First Results*. Bonn: Federal Ministry of Education and Research (BMBF).
Chow, William, David Block-Schachter and Samuel Hickey. 2014. "Impacts of Real-Time Passenger Information Signs in Rail Stations at the Massachusetts Bay Transportation Authority." *Transportation Research Record: Journal of the Transportation Research Board* 2419: 1–10.
Cresswell, Tim. 2012. "Mobilities II: Still." *Progress in Human Geography* 35 (5): 645–653.

Cresswell, Tim. 2014. "Friction." In *The Routledge Handbook of Mobilities*, edited by Peter Adey, David Bissell, Kevin Hannam, Peter Merriman and Mimi Sheller, 107–115. Milton Park: Routledge.

Dubé, Laurette, Bernd H. Schmitt and France Leclerc. 1989. "Consumers' Reactions to Waiting: When Delays Affects the Perception of Service Quality." *Advances in Consumer Research* 16: 112–125.

Dziekan, Katrin and Karl Kottenhoff. 2007. "Dynamic at-Stop Real-Time Information Displays for Public Transport: Effects on Customers." *Transportation Research Part A* 41: 489–501.

Ehn, Billy and Orvar Löfgren. 2010. *The Secret World of Doing Nothing*. Berkeley: University Press of California.

Gasparini, Giovanni. 1995. "On Waiting." *Time & Society* 4 (1): 29–45.

Infopolis2. 1998. "Review of Current Passenger Information Systems (Deliverable 1)." Commission of the European Community.

Mann, Leon. 1969. "Queue Culture: The Waiting Line as a Social System." *American Journal for Sociology* 75 (3): 340–354.

Mead, George Herbert. 1929. "The Nature of the Past." In *Essays in Honour of John Dewey*, edited by John Cross, 235–242. New York: Henry Hall.

Osuna, Edgar Elias. 1985. "The Psychological Cost of Waiting." *Journal of Mathmetical Psychology* 29: 82–105.

Schwartz, Barry. 1974. "Waiting, Exchange, and Power: The Distribution of Time in Social Systems." *American Journal of Sociology* 79 (4): 841–870.

Schwartz, Barry. 1975. *Queuing and Waiting: Studies in the Social Organization of Access and Delay*. Chicago: University of Chicago Press.

Schweizer, Harold. 2008. *On Waiting*. London: Routledge.

Sekara, Vaso and Mari Anne Karlsson. 1997. *A Field Evaluation of Real-Time Information at Tram and Bus Stops. Part 2*. Gothenburg: Traffic & Public Transport Authority City of Gothenburg.

Sheller, Mimi and John Urry. 2006. "The New Mobilities Paradigm." *Environment and Planning A* 38 (2): 207–226.

Taylor, Shirley. 1994. "Waiting for Service: The Relationship Between Delays and Evaluations of Service." *Journal of Marketing* 58 (2): 56–69.

Urry, John. 2003. *Global Complexity*. Cambridge: Polity Press.

Vannini, Phillip. 2011. "Mind the Gap: The Tempo Rubato of Dwelling in Lineups." *Mobilities* 6 (2): 273–299.

Vozyanov, Andrey. 2014. "Approaches to Waiting in Mobility Studies: Utilization, Conceptualization, Historicizing." *Mobility in History* 5 (1): 64–73.

4 Bus Stops Matter

An Ethnography of the Experience of Physical Activity and the Bus Stop Design

Anne Victoria

Bus stop consolidation measures assert that bus users will not have to wait long at the bus stop. These initiatives are becoming more common within transit agencies as an economical way to increase vehicular efficiency and passenger ridership. The goal is for *on-time* performance, which means buses arrive and depart on schedule. This wait is in relation to active transportation, which refers to any form of travel that is non-motorized, such as walking, and which many consider a reasonable way for everyone to meet the daily recommended physical activity (Pate et al. 1995). Studies have estimated that public transit users, compared to those who depend on a car, walk 30% more steps (Besser and Dannenberg 2005; Lachapelle 2010). Therefore, bus users appear most likely to meet the recommended daily activity. My research investigated whether the design of the bus stop is becoming less valued because users do not have to wait long and know exactly where the bus stops will be and, in that case, whether they are less likely to meet national recommendations (Victoria 2014a). The findings of that study showed that the bus stop design strongly contributes to the experience of active transportation. In this chapter I will focus on a predictive health perspective from my research on public transportation and research on the relation between mobilities and health to inspire the design of a better bus stop.

Being There

I chose participant observation and collected 26 in-depth interviews to examine the bus users' experiences of getting to, waiting at, and using multiple bus stops (Hutchinson 2000; Bissell 2007). I acquired insight to the bus users' experience by taking part in their everyday activities—talking with and observing people while they rode the bus, waited for the bus, boarded the bus, or after they alighted the bus. At the same time, the Knoxville Area Transit in Knoxville, Tennessee, was implementing a bus stop consolidation program. I intersected that event with the international appeal for active transportation. By collecting data from the insider's point of view or from the bus users who actually experience the event, I came to see the movement of walking through the lens of predictive health and argued that traditional health measurements for active transportation such as cardiovascular fitness and energy expenditure for weight loss do not capture the importance of a bench in *being there* for the bus, whereas predictive health indicators, such as dependent edema, shoulder joint dysfunction, and weather effects, do. This examination on the relationship of the armatures to movement provides a more complete health profile.

Armatures in Relation to Lived Moment

Mobilities research has examined the in-between places and structures associated with movement (Jensen 2009, 2015). These armatures of mobility are networked: with potential social meaning and practices, a lived movement that is also bodily sensed. In the sense that a bus stop—a meeting/stopping place—is the point where a pedestrian becomes a passenger, permission to care for oneself has been underappreciated in transit planning.

Therefore, attention could be directed away from a technocratic approach as an *on-time* performance to the lived experience of the individual bus users in the everyday process of navigating the bus stop (Figure 4.1). I came to

Figure 4.1 Bus user walking to the bus stop identified by the white sign on the pole, far right

Source: Anne Victoria.

see the lived movement of predictive health in the form of functional health. Functional health can be defined as the structure and function of muscles *and* joints in conjunction with the ability to perform activities of daily living or the *maintenance* of the physical condition of muscles and joints. Therefore, actual poorer health may result in the form of shoulder joint dysplasia (carrying packages), weather effects (cold, heat, and rain), and fatigue (standing). Furthermore, the outcomes often covertly accumulate in small doses over an extended period of time rather than in one acute incident. This scenario is similar to the way in which some medical practices have begun to look at and treat low back pain. The implication is that the result has an impact on all ages and may not seem to matter if the bus user was initially in a state of good or bad health. Therefore, a valid marker of future health would measure shoulder strain and the effects of weather and standing.

Ten Minutes Is a Long Time to Wait

Although the buses now connect to each bus stop with more reliable on-time performance, bus riders often must wait five to ten minutes before boarding. Without amenities, such as benches or shelters, the decision to maneuver to a bus stop is bodily felt as *weighted*. This composite of the lived mobility is similar to how the body is examined as both an object of study as well as the focal point of experiencing the natural world (Csordas 1994, 2011). For example, Victoria (2014b) applied a gendered perspective to understand moving to the bus stop and waiting at the bus stop. The thematic descriptions of *holding on* and *wearing down* show that men and women experience bodily senses differently and suggested the value of armatures and structures to personal health. The lived mobility is in contrast to the numbers valued by transit planners' technocratic viewpoint. There is a difference in meaning of *buses will be on time*, as in bus stop consolidation, and the bus user *times herself exactly* before the next bus, as in the following scenario where an interviewee responds to the question on how they prepare for their day by pointing out that:

> I time myself exactly seven minutes before the arrival of the next bus. Then I leave my place. [I] don't want to be [outside] long because it may be hot, humid or rainy plus there is nowhere to sit; so, I leave just those one to two minutes extra because [I] may be held up by the traffic light, waiting to cross.

The first viewpoint, *buses will be on time*, sends a message that amenities do not matter and the latter perception, *times herself exactly*, indicates a bench and a shelter certainly do matter. There is a reaction—not to stand and wait—to get out there *just at the right time*. The experience of mobility is sensed as *wearing down* because the cumulative effect of even brief waits outside wears the body down (Figure 4.2).

Figure 4.2 Bus users waiting at the bus stop
Source: Anne Victoria.

Concluding Remarks

My study explored a different perspective of walking and health; focusing on the armatures in relation to movement demonstrates the multiple and interconnected ways that a bus stop can be experienced. This attention makes visible a more effective active transportation program. Otherwise, while a program might appear to succeed, actual better health may not be obtained. Several recommendations are noted. First, use language that expresses the bodily ability to maintain mobility. Networked mobilities introduce human agency into everyday health behavior or the permission to care for oneself. Second, add functional health to transport performance. Measuring functional health can be a valid register of social justice. Last, require standard structures to all bus stops. Minimal structural requirements, such as a shelter and bench, even if the bus user only has to wait ten minutes at each bus stop, discourage bus users from experiencing a weakened physical state. They encourage the maintenance of good health and sends a message that bus stops matter.

References

Besser, Lilah M. and Andrew L. Dannenberg. 2005. "Walking to Public Transit: Steps to Help Meet Physical Activity Recommendations." *American Journal of Preventive Medicine* 29 (4): 273–280.

Bissell, David. 2007. "Animating Suspension: Waiting for Mobilities." *Mobilities* 2 (2): 277–298.

Csordas, Thomas. 1994. *Embodiment and Experience: The Existential Ground of Culture and Self*. Cambridge, England: Cambridge University Press.

Csordas, Thomas. 2011. "Cultural Phenomenology." In *A Companion to the Anthropology of the Body and Embodiment*, edited by Frances E. Mascia-Lees, 137–156. Oxford, England: Wiley-Blackwell.

Hutchinson, Sikivu. 2000. "Waiting for the Bus." *Social Text* 18 (2): 107–120.

Jensen, Ole B. 2009. Flows of Meaning, Cultures of Movements—Urban Mobility as Meaningful Everyday Life Practice." *Mobilities* 4 (1): 139–158.

Jensen, Ole B. 2015. *Staging Mobilities/Designing Mobilities*. London: Routledge.

Lachapelle, Ugo. 2010. "Public Transit Use as a Catalyst for an Active Lifestyle: Mechanisms, Predispositions and Hindrances." PhD diss., University of British Columbia.

Pate, Russell R., Michael Pratt, Steven N. Blair, William L. Haskell, Caroline A. Macera, Claude Bouchard, David Buchner, Walter Ettinger, Gregory W. Heath, Abby C. King, Andrea Kriska, Arthur S. Leon, Bess H. Marcus, Jeremy Morris, Ralph S. Paffenbarger Jr., Kevin Patrick, Michael L. Pollock, James M. Rippe, James Sallis, and Jack H. Wilmore. 1995. "Physical Activity and Public Health: A Recommendation from the Centers for Disease Control and Prevention and the American College of Sports Medicine." *Journal of American Medical Association* 273 (5): 402–407.

Victoria, Anne. 2014a. "Bus Stop Matters." In International Association for the History of Transport, Traffic and Mobility, 12th Annual Conference, Spinoffs of Mobility: Technology, Risk and Innovation (Archived).

Victoria, Anne. 2014b. "Bus Stop Matters: Exploring the Gendered Perspective of Functional Health." In *5th International Conference on Women's Issues in Transportation*, 403–412. Washington, DC: Transportation Research Board.

5 Solid Urban Mobilities
Buses, Rhythms, and Communities

Katrine Hartmann-Petersen

Many important analyses of mobilities in urban life are analyzed in relation to issues such as postmodern lifestyles, urban planning, and sustainable praxis. In this chapter, I approach this subject from a less commonly used perspective: I'm telling positive stories about the use of buses in the city. Identifying the bus as a moving anchor in a lot of people's everyday lives, we learn about networks, rhythms, and variations in urban life. Understanding these optimistic elements of networked urban mobilities can generate not only new developments but also ambitious future mobile urban planning. Many citizens (mainly car drivers and cyclists) have an opinion about buses and bus transport in everyday life. For many people, buses are uncomfortable, slow, and force you to sit far too close to other passengers than is often comfortable—they are low status. But stories from both passengers and drivers *also* show that the bus works as a moving community, connecting the multiple dots that everyday life consists of (Hartmann-Petersen 2009).

In Copenhagen, one of the backbones of the city's mobility infrastructure is the 5A bus route. It is the busiest route in Denmark, having 65,000 passengers daily. It travels between the northwestern part of Copenhagen, through the city center, and then on to the airport in the southeastern area. This specific bus route has an iconic standing among many Copenhageners—whether they use it or not. The outset for the chapter is a research project mainly focusing on flexibility and volatility (Sennett 1998) in the everyday lives of bus drivers (Drewes Nielsen et al. 2010). The theoretical outset—and the gateway into understanding the role of the buses in urban life—stems from this project that methodologically builds upon qualitative in-depth interviews (Kvale 1996), focus groups (Halkier 2010), and an action research approach (Nielsen and Svensson 2004). In this chapter, I mainly draw empirically on a radio montage made by the Danish Broadcasting Corporation (DR 2015). The radio montage collects stories from the 5A bus line in order to show what experiences and perceptions of urbanity passengers and bus drivers have. I quote the anonymous passengers who tell the reporter how they sense traveling with the bus, and how they feel like an integral part of urban life by using this mode of transport.

Fluidity in Urban Life

According to Bauman's (2005, 2006) notion on liquidity, late modern individuals are integrated into liquid everyday lives. The characteristics of modernity have been the disintegration or corrosion (Sennett 1998) of solid and predictable conditions. Bauman claims that the disintegration of solid structures leads to de-institutionalization at multiple societal levels. He argues that this is an inevitable consequence of individualization:

> now, as before—in the fluid and light as much as in the solid and heavy stage of modernity—individualization is a fate, not a choice. In the land of individual freedom of choice the option to escape individualization and to refuse participation in the individualizing game is emphatically not on the agenda.
>
> (Bauman 2006, 34)

With this interpretation of the metaphor of liquid modernity in mind, it is important to focus on the implied notion that liquid relations and 'ties' are only temporary. Bauman indicates that they will re-configure and solidify over time. However, this leaves us with the open question of how these radical changes take shape. How will these 'fluids' become 'solid'?

The main argument in this chapter is that the bus is a kind of moving 'solid' structure to many citizens in urbanity. Things happen in the bus—things are going on in the bus. Traveling by bus, we are part of a networked urban mobile system that is more than just a means of getting from A to B (Urry 2000, 2007; Hannam et al. 2006; Freudendal-Pedersen 2009; Hartmann-Petersen 2009).

In the following, I suggest that the 5A bus in Copenhagen seems to reflect the interconnectedness between the city and its citizens in at least three different relations: *rhythms* in the bus, *community* in the bus, and *connecting the dots* within the bus.

Rhythms in the Bus

Listening to the passengers' anecdotes, we hear a lot about urban rhythms related to time, to seasons, to life stages, and to specific areas, etc. In mobilities research, rhythms of mobilities have been increasingly investigated (Lefebvre 2004; Simpson 2008; Creswell 2010; Edensor 2010a, 2010b; Edensor 2011). Urban life is interconnected with multiple rhythms and these rhythms also influence the bus journey. The passengers—as well as the drivers—perceive the bus window as the screen through which they sense multiple urban rhythms (Hartmann-Petersen 2009).

In the radio montage, a female artist talks about the way she recognizes the city's plurality on the bus journey and how it inspires her art: "I'm inspired by diversities. Certain places in urban space have certain colors.

34   Katrine Hartmann-Petersen

When the light falls across a wall, I suddenly see corrosion or moss that I can recreate [in my art]." She also considers the bus as a solid marker and a silent witness to her personal life through the years:

> My personal life has—for better or worse—been taking place in and around the bus. Starting from the time where I had small kids and we were a nuclear family. Continuing to the point where my marriage broke up and we became a 'part time family.' I also go to work every day on this bus.

Another passenger, a middle-aged male, loves to observe the differences as the bus moves throughout the city. He studies the rhythms related to cultures:

> Culture-wise, this bus line is very mixed. It is so different whether you enter the bus in the northern part of the route or in the southern part. By Kastrup [south] there are a lot of school kids and people working in the airport. Here at Norrebro [further north] it is much more mixed ethnically. Here we have shops selling gold and kebab joints.

A student observes urban changes through the bus window and relates differently to the bus journey depending on time of day:

> If a billboard has been moved or a lamppost is bent, I see it. When it is dark at night, it is not that interesting to be staring out of the window. Then I only see myself—blue eyes, brown hair and maybe a little beard [laugh].

Community on the Bus

Another perspective of the bus, as a moving solid structure in urban space, is in the stories of the bus as platform for community engagement (Freudendal-Pedersen and Hartmann-Petersen 2006). The passengers often interact in numerous ways. In the radio montage, a retired woman says:

> If a young mum with a baby carriage wants to enter I help her. Except from [the joy of] helping her, it also reminds me of my own time as a young mum when I went with the bus alone and needed help from other passengers. That's the way my thoughts turn [when going by bus].

A young woman talks about her meeting with the bus authorities in an unexpected way:

> It was Christmas day and there were no other passengers on the big bus. I almost felt that I was in a major taxi. I snap-chatted [to my friends]

that I was alone on this big Christmas bus. Then I came across the funniest YouTube video that I had ever seen. I was sitting there in my own world laughing out loud. And then suddenly a man tapped my shoulder asking what I was laughing at. I offered to show him the video. And then we watched the video together guffawing. Then I suddenly looked at him and saw that it was a ticket inspector. And I had forgotten to clip.

The woman's story is an example of how people connect in unpredictable ways because they are at the same place at the same time inside the bus. Another woman tells us about a situation where the bus driver helped her buy a ticket because she misunderstood the new ticket system: "It was fantastic. He made my day. Afterwards, I felt I had an obligation to help other people that day because he helped me [in the morning]." Another way of building communities appears in this quotation from the middle-aged woman; she talks about being together while being apart: "Time in the bus gives me rest and time. I'm having a cozy time. I'm often smiling. . . . It gives me the feeling of being together [with the other passengers] and still in your own, private world."

Connecting the Dots Within the Bus

Of course the bus is literally providing a logistical service by moving the passengers from A to B in the city. But figuratively speaking, the time spent within mobilities in busy urban everyday lives are also considered as the in-between that provides a much-needed break between daily activities (Freudendal-Pedersen 2009; Jensen 2012). You can observe other people, you can daydream (Ehn and Löfgren 2010), or you can prepare yourself for the next task ahead. A passenger says:

> You can't hurry in a bus. It takes the time it takes. It is very healthy, I believe. You can think in a bus. I am sure it is good for your mental health that you are mobile and are moving in ways that you can't control. You are not in charge [in the bus].

The female artist considers the bus journey as a time for recharging her creative batteries: "It is a kind of meditation for me. I'm visualizing paintings and pictures. Maybe I'm in a state of dreaming."

In a more material, practical way, she also finds the 5A bus identifiable in order to make new routes in the city. She talks about the challenges she has when getting used to the fact her daughter moved away from home and settled in her own apartment. She finds it reassuring that her daughter still lives on the 5A line. It makes her mentally closer to home, she argues: "I'm so lucky that [the apartment] is placed next to this bus line. You only have to cross Dronning Louises Bridge—and then you are at Sophie's place."

36 *Katrine Hartmann-Petersen*

Concluding Remarks

The 5A bus passes through different neighborhoods every day, moving thousands of people around multiple urban spaces from one place to another. I have argued that the stories from the passengers show that the bus is figuratively a moving, and yet still solid, point of reference for many passengers in their everyday lives. The bus line is providing logistical, cultural, and mental meaning to the passengers by facilitating rhythms, communities, connections, and recognition in a fluid society. This also relates to Bauman's metaphor of liquidity. Not everything is liquid. The bus is an example of a structural solid in urban life.

The three aspects above overlap and more could definitely be added. Stories from a bus perspective offer an insight into mobile, urban, everyday life that additionally should inspire future planning of networked urban mobilities. On the one hand, regulating and developing mobilities systems within urban traffic has to take rational and efficient parameters into account; on the other, the perceptions above can inspire the development of methodologies and theories to understand the interconnectedness between everyday life and urban mobilities.

References

Bauman, Zygmunt. 2005. *Liquid Life*. Cambridge: Polity Press.
Bauman, Zygmunt. 2006. *Liquid Modernity*. Cambridge: Polity Press.
Creswell, Tim. 2010. "Towards a Politics of Mobility." *Environment and Planning D: Society and Space* 28: 17–31.
Danish Broadcasting Corporation (DR). 2015. "Livet I Bybussen." edited by Ane Skak and Torben Brandt. Broadcasted first time 30.05.2015. www.dr.dk/p1/livet-i-bybussen/.
Drewes Nielsen, Lise, Kurt Aagaard Nielsen, Eva Munk-Madsen and Katrine Hartmann-Petersen. 2010. *Fleksibilitet, flygtighed og frirum—en kritisk diagnose af det senmoderne arbejdsliv*. Frederiksberg: Roskilde Universitetsforlag.
Edensor, Tim. 2010a. *Geographies of Rhythm: Nature, Place, Mobilities and Bodies*. Aldershot: Ashgate.
Edensor, Tim. 2010b. "Walking in Rhythms: Place, Regulation, Style and the Flow of Experience." *Visual Studies* 25 (1): 69–79.
Edensor, Tim. 2011. "The Rhythms of Commuting." In *Mobilities: Practices, Spaces, Subjects*, edited by Tim Cresswell and Peter Merriman, 189–204. Aldershot: Ashgate.
Ehn, Billy and Orvar Löfgren. 2010. *The Secret World of Doing Nothing*. California: University of California Press.
Freudendal-Pedersen, Malene. 2009. *Mobility in Daily Life: Between Freedom and Unfreedom*. Aldershot: Ashgate.
Freudendal-Pedersen, Malene and Katrine Hartmann-Petersen. 2006. "Fællesskaber som udgangspunkt? Refleksiv mobilitet og human security i mobilitetsforskningen." *Nordisk Samhällsgeographisk tidsskrift* 41/42: 175–196.

Halkier, Bente. 2010. "Focus Groups as Social Enactments: Integrating Interaction and Content in the Analysis of Focus Group Data." *Qualitative Research* 10 (1): 71–89.

Hannam, Kevin, Mimi Sheller and John Urry. 2006. "Editorial: Mobilities, Immobilities and Moorings." *Mobilities* 1 (1): 1–22.

Hartmann-Petersen, Katrine. 2009. "I medgang og modgang. Fleksibilitet og flygtighed i buschaufførers mobile liv." PhD diss., Department of Environmental, Social and Spatial Change, Roskilde University.

Jensen, Hanne Louise. 2012. "Emotions on the Move: Mobile Emotions Among Train Commuters in the South East of Denmark." *Emotion, Space and Society* 5: 201–206.

Kvale, Steinar. 1996. *InterViews: An Introduction to Qualitative Research Interviewing*. Thousand Oaks: Sage.

Lefebvre, Henri. 2004. *Rhythmanalysis: Space, Time and Everyday Life*. London: Continuum.

Nielsen, Kurt Aagaard and Lennart Svensson. 2004. *Action and Interactive Research: A Nordic Approach*. Stockholm: Arbetslivsinstituttet.

Sennett, Richard. 1998. *The Corrosion of Character: The Personal Consequences of Work in the New Capitalism*. New York: W. W. Norton & Company.

Simpson, Paul. 2008. "Chronic Everyday Life: Rhythmanalysing Street Performance." *Social and Cultural Geography* 9 (7): 807–829.

Urry, John. 2000. *Sociology Beyond Society—Mobilities for the Twenty-First Century*. London: Routledge.

Urry, John. 2007. *Mobilities*. Cambridge: Polity Press.

6   On Social Cracks in Train Commuting

Hanne Louise Jensen

At 6:40 A.M. Trine enters the train carriage where I am sitting with Henry and Emil. She is rushing in, having made an effort to connect her two morning trains. As she arranges her bags on the luggage rack above her usual seat, Henry asks her from the other side of the aisle, "Did you remember to buy the herbal medicine for my neighbor?" Trine confirms and immediately asks, "Will you help me remember my bags?" Henry replies, "I'm sure you will remember them yourself—what's in them?" "Wine and crisps for our afternoon travel—it's the last day before the holidays that I'm sure everyone is on the 15:58 train home," Trine replies (Field notes).

Trine, Emil, and Henry are members of a group of six to ten train commuters. They meet in the same location in the train every morning, where they are almost guaranteed a seat due to the small number of fellow travelers boarding the train at the first station of the service connecting the outskirts of Zealand with Copenhagen. In the afternoon, they compete with many other fellow commuters to get the same seats as the train is crowded when leaving the capital. As is the case for many other commuter friends, they did not know each other before they started commuting on the same train. Now their relationship reaches beyond the train and into their everyday lives in their local neighborhoods. This chapter explores the inductively generated concept of *social cracks*, focusing on the potentials in train commuting that help us understand how mobile friendships develop amongst commuters who otherwise are socially diverse and live relatively segregated lives. By focusing on these social possibilities of the growing networked urban mobilities, this chapter shows the ways in which trains can become an important place for forming various types of social relations.

Inspiration and Fieldwork

To a great extent, this study is inspired by the work on car-sharing conducted by Eric Laurier and colleagues at the University of Edinburgh. They describe the car-sharing relation as "peculiar: not quite flat mate, not quite friend, not quite neighbor, nevertheless in instances exemplifying qualities associated with each" (Laurier, Brown, and Lorimer 2007, 8). This is in line

On Social Cracks in Train Commuting   39

with Malene Freudendal-Pedersen's (2009) finding that commuting time can be a valuable time between different and very busy everyday arenas—a time when it is possible to recharge and relax. It was with this in mind that I went into the field, but the life that unfolded in the trains did not fail to surprise and amaze me with regard to the abundance of diverse micro practices and their importance in the everyday lives of the commuters.

This chapter is primarily based on participatory mobile ethnographies carried out in 2010–2011 amongst commuters traveling by train on two different train services connecting the Danish capital region with its outskirts (see more on the study in Jensen 2012a, 2012b). The practice of commuting is readily accessible as a research field—it is merely a question of boarding the early morning and the late afternoon trains where the field unfolds as the train connects the commuters' homes with their work. Indeed, Bissell's (2010) call for *less hasty research styles* within the field of mobile sociology readily applies here. For two weeks I commuted with the group to which Trine, Emil, and Henry belong. They spend between 10 and 20 hours a week together on the train service connecting the seaport town Rødby with Copenhagen. Commuting and talking for hours about the banal everyday journeys caused some of the commuters participating in the research to start wondering about the particularities and qualities of the micro situations in the train, even during the periods between my meetings with them. Taking part in their commuter lives, sweating with them in the summer, drinking beer with them on Fridays, and standing or sitting on the floor with them in overcrowded train carriages gave me great insight into the bodily and social challenges and benefits of train commuting. Commuting an additional two weeks on the Kalundborg–Copenhagen service provided an opportunity for relatively short semi-structured interviews, biographical interviews, and observations. Thus, the fieldwork allowed the participants to both show and narrate to me their everyday lives on the trains.

Findings

Asked how they got to know each other, several commuters pointed to the existence of a *social crack* in situations of delay and situations of unpleasant weather. But this is not where the story starts. Knowing where the train stops and which carriage will allow them to make the fastest exit and reach their connecting train or final destination with least effort, causes most commuters to wait in almost the same spot on the departing platform every day. Often there is no interaction on the platforms, and the commuters treat each other as anonymous others during their routinized daily journey, or, in the vocabulary of Ole B. Jensen, they are *Mobile Others* (Jensen 2010b). But when a situation occurs in which they are certain to have the same opinion as their fellow commuters, a talk might be initiated. As a card-playing commuter group told me, "For months we said hey and hello and hey and hello and then something was wrong with the train—you can always talk about

40   Hanne Louise Jensen

the train and the weather—and following that we started to talk together on a regular basis" (Field notes). In this way, the routines regarding the selection of train carriage combined with the certainty of shared opinions opens a *social crack* in which it is socially acceptable to break the anonymity. Moreover, many of the talks about the train relate to disruptions in the travel time and delays; and as Ehn and Löfgren (2010) point out in their excellent work on banal everyday practices, social waiting situations increase the quality of the waiting experience compared to individual waiting situations—hence it is both socially acceptable and desirable to break the anonymity in these situations. This can be the first step in forming a much tighter social bond when you dwell within the same community of commuters every day for long periods of time—for some commuters until the end of their working lives.

Once the anonymity of the *Mobile Other* relationship is broken, it will take a great effort to reconstruct this, and it is more likely that a period will follow in which the members of the relationship can be characterized as *Mobile Acquaintances* who know a little about each other and are free to initiate a conversation on the platform or in the train. But then, as Emil tells me, "somebody starts talking and others join the conversation, then you start sitting together in the train, and from then on the ball starts rolling and you stay around the group you have found" (Field notes).

Using a term borrowed from Ole B. Jensen (2010a), the groups of commuters who purposely sit together in the train can be described as *Mobile Withs*. They are mobile with each other and often form very engaging social situations on board the train. If we look at the group of commuters from the station in Rødby through the perspective of Randall Collins (2004), part of the group's social success has to do with the bodily proximity while sitting in the train. The bodily proximity allows for successful ritual interaction, where the commuters share a mutual focus of attention as well as their moods with each other. When a train carriage contains one or more groups of *Mobile Withs*, the noise level increases as laughter and conversations are shared. And a conversation that begins within the group of *Mobile Withs* may be experienced as an invitation to non-members to participate by commenting, due to the public character of the train. The *social crack* opened by this collective effervescence can become a way of entry into an already constituted group of *Mobile Withs*.

As the relation intensifies, some commuters who commute in groups of *Mobile Withs* start to interact outside the train as well. This happened for a group of women whose interaction consisted in talking and exchanging favors like knitting patterns or slips from plants on the train. When a husband to one of the women dies a *social crack* develops. A few weeks after his death the wife did not turn up for several days, leaving the rest of the group worried; they were unable to take care of her because they did not know where she lived, nor did they know her phone number. When she finally turned up in the train again, after what turned out to be a bad flu, the women decided to exchange phone numbers and started to visit each other. When exchanging favors such as minding each other's chickens, giving each other lifts to and from the train, sending postcards, lending out holiday homes, delivering hedge plants to each other, buying herbal medicine for each other's neighbors and so forth, the commuters' social relationships change from *Mobile Withs* to *Mobile Friends*. The forming of friendships which are sustained both inside and outside of the train is a way of allowing for friendships to take up a lot of time in a busy everyday life, despite commuting for up to 20 hours a week. By turning *Mobile Withs* into *Mobile Friends* the train becomes a place where commuters can sustain and develop their friendship relations (see Jensen 2012a and 2012b for an elaboration of the emotional thrive and struggle on board the trains).

Concluding Remarks

There are many *social cracks* in train commuting. This chapter has showed some of those that are important in order to transform strangers or *Mobile Others* into *Mobile Acquaintances*, *Mobile Withs*, and *Mobile Friends*. By allowing for an increase in the intensity of the social relation, the *social cracks* help improve the experience of the commute and facilitate deep meetings amongst commuters who otherwise live diverse and relatively segregated lives. It is almost like magic. I hope these findings will participate in inspiring more studies into how otherwise trivial daily activity can be enchanted and made meaningful.

References

Bissell, David. 2010. "Narrating Mobile Methodologies: Active and Passive Empiricisms." In *Mobile Methodologies*, edited by Ben Fincham, Mark McGuinness and Lesley Murray, 53–68. Basingstroke: Palgrave Macmillan.

Collins, Randall. 2004. *Interaction Ritual Chains*. Princeton: Princeton University Press.

Ehn, Billy and Orvar Löfgren. 2010. *The Secret World of Doing Nothing*. Berkeley: University of California Press.

Freudendal-Pedersen, Malene. 2009. *Mobility in Daily Life: Between Freedom and Unfreedom*. Farnham: Ashgate.

Jensen, Hanne Louise. 2012a. "Emotions on the Move: Mobile Emotions Among Train Commuters in the South East of Denmark." *Emotion, Space and Society* 5: 201–206.

Jensen, Hanne Louise. 2012b. *Hverdagslivets kollektive mobilitet—om at pendle med tog og skabe et mobilt sted*. Roskilde: Roskilde Universitetstryk.

Jensen, Ole B. 2010a. "Erving Goffman and Everyday Life Mobility." In *The Contemporary Goffman*, edited by Michael Hviid Jacobsen, 333–351. New York: Routledge.

Jensen, Ole B. 2010b. "Negotiation in Motion: Unpacking a Geography of Mobility." *Space and Culture* 13 (4): 389–402.

Laurier, Eric, Barry Brown and Hayden Lorimer. 2007. *Habitable Cars: The Organisation of Collective Private Transport.* Full Research Report ESCR End of Award Report, RES-000–023–0758. Swindon: ESCR.

7 *Road Radio*
Taking Mobilities Research on the Road and Into the Air

Aslak Aamot Kjærulff and Kaare Svejstrup

During the summer of 2013 we (a mobilities researcher and a radio journalist) recorded, edited, and aired four episodes of *Road Radio* on a month-long road trip across United States. We drove from coast to coast, visiting cities, rural areas, and national parks, capturing stories, conversations, and sounds. *Road Radio* is radio about mobility and mobilities studies—produced on the move and an experiment with radio formats used to document research processes. It consists of four episodes broadcasted on a Danish national public radio station, combining the features of a travel and a science program.

In this chapter we discuss the experiences from making representations of research in a more 'dense' way than the usual written text and argue for further experimentation in presenting research agendas to public audiences (Vannini 2012, 2015). *Road Radio* was a way of unfolding our interests in using radio to bring many more voices, sounds, and atmospheres to the often very text-based vocabularies of research (Bessire and Fisher 2013). From a radio journalistic perspective *Road Radio* was also an attempt to convey personal narratives tied to the field of mobilities research to a broader audience.

Why Did We Make *Road Radio*?

The guiding question for the show was: What is happening to the mobilities of people who are trying to live outside of the American dream of cars, family homes, career jobs, and urban-style consumption? The question involves a deeper interest in how different people react to a modern culture, and seems to hollow out the natural and human resources on which it is based (Steffen et al. 2015; Urry 2013; Wells 2013). This question also involves a journalistic interest in how to report from research and lived experiences to generate new or alternative angles on broad concerns. In the following, focus is on some of the characteristics of *Road Radio* most inspiring to us, in the hope of creating affinity between empirical research methods and production of public radio.

On-the-Road Production

Typically, radio documentaries are produced over great distances in time and space. The producers conceptualize stories, gather field recordings, and edit programs in different environments, with the immediate sensations and emotions of the fieldwork long gone. In *Road Radio* we tried to bring our own journey and our own immediate thoughts, feelings, and sensations into the program. The interviews, sound collecting, and editing process took place on the move and almost concurrent, thereby mobility and mobilities research was brought into the production of the program (Lury and Wakeford 2012).

We wanted the program to be a 'dense' auditive experience, in order to make the audience's encounter both an informative and sensory experience. In an interview Anne Fernald, head of Stanford Institute's Center for Infant Studies, explained the cognitive importance of hearing: "Sound is like touch at a distance." The communication of complex information is easier when supplied by a dense set of sensations and feelings connected to a topic, rather than a linear abstract message (Manning and Massumi 2014; Manning 2015).

In order to create this 'dense' auditive experience, the programs include a multitude of different sounds. Most important are the interviews. But we also recorded a lot of other sounds, such as:

- site recordings of the places our interviews were conducted (birds chirping, wind blowing through a garden, acoustics of a shipping container)
- atmospheric sounds of the places we visited (sounds of the Mississippi River, commercials at a gas station)
- our own reactions or associations to what we encountered (being shocked by the vast industrial landscapes outside of Detroit)
- informal conversations between us during the journey (coincidently documenting a car crash we were involved in)
- unplanned or coincidental interactions with people (rolling down the window to talk to other drivers on the freeway)
- music we listened to while traveling (used as soundtrack for the shows)

We composed our edited stories, corresponding field recordings, and selections of musical tracks using a multilayered sound editing software (Heisenberg). After the raw material was composed, we recorded ourselves as hosts 'gluing' the stories, interviews, and sound bites together in silent locations: a car, a hotel room, a deep forest, or an abandoned airport.

Four Themes; Four Radio Shows

The chronology of the first few days of our journey was directly incorporated into the first show, titled *The Family Tank*. The show starts in an airplane, continues in an airport and a car rental agency, and eventually follows us driving a car in Philadelphia. We had interviews with Mikkel Thomsager, a Danish expert on American car culture; mobilities researcher Mimi Sheller, who had just finished a book on the material history of aluminum (2014); and curator Jody Roberts, working with public awareness around climate change (2014). We mixed the personal experience of starting a journey with conversations about mobilities research and escalating environmental crises. The first show became both an introduction to our journey and the field of mobilities research.

The second show, titled *Not Just 'From A to B'*, connected stories involving critique of the inequalities of US transportation. The show geographically moves in and out of New York and to Chicago. This involves a music producer telling about his experience of traveling as a soldier, a geographer explaining how public transportation becomes a focal point for social struggles, and a group of kids explaining the internal working of a bike shop they help run in a rough Chicago neighborhood. The show illuminates the personal significance of traveling and different experiences of struggling or working with mobility justice.

The third show, titled *Motor City, Animal Farm*, moves geographically from urban Detroit to rural Massachusetts. Here we were thematically juxtaposing post-industrialist urban projects (shipping containers containing local community centers and making artworks out of materials from foreclosures) with biodynamic farming and rural religious communities (spiritual connectivity of humans working with plants and animals and social ties created at childbirth in a Christian congregation). The show opens up for the differential yet very embedded and relevant reflections on mobilities from urban to rural areas.

The fourth show, titled *Nature, Future and Death*, aimed to push existential and futuristic themes to the forefront of mobilities research. It moves from the Mississippi River and prairies, to the Badlands in South Dakota, to urban areas of Chicago and Los Angeles. The show focused on ecological and cultural temporalities of rivers and bridges as well as planetary and cosmic temporalities of landscapes and light traveling from stars. It recaptures perspectives on future societies from earlier conversations with researchers, curators, and children. The show ends with an interview on the final journey everybody takes with a Los Angeles-based death expert. As a part of the interview we played a recording of a traffic accident we were involved in on a freeway in Philadelphia during our first hour in our newly rented car. The show thus points towards the contingent and uncontrollable character of mobilities, in longer stretches of time and in the here and now.

The four shows create entry points and openings to the meaning of mobilities to a wide range of people. This diversity explores criteria by which some things are considered knowledge and others not—not by questioning mobilities research authorities, but by showing how the interest in mobilities is present in a range of ways in people's lives.

Concluding Remarks

During our journey we met with academics, curators, artists, musicians, farmers, priests, publishers, bike-mechanics, primary school children, literary historians, and activists. Some people we spent a couple of hours with, others we stayed with for several days.

Focusing on each person's personal perspective on mobility was of great importance to us, especially when we talked to academic authorities in the field of mobilities research. Often in media, researchers are treated in formal and impersonal ways. In *Road Radio* the narratives of researchers and curators are not only tied to stories about their professional experiences, but also involve aspects of their personal lives. This emphasizes the more-than-professional aspects of cultural and academic work and allowed for couplings between research topics and lived experiences.

The collaboration between a scientist and a journalist is not without difficulties. During the production arguments arose from different perspectives on communicative roles, explanatory level, and especially the relation between us as producers and the people we interview and portrait. From a traditional journalistic point of view the relation between the source and the producer is one-way: The producer observes and interacts with the sources in their environment and collect data with the sole purpose of constructing a narration to be published. After the collection of data, the role of the source is outplayed. As a journalist you regard the collected data as your property and the editing process as a creative process that you hold the exclusive right to. The final product only has one purpose: to convey the constructed story to the audience. As an academic the relationship between producer and source is different. Here research is carried out with more than a final conclusion in mind. There is a commitment to tell the sources stories as they emerge on the research journey. As producers of a highly edited media piece, a responsibility for the quality of the context and the subjectivities composed from interviewees are central. Statements that might be journalistically interesting for their controversial qualities can be hard to accept as the only side shown of a person.

These dilemmas led to editorial conflicts but we found common ground in embedding the value of multiplicity and associations that lead in multiple directions into the production. In this regard the quality of a journalistic radio format is the ability to present several types of entry points to the same topic, and thus at once destabilizing the idea that the mobilities research field is composed on one grand narrative and at the same time illuminating how travels and flows change over time and between lives and contexts.

References

Bessire, Lucas and Daniel Fisher. 2013. "The Anthropology of Radio Fields." *Annual Review of Anthropology* 42 (1): 363–378.

Lury, Celia and Wakeford, Nina, eds. 2012. *Inventive Methods: The Happening of the Social*. Abingdon: Routledge.

Manning, Erin. 2015. "Against Method." In *Non-Representational Methodologies*, edited by Phillip Vannini, 52–71. New York and London: Routledge.

Manning, Erin and Brian Massumi. 2014. *Thought in the Act*. Minneapolis: University of Minnesota Press.

Roberts, Jody. 2014. "Sensing Change Exhibition." September 1, 2015. http://sensingchange.chemheritage.org/.

Sheller, Mimi. 2014. *Aluminum Dreams—The Making of Light Modernity*. Cambridge: MIT Press.

Steffen, Will, Wendy Broadgate, Lisa Deutsch, Owen Gaffney and Cornelia Ludwig. 2015. "The Trajectory of the Anthropocene: The Great Acceleration." *The Anthropocene Review* 2 (1): 81–98.

Urry, John. 2013. *Societies Beyond Oil: Oil Dregs and Social Futures*. New York and London: Verso.

Vannini, Phillip. 2012. *Ferry Tales: Mobility, Place, and Time on Canada's West Coast*. New York: Routledge.

Vannini, Phillip. 2015. *Off the Grid—Re-assembling Domestic Life*. New York and London: Routledge.

Wells, Jennifer. 2013. *Complexity and Sustainability*. New York: Routledge.

8 Managing Mobilities in the Working Context

Sarah Nies, Katrin Roller, and Gerlinde Vogl

Against the backdrop of increasing globalization and the growing web of worldwide transportation and information networks, the 'mobilization of labor' (Voß 2010) is an essential part of networked urban mobilities. To be mobile—that is, to move, to connect, and to be flexible—is becoming an inherent part of the working experience of an increasing number of employees (Kesselring and Vogl 2010; Kesselring 2015).

In our research we have asked how employees have engaged in work and private life practices under increasingly mobile conditions. Our work is grounded in and builds upon research on corporate mobility regimes (Kesselring and Vogl 2010; Kesselring 2015).

In the following, we describe how we went about analyzing these processes and spotlight some of the central findings from our research project[1] on the mobility patterns of highly qualified business travelers of a vehicle manufacturing enterprise and construction workers who commute weekly in the Metropolitan Region of Munich.

An Analytical Scheme for Studying Spatial-Temporal Structures

Seeing mobility at work as an everyday practice, we conducted 46 in-depth interviews with employees, workers, and executive managers as well as additional expert interviews with human-relation managers, business managers, and employee representatives. The analytical scheme we developed in the course of our research project distinguishes between the following spatial-temporal categories: transition (*'being on one's way'*), presence (*'being there'*), absence (*'being away'*), and relocalization (*'being back'*). For each of these dimensions we were able to highlight a set of specific requirements mobile individuals must deal with:

- First of all, mobility comprises physical movement as such, the act of *'being on one's way'* from one place to another. This dimension is defined by movement in space and is characterized by a state of transition from one place to another that can be referred to as 'transition time.'

Managing Mobilities in the Working Context   49

- The process of *'being on one's way'* serves the purpose of being present at a specific destination. Every business trip and every commute is related to a task that is bound to a specific place. As an important aspect, this form of mobility involves *'being there.'* This includes the social situation in which a person puts him- or herself, the tasks that await the person at his or her destination, the uncertainties that the person is faced with there, and so forth.
- An important element of the experience of mobility is the absence from home—*'being away.'* This refers to the absence from home and the personal social relationships associated therewith as well as to the absence from one's regular work and workplace. In both cases, time appears as 'missed time'—missed time with one's family and, in the case of business trips, missed time to complete one's regular tasks at work.
- Business trips and commutes are both a form of 'circular mobility' (Schneider et al. 2002, 2008) that returns to its starting point, from which it then begins again. Mobility at work does not end once the individual has returned home; from this perspective, mobility also always begins prior to the actual trip. The experience of mobility therefore also comprises (the moment of) *'being back,'* the act of relocalization. This is where the prerequisites of mobility are created, while the sphere of life and work back home is shaped by periods of absence and the experiences of mobility. Under circumstances of regular mobility, this makes the time back home appear as 'condensed time.'

This briefly outlined analytical scheme enables us to describe different mobility demands, strains, and practices, each of which can be appropriately understood only by taking the interplay of the various dimensions into consideration. For instance, *'being there'*—at one's destination—can be fully grasped only if we take into account that this involves *'being away'* from colleagues, family, and other social spaces.

Mobility Experience of Commuters and Business Travelers

The mobility experience of weekly commuters stands in sharp contrast to common perceptions of mobility in terms of flexibility and the dissolution of boundaries. The reality of the mobility, work, and lives of these commuters is defined by sharp boundaries as well as by firmly established routines and strong obligations. Their scope of individuals' flexible, self-determined decision-making is limited, both during the week (they can neither individually determine their working hours, nor does the available infrastructure allow them to move about as they please) and on weekends. For the 50-year-old construction foreman and father of a four-year-old daughter the time being away from home is completely dedicated to work:

> The reason I'm here is to work. I don't care whether I come in at seven or at eight. It's simply . . . well, I am here to work. I don't have my

> family here now. . . . I really honestly spend zero money here . . . I'd rather spend my money with my wife and child at home. I don't need any Wi-Fi here, I don't need to go in the park in the afternoons or evenings, because all this . . . I can do all this with my wife and child at home. I get more out of doing these things at home.
>
> (B2–04)

Life back at home follows a strict script. Limited time resources and missed activities while absent during the week define '*being back*.' The fact that this mobility situation is not an exclusively negative experience primarily has to do with the *opportunities* that arise *by existing boundaries.*

The mobility experience of the *business traveler* is shaped primarily by the experience of '*being away*.' However, in those cases in which the experience of commuting revolves around being separated from one's family, business travelers define mobility in terms of the challenge of dealing with the job tasks left behind at the regular workplace.

> Well, being on the road isn't really that bad. The real problem is that you have even more work than you had before because you know exactly that when you've been gone for eight days, all that work remains unfinished. Or I have to take care of it beforehand. Or afterwards, knowing exactly that, well, time, that time will be missing somewhere.
>
> (B4–02)

Business travelers tend to emphasize less the burdens of mobility on their private life than the challenge of having to manage their work under conditions of mobility. At the same time, they face the task of having to adapt their private life to the demands of a flexibilized working world—both in terms of time and place. This constellation results in a trade-off between absence from one's regular workplace, the time resources at one's destination, and absence from home. If the person is absent from the regular workplace for too long, work accumulates there; if the time planned for the trip is too short, there is the risk of an intensification of work and too much immediate stress at the destination. The promise of a solution seems to be in extending the trip at the expense of the time devoted to one's private life—with all the problems that this entails for the latter.

As opposed to the situation of commuters, whose mobility patterns hinge on drawing a sharp boundary between work and private life, in the case of business travelers this boundary breaks down at home as well. Although many make a deliberate attempt to maintain this boundary and keep work from intruding into private life after the end of the workday or on weekends, permanent availability, at least occasional weekend work, or private appointments that are postponed on short notice are very common.

Concluding Remarks

We have shown that the dissolution and (re-)drawing of boundaries between work and private life cannot be adequately understood without including space, time, and physical movement into the analysis. By taking into account the genuine perspective of the ones experiencing mobility at work on a regular basis, we were able to distinguish different dimensions of spatial-temporal mobilities and to analyze their interconnectedness. Paying respect to these different dimensions allows for a richer understanding of stresses and strains of mobility practices as well as their enrichments and trade-offs. Coming from this perspective a close relation between the current mode of control—regarding the labor process—and specific mobility practices can be observed. Therefore, our empirical findings are a small contribution to bring the mobility turn into the sociology of work, particularly in the German context, where—despite growing importance of mobility practices—most approaches still remain to be largely 'a-mobile' (Sheller and Urry 2006) until today.

Note

1. The research project Mobility in the Working World—a Catalyst of Social Inequality (Mobilität 'rund um die Arbeit'—Katalysator sozialer Ungleichheit; duration: 10/12–5/15) was funded by the Hans Böckler Foundation.

References

Kesselring, Sven. 2015. "Corporate Mobilities Regimes: Mobility, Power and the Socio-Geographical Structurations of Mobile Work." *Mobilities* 10 (4): 571–591. doi:10.1080/17450101.2014.887249

Kesselring, Sven and Gerlinde Vogl. 2010. *Betriebliche Mobilitätsregime*. Berlin: edition sigma.

Schneider, Norbert F., Ruth Limmer and Kerstin Ruckdeschel. 2002. *Mobil, Flexibel, Gebunden*. Frankfurt am Main: Campus.

Schneider, Norbert, F., Silvia Ruppenthal, Detlev Lück, Heiko Rüger and Andrea Dauber. 2008. "Germany—A Country of Locally Attached but Highly Mobile People." In *Mobile Living Across Europe I*, edited by Norbert F. Schneider and Gerardo Meil, 105–148. Opladen: Barbara Budrich Publishers.

Sheller, Mimi und John Urry. 2006. "The New Mobilities Paradigm." *Environment and Planning A* 38 (2): 207–226. doi:10.1068/a37268

Voß, G. Günter. 2010. "Subjektivierung und Mobilisierung: Und: Was könnte Odysseus zum Thema 'Mobilität' beitragen?" In *Mobilität und Mobilisierung: Arbeit im sozioökonomischen, politischen und kulturellen Wandel*, edited by Irene Götz, Katrin Lehnert, Barbara Lemberger and Sanna Schondelmayer, 95–135. Frankfurt am Main: Campus.

9 Tracing Trans-Atlantic Romani Im/Mobilities

Doing Ethnography in a Hyper-Mobile Field

Esteban C. Acuña

During early explorations on Romani trans-Atlantic im/mobilities,[1] I helped a Paris-based colleague to carry out her linguistic research on the variants of Romani language spoken in Bogota and their contact with variants of Spanish in the Americas. Helping me with this endeavor was Toza Cristo, a patriarch and active participant in negotiations between Rom families and the Colombian State, who recommended me to join him in visits to a couple of houses. On one of those occasions we visited his daughter and son-in-law. Conversation got exciting when they reminded me that among the people in the room there were several ways of speaking (in both Spanish and the Romani language): Toza's wife, Nubia, had been raised on the Venezuelan border; his son-in-law used to live in the city of Medellin; and Toza and his daughters had lived most of their lives in the Colombian capital. They all shared physical and emotional connections to all of those places, materialized in the presence of family members all over.

After recording answers to the linguistic questionnaires, conversation shifted to an important celebration: the wedding of one of the young men in the family. The groom had spent the last few years recovering after a failed marriage with a Romani woman from the United States, where many families had migrated in the 1980s and 1990s. Finally the elders agreed that his dues were done and a new wedding with a bride from Venezuela was being planned. The whole extended family was expected to go with him and join the rituals and celebrations. However, not everyone had the time or the resources to fly or drive to the border city of Cucuta, where the wedding would take place. The ones who were fortunate to do so were eager to send pictures and text messages describing every detail of the event. Toza's daughter continuously received *Whatsapp* messages on her smartphone. She read them aloud and the others listened, commented, and asked for more pictures or videos of the bride who was joining the family, her entourage, and the multiple parties and gatherings.

This encounter embodies several of the challenges that arose from the explorations of various translocal connections and mobile practices across and beyond the Atlantic in the daily life of Romani groups, families, and individuals. This chapter aims to give a concise overview of how the act

Tracing Romani Im/Mobilities 53

of doing fieldwork guided my own research. The meeting with Toza and Nubia's family is a telling example of how a single moment can become a complex cluster of diverse im/mobilities; the reason I judge this 'field' as hyper-mobile. The moment was at the same time a daily neighborhood visit, a reunion, and a confluence of academic and activist collaborations. The simultaneous wedding preparations were attended in person, traveling by plane (or car), and through text messages. The several languages in use made matters even more complex. Although the need for an approach that went beyond localized ethnographies was palpable even before the project started, particular encounters made me realize the urgent need to incorporate critical insights on how to approach processes of emplacement and displacement, mobilities and immobilities. Finally, it was necessary to reflect not only on how to grasp them, but also on the importance of maintaining awareness of how I was positioned in this confluence of circumstances, how ethical considerations multiplied as connections extended, and how particular contexts affected these movements.

The Research Process and Its Challenges

In order to get a hold of these mobile/immobile phenomena, I chose to explore three central sites that could help describe the translocal, transnational, and trans-Atlantic exchanges that composed the backbone of these Romani connections: Toronto, Budapest, and Bogota. These were the zones in which I spent most of 2013 and the beginning of 2014, my multi-sited field year. For each one a minimum of three months was allotted, even though comings and goings and staying in contact have been an intrinsic part of the endeavor before and after.

The possibility to explore these connections implied a change of perspective. There was a need to focus on "multiple connections rather than multiple sites" (Robben 2007, 331). Comparative research has usually centered on emitting locations and receiving locations, an approach that tends to fall back on an "isomorphism of space, place, and culture" (Gupta and Ferguson 1992, 7), and has been heavily criticized for over two decades by contemporary anthropological work. New trends in ethnography have tried to overcome this limitation, conscious that this assumption is a cornerstone of 'Western imagination' that should be de-constructed (e.g. Coleman and von Hellermann 2011).

The most noticeable attempt to apply these insights to the ethnographic craft has been George E. Marcus' work, which arose precisely from trends of thought about world configurations beyond the locale, namely anthropologies of globalization(s) and intakes on networks as central units for social theory (Marcus 1995, 102; Candea 2007, 169). Ulf Hannerz (2003, 206) notes how the term might be misleading because 'translocal' ethnography seems to be a better fit when one focuses on linkages and connections in between 'places.' Marcus pushed for a set of methods that, while

54   Esteban C. Acuña

tracing phenomena "across and within different sites" (1995, 96), had the potential to destabilize binary distinctions criticized by the spatial turn that was in progress. In the case of Romani im/mobilities, as exemplified by the described encounter, it was necessary to amplify the scope, since localized ethnographies had not been able to account for how translocal relations affected quotidian practices.

Towards an Im/Mobile Ethnography

I have chosen to describe the eventual set of methods that resulted from the field experience as im/mobile ethnography; an adaptable, context-sensitive combination that, in time, arose from involvement, engagement, and collaboration in/among/between mobile networks and connections. As a starting point, the cities were conceptualized as 'contact' or 'friction' zones (Pratt 1991, 34; Tsing 2005, xi), hubs that were not mere contexts, but vibrant settings in which kinship, activism, business, religiosity, and other forms of expression crisscrossed Romani lives and routes. It became routine to be prepared for these changing settings, this richness in uncertainty in which a daily visit could turn into a translocal or national event. From its early stages the project focused on biographical narratives, originally as a main technique for its development of semi-structured, in-depth interviews: "a conversational meeting with at least one other self" (Skinner 2012, 6), but usually more than one, given tight family structures and my own situation as a single young male traveling alone.

Participants were encouraged to tell their life stories by reflecting on their histories of travel and being at home. Narratives included various mobilities: border crossings, changes in residence, family or friend visits, business and economic tactics and strategies, activism or educational journeys, virtual travel, among others. Respondents in general preferred to actually show me part of their life through walking through their neighborhood, eating together, working together, watching pictures or videos together, surfing Google Maps, doing errands, among other daily practices (in a similar way that had occurred in the encounter described). Several interviews spanned two, three, or even four sessions. In each setting I used one month's worth of time to build up relations, rapport, and trust. Processes of displacement and emplacement, including my own, became object of discussion and analysis as well. That very day I talked with Toza's family not only about their own trips, but also my own trans-Atlantic travel. My own movements had to adjust to those of actual connections and exchanges that occurred at the same time.

Im/mobile ethnography seems like an oxymoron: a multi-sited, grounded but mobile fieldwork. An oscillating continuum between techniques, similar to 'go-alongs' (Kusenbach 2003) or 'shadowing' (Jirón 2011). Each talk, or 'walk-along,' 'ride-along,' or 'work-along,' was accompanied by diary entries that described its context. The interviews were part of longer informal periods of contact, where participant observation was indeed the best way to register events that could span for hours, days, weeks, and even months. The interview acted as a bridge between these daily occurrences and the historical relations that produced them.

Despite being limited by constant movement, prolonged contact allowed a better understanding of the context of each encounter, and provided a scenario where the interview itself was negotiated and reflected upon. As the settings multiplied, new considerations had to be brought to the table, especially during the moments in preparation and in between the times when the recorder was on.

Concluding Remarks

Methodological adaptiveness had its limits. Such a project would have been impossible as a 'lone-ranger.' It was a collective endeavor, in which researcher, interpreters, respondents, scholars, and intellectuals were roles taken by several of the protagonists according to specific contexts and limitations (time, language, social and physical boundaries, ethical requirements, etc.). This also implied that it was an interdisciplinary effort which had to gather reflections that came from various bodies of knowledge in order to make sense of the wide exchanges and connections described.

In practice, it reflected the need for trust: relying on previous academic explorations and patience and serendipity (Rivoal and Salazar 2013) when deciding to let go of the security of localities, instead of tracing mobilities and connections. It has also deeply affected the writing process which, far from being smooth, needs to reflect the intense shifts and complexities that were an intrinsic part of the mobile lives of individuals and families like Nubia, Toza, and their relatives. Experiencing these connections, networks, and exchanges became not only a methodological standpoint, but a cornerstone of the dissertation's conceptual framework.

Note

1. This article is based on an ongoing doctoral dissertation project part of the Cultures of Mobility in Europe (COME) research group at Freiburg University, financed by the Excellence Initiative of the German Research Foundation.

References

Candea, Matei. 2007. "Arbitrary Locations: In Defense of the Bounded Field-Site." *Journal of the Royal Anthropological Institute* 13: 167–184.

Coleman, Simon and Pauline von Hellermann. 2011. *Multi-Sited Ethnography: Problems and Possibilities in the Translocation of Research Methods*. New York and London: Routledge.

Gupta, Akhil and James Ferguson. 1992. "Beyond 'Culture': Space, Identity, and the Politics of Difference." *Cultural Anthropology* 7 (1): 6–23.

56 Esteban C. Acuña

Hannerz, Ulf. 2003. "Being There . . . and There . . . and There! Reflections on Multi-Site Ethnography." *Ethnography* 4 2: 201–216.

Jirón, Paola. 2011. "On Becoming 'la sombra/the Shadow'." In *Mobile Methods*, edited by Monika Büscher, John Urry and Katian Witchger, 36–53. London and New York: Routledge.

Kusenbach, Margarethe. 2003. "Street Phenomenology: The Go-Along as Ethnographic Research Tool." *Ethnography* 4: 455–485.

Marcus, George E. 1995. "Ethnography in/of the World System: The Emergence of Multi-Sited Ethnography." *Annual Review of Anthropology* 24: 95–117.

Pratt, Mary Louise. 1991. "Arts of the Contact Zone." *Profession* 91: 33–40.

Rivoal, Isabelle and Noel B. Salazar 2013. "Introduction: Contemporary Ethnographic Practice and the Value of Serendipity." *Social Anthropology* 21 (2): 178–185.

Robben, Antonius C.G.M. 2007. "Multi-Sited Fieldwork." In *Ethnographic Fieldwork: An Anthropological Reader*, edited by Antonius C.G.M. Robben and Jeffrey A. Sluka. Blackwell Anthologies in Social and Cultural Anthropology, 331–335. Malden: Blackwell Publishing.

Skinner, Jonathan. 2012. *The Interview: An Ethnographic Approach*, Asa Monographs. London: Bloomsbury.

Tsing, Anna L. 2005. *Friction: An Ethnography of Global Connection*. Princeton and Oxford: Princeton University Press.

Part II

Communities and Collaborations

10 The Little Mermaid Is a Portal
Digital Mobility and Transformations

Lilyana Petrova

Once upon a time there was a young mermaid, half girl half fish, who lived in the underwater kingdom and emerged from time to time to observe the world of humans. She eventually fell in love with a beautiful prince who often went for walks along the seashore. Most probably she loved him for his two legs, which allow him to move on the ground of humans. With the help of an underwater witch, she eventually bartered her fish tail and her voice for a pair of legs. Transformed, she escaped to the terrestrial world where she discovered the feeling of its infinite possibilities, designed borders, and limitless emotions. So goes the famous story of Hans Christian Andersen, *The Little Mermaid*.

This classic tale speaks of our modern-day mobility in today's networked cities. Immersed in our urban environment, do we not strive for a different way of moving within this environment? Boundaries? The transformation of the little mermaid is not a separated fictional event, stranded in literature, but rather a part of an actual process of alterations that closely parallels the mobility experience itself. By its inherent attractiveness, mobile technology transforms our way of walking, talking, and being together. In the tradition of the mobility turn (Urry 2000; Castells et al. 2007), this paper will reflect on how digital mobility has influenced our way of experiencing movement within the city and the related transformations that take place in this process in three steps (the story, the statue, and the *portal*). The particularity of the research stands in the chosen research field, the alternate reality game called *Ingress*, which walks us through the little mermaid metamorphosis.

Parcours Project and Parkour Method

Since its arrival, the mobile phone has provided numerous practical tools such as personal road navigators, hand-held cameras, video phones, and constant Internet connection (3G, 4G). More than just tools, these items stand for everyday practices, from personal hobbies to social interactions, to love relations, to ways of seeing, ways of reading, ways of talking, ways of playing, and ways of moving. In fact, on its pedestal, in a clean and bright spot, the mobile phone has made us desire a totally different way of being

60 Lilyana Petrova

and existing. In this context, the notion of *parcours* helps to spread light on the relation between communication and mobility. The transformation happens on the path between the sublime depths of our routine lives and on the on-ground promise of a different and more fulfilling mobility. *Parcours* is a French word for path and a verb for walking, browsing, roaming, skimming. As such it is a perfect blending of both, the physical movement from one side and all its affective dimensions from the other. In that sense, this particular notion is helpful to consider the intersections between the different layers of mobility as a whole, and consequently, the networked urban mobility.

The choice of the research field is of great importance, and Google's GPS-based game *Ingress* has proved to be a very fruitful one. *Ingress*[1] is a mobile online game, which uses the actual world surface as a playground. The mobile app invites the user to choose between two factions (green or blue) granting him access to a 'secret' map on which the locations of public sculptures, statues, or cultural places are indicated as green or blue dots, called *portals*. The player's 'mission' is to gain more portals for its own team but in order to do so he has to physically move and experience the world around him. The ultimate goal lies in gaining as much territory as possible and in progressing in the personal statistics such as distance walked, number of portals visited, or areas controlled amongst others.

As for the methodology perspective, empirical methods such as virtual, visual, and sensory ethnography (Hine 2001; Pink 2009), as well as mobile methods (Büscher and Urry 2009) and performative research (Denzin 2001; Diebner 2012) have been helpful and instructive. Nevertheless, we sensed the need to improve these methods in order to address the particular issue of the mobile users' *parcours*. This resulted in what we will define as the *Parkour Method* (Petrova 2015), a combination of methodological procedures that target the use of the mobile phone within the movement. It builds as follows: 1) analyzing the subject matter and pointing out problematic notions; 2) creating art/research installations, designed to query heterogeneous data about those notions; and 3) analyzing and manipulating the collected data in a visual and/or interactive manner to extract and to present findings as well as to make them open and accessible for further research. The following example of the *Operation (OP): The Little Mermaid* (Figure 10.1) is one of the research/art pieces conceived for the notion of *transformation*.

OP: The Little Mermaid

For the conference Networked Urban Mobilities, 5–7 November in the city of Copenhagen, we organized a research performance designed to carve and explore the experience between different mobilities. The *OP: The Little Mermaid*[2] confronts views of ordinary citizens with those of *Ingress* players, focused on a single urban element—the little mermaid—and elaborates on three of its main dimensions/transformations—the story, the statue, and the *portal*.

Figure 10.1 OP: *The Little Mermaid*
Source: Lilyana Petrova.

a) The Little Mermaid Is a Story

The first transformation is from the body of the mobile user as a mermaid, to the story of it; from the walking to the feeling of walking; from the physical experience to its narrated representation. As our body is strolling the streets of Copenhagen, it perceives itself as a being within a particular architectural setting: a screen (Google Street), a city (Copenhagen), an image (dreams, souvenirs, videos, sounds, GPS traces), or a game (*Ingress*). Each of these frameworks sets corresponding 'mobile embodied performances' to a particular environment to which it belongs (Jensen 2013). The act of transitioning from one to another is not a neutral one. In the case of the little mermaid, she decides to switch from her default swimming to a different kind of corporeal movement (walking). In fact, we are somehow locked in the stories of our bodies, and we can transform the scenario only by escaping the limits of their original shape and predisposition. But how?

b) The Little Mermaid Is a Statue

In a sense, the statue of the little mermaid is a fixed entity in space and time, designed to structure the urban mobile experience around itself. This is true for Copenhagen, as a tourist city. This is also true for *Ingress*, as a geolocated game in which all statues and other urban constructions transform into representations on a map (*portals*). As such, they become gravitational points and generate movement around themselves. Therefore, the second transformation of our urban rules of motion is the one from a story into a statue. Seen from the Cosmobilities perspective, cities need a strong and socially inclusive mobility system.[3] Said in other words, there is a need for a shift from the practice of a one directional free-flowing movement into the practice of what we can define as '*parcours*,' a complex and multiple directions movement within a symbolic environment.

62 *Lilyana Petrova*

While observing the practices of any smartphone user, whether being an *Ingress* player or not, we understand that the space-centered experience of contemporary cities transposes a dictatorial setting from the urban territory to the digital one. The statues serve as symbols around which rises a mobile social order. In the same way the prince is the symbol of a specific status, enabling a different kind of mobility, yet inaccessible and not part of its environment. In a way, the desire to belong to 'the other side' is almost a sign of resistance to an established order, which limits the bursts of our potential movements. Consequently, simple acts such as taking a photo of the statue of the little mermaid, 'hacking' it in *Ingress,* or 'checking-in' in *Foursquare,* become gestures of rebellion and desire to go beyond one's own capability. We can think of them as Condillac's sensations, bringing us increasingly closer to the status of 'statue' of a perceptive being (Condillac 1798).

c) The Little Mermaid Is a Portal

In conversation, *Ingress* agents claim that they can 'feel the portals,' which means that they are in communication with the images displayed on the screens. Thus they can perceive themselves in a different immersive environment. Nevertheless, a mediator is needed in this transformational adventure, a 'witch' who can help transform from an occasional mobile state into an existential state of digital mobility.

During the *OP: The Little Mermaid*, we drew a line on the ground, encircling the beautiful statue in an imaginary showcase. This circle was drawn with a diameter of 40 meters, thereby materializing the in-game geolocated representation of the *portal*. We invited Copenhagen agents to participate and in parallel approached passersby and questioned their perceptions of this delimited space. We introduced them to *Ingress* as a different point of view of the statue and filmed the conversations and their reactions. Observation shows that the little mermaid is a *portal* not only because the statue is a part of a game, but also because the *Ingress portals* are pillars for a digital urban structure, accessible only through the application and the related community of users. Owing to this connectedness, the city transforms into an alternate environment, allowing us to move differently inside of it. Here, a third transformation happens within the same geographical space, perceived differently according to the actual alteration of the designated mobility.

Concluding Remarks

According to Andersen, the little mermaid leaves her original milieu because she falls in love. Ultimately, the object of her desire is not the beautiful prince but rather his legs. Attracted to the possibility of moving and communicating differently, she endures all the transformations in the hope of surpassing her mermaid condition. Indeed, 80% of *Ingress* players say that what hooked them in the game is the obligation to move. It would be particularly interesting to research further in this direction, to insist on the movement as experience and to observe the perceptive differences brought by the use of the smartphone application. With its million clicks, thousand hacks, and hundred *gates* to Thebes, the smartphone is like a Japanese *torii*, a symbol of a border between a profane and a sacred space. With a leap of faith, one has to walk through it as an engagement to one's reinvented mobile self (Goffman 1956). It stands for a relational mobility, one where movement is used as a stage on which one performs their everyday reality, and by doing so, changes the ontology of their world. Perhaps this is what Spinoza calls an 'affect'—the acting power of the body to believe in images, to obey fantasy.

Notes

1. Link to the *Ingress* game website: http://ingress.com/.
2. The event web page: http://digitalparcours.org/thelittlemermaid.
3. The actual topic of the tenth conference of the Cosmobilities Network, 'Networked Urban Mobilities,' was focused on the urban mobility subject matter, inviting scholars from social sciences and other mobility-relevant disciplines to investigate and assess the impact of networked urban mobilities on the urban condition (Cosmobilities, 2014).

References

Büscher, Monika and John Urry. 2009. "Mobile Methods and the Empirical." *European Journal of Social Theory* 12: 99–116.
Castells, Manuel, Mireia Fernandez-Ardevol, Jack Linchuan Qui and Araba Sey. 2007. *Mobile Communication and Society: A Global Perspective*. Cambridge: MIT Press.
Condillac, Etienne Bonnot de. 1798. *Traité Des Sensations: Augmenté de L'extrait Raisonné*. Corpus Des Oeuvres de Philosophie En Langue Française. Paris: Librairie Arthème Fayard.
Cosmobilities. "Networked Urban Mobilities Conference and Mobile Art Exhibition." Aalborg University Campus in Copenhagen, 2014. www.cosmobilities.net/2013/12/10/networked-urban-mobilities-conference-2014/.
Denzin, Norman K. 2001. "The Reflexive Interview and a Performative Social Science." *Qualitative Research* 1 (1): 26–46.
Diebner, Hans H. 2012. "Performative Science—Reconciliation of Science and Humanities or the End of Philosophy?" *Studia UBB. Philosophia* 57 (April): 3–7.
Goffman, Erving. 1956. *The Presentation of Self in Everyday Life*. Edinburg: University of Edinburg. Social Sciences Research Center. Monograph No.2.
Hine, Christine. 2001. *Virtual Ethnography*. London: Sage.
Jensen, Ole B. 2013. *Staging Mobilities*. New York: Routledge.
Petrova, Lilyana Valentinova. 2015. " 'OP Petit Poucet': Propositions méthodologiques adaptées à la communication géolocalisée." In *Doctoriales de la SFSIC*, edited by Dominique Carré and Françoise Pequienséguy, 271–229. Lille: SFSIC.
Pink, Sarah. 2009. *Doing Sensory Ethnography*. London: Sage.
Urry, John. 2000. *Sociology Beyond Societies: Mobilities for the Twenty-First Century*. London: Routledge.

11 Viscosities and Meshwork
Assembling Dynamic Pathways of Mobilities

Lauren Wagner

{network} Lubna who recognised me from the road—how circuitous and closed these networks are, even I can insert . . . {/network}

In this chapter, I want to reflect on how working from an assumption of humans as materially and affectively mobile configures *viscosity* and *meshwork* as useful theoretical dynamics for approaching networked urban mobilities. I use *viscosity* as a means for imagining how expressive human social networks stick together and keep others out, even while not remaining in fixed physical spaces; and *meshwork* to recognize how all sorts of political, technological, and material infrastructures engage these expressive networks, shaping their potential and actual pathways. These concepts became necessary to me in the midst of my PhD research, as my own ontological framing shifted from humans-as-static to humans-as-mobile—rendering the presumptions of much social science theory inoperable with my fieldwork observations on diasporic circulation.

The fieldnote above demonstrates how I encountered my problematic ontological presumption of humans-as-static. In the course of 'following the people' to learn about how summer vacations in a diasporic homeland are part of practices of 'being diasporic,' I crossed the Netherlands, Belgium, France, Spain, and into Morocco along with one participating family making their annual trajectory from one home to another (Wagner 2011). I encountered many other families following the same path along the same road, and making the same stops at gas stations, rest areas, and tourist sites to break the journey and reunite disparate cars in their caravans. As an ethnographer, I cold-approached passengers in other cars in those stops, in the constant pursuit of new and extended contacts that would contribute to the empirical data on this holiday experience. I must have introduced myself to Lubna in one of these rest-stop encounters, because a month later she recognized me in the bathroom at a hotel pool in Meknes. Standing at the sink, washing my hands, she exclaimed a hello and reminded me that we had met on the road in Spain somewhere.

This first experience of re-encounter came as a surprise. The quoted field-note reflects surprise (and perhaps some anthropologist pride?) both that I had inserted myself into these social networks appropriately enough to be a recognizable person, and the shock of encountering her at all—someone from the road, rediscovered in a new location. As my fieldwork progressed, I noticed other 'coincidental' meetings with participants in disparate places, and began to pay closer attention to how these seeming 'coincidences' occurred. They were generally not in physical proximity to each other, nor in what would normally be defined as a locatable spatial 'community' (even for these mobile, diasporic visitors) with two polarities defined by their resident and ancestral hometowns. Yet, the empirical preponderance of this and other 'random' re-encounters during fieldwork required some way to understand how these locations *must* be linked to each other in a way I had not yet conceptualized. That, despite their seemingly self-evident physical and temporal distance, these mobilities were networked in some kind of tangible, durable form that allowed even an outsider like me to enter their flow, in the same way other ethnographers spend time in a fixed, physically located 'community.'

Viscosity and Meshwork

This sense of flow pulled me decisively away from traditional framings of transnationalism and diaspora, in that these persistently depend upon an underpinning spatial framework of nations and their boundaries, and towards the fluidity of mobility and network. More specifically, as I began coding and analyzing this fieldwork, my supervisor handed me the book *Psychedelic White* (Saldanha 2007), which became instrumental in conceiving of how these re-encounters might be predictable as *viscous* events across a socially-networked leisure *meshwork*. In exploring Goa as an international rave 'scene' producing machinic geographies of race, Saldanha describes practices of participants and aspirants to the 'scene' tending to cluster together into certain locations, atmospheres, and groupings so that some are able to integrate while others are—unforcefully, yet palpably—kept out. These groupings are characterized by their stickiness and collective movement—as he calls it, their *viscosity*—in their nightly pursuits as they disassemble from one location and travel, reassembling almost magically in a new leisure activity.

By imagining Lubna's and my movements as what Saldanha calls a 'political geography of many bodies' (2008), I was able to step back to observe viscosity as a dynamic mobility, describing the movements of a material mass of actors along with the agentive affordances of their consumption environments, predictably magnetizing towards and away from each other between certain locations. This ontological shift focused my attention on how these networked collectivities of like-minded individuals are primarily

66 *Lauren Wagner*

and profoundly mobile. Inherent to that ontological reframing in mobility is my re-encounter with Lubna (or someone like her): In these terms, it is only natural that we would re-encounter each other as I became embedded in leisure consumption practices and their predictable spaces for European Moroccans on holiday in Morocco.

The notion of *meshwork* pairs with viscosity as an equally mobile infrastructure supporting it. Saldanha takes note of political and technological actors that tend to congeal viscous groupings—like the motorbike as a mode of transport for his Goa 'freaks,' or, in my case, the family car as a mode of transport for diasporic Moroccans. Such technologies and their concomitant trodden pathways (Ingold 2007, 2008) are the interwoven fabric of structures that become a layer of support (De Landa 1997), creating infrastructural meshworks for viscosities of moving bodies. Meshwork may be latent in existing material and political structures—like transport, communicative transmission, trust networks, and built infrastructures for human life—and become enlivened in the viscous seeking of collectivities at certain nodes or along certain pathways. This enlivening happens in how neither the gas station in Spain nor the hotel pool bathroom in Meknes were created for me and Lubna to meet, yet they both have become enmeshed into viscous geographies of diasporic Moroccans traveling to Morocco over summer holidays. In order for us to meet, their material affordances and latencies—their provision to take a break from the road and fill one's tank, or to wash away one's waste, sweat, and dirt—have become indispensable as infrastructural nodes along this well-trodden pathway, supporting the 'alongness' of assembling, dispersing along a trajectory, and predictably reassembling elsewhere.

Concluding Remarks

Combining these terms allows me to approach human-life-as-mobile, and then interrogate how material and affective conditions that may seem very solid and static encourage us to slow down in certain nodes long enough to encounter each other. This change of perspective, in particular, helps me reconceive some of the assumptions that dominate migration, diaspora, and transnationalism as research areas and policy topics—such as the focus on examining individuals in terms of 'belonging' or 'not belonging' that happens in fixed, immutable, and spatially-configured 'homes,' defined through community, ethnicity, nationality, or citizenship, and their borders. For the participants in my research, rather, I observed a sense of belonging that happened in mobility, specifically in interaction with like-minded (yet diverse) others who were viscously engaged in parallel assemblings of leisure consumption practices. The 'borders' that became activated through their viscosities were not necessarily ones defined by an ethnic or national label, but more potently ones of economic power; borders that echoed in Saldanha's research as geographies of consumption distinction, which happen to coincide with and perpetuate divisions of (racialized, ethnicized) citizenship.

My analytical experience of mobilities, then, was as ongoing dynamics: meshworks of structures allowing and disallowing passage along certain pathways, and collectivities becoming palpable as viscous movement that attract some and push others out. These dynamics emerged in the meetings I had with Lubna—now configured as predictably likely rather than a surprise—and in the ways, as I argued in the Networked Urban Mobilities conference (Wagner 2014), this experience of 'going on holiday' is not so much a departure from 'normal' life as it is a site in which 'normal' diasporicness is perpetuated, reinforced, and iterated for future generations. In short, in order to take mobility as a starting point, and to take seriously the 'alongness' of mobilities, I put forward viscosity and meshwork for further research in networked urban mobilities, as two interdependent dynamics describing assemblage that make belonging something that happens along the road as much as something that happens at its destination.

References

De Landa, Manuel. 1997. *A Thousand Years of Nonlinear History*. New York: Zone Books.

Ingold, Tim. 2007. *Lines: A Brief History*. London and New York: Routledge.

Ingold, Tim. 2008. "Bindings Against Boundaries: Entanglements of Life in an Open World." *Environment and Planning A* 40 (8): 1796–1810. doi:10.1068/a40156

Saldanha, Arun. 2007. *Psychedelic White*. Minneapolis: University of Minnesota Press.

Saldanha, Arun. 2008. "The Political Geography of Many Bodies." In *The SAGE Handbook of Political Geography*, edited by Kevin R. Cox, Murray Low and Jennifer Robinson, 323–333. London: Sage.

Wagner, Lauren. 2011. "Negotiating Diasporic Mobilities and Becomings: Interactions and Practices of Europeans of Moroccan Descent on Holiday in Morocco." Doctoral thesis, Geography, University College London. http://discovery.ucl.ac.uk/1317815/.

Wagner, Lauren. 2014. "Hypermobility on Holiday: Networked Affective Densities in Leisure Trajectories Through Morocco." Presented at the Cosmobilities 10th Anniversary Conference: Networked Urban Mobilities, November 5–7.

12 Parked Students, Surfing Workers, and Working in Third Places With Mobile Technology

Michel Després

"Can I access the Wi-Fi here, please?" said the student while sitting in the café and opening his laptop. Just at that moment a businesswoman asks for the same thing while swiping her fingers on her smartphone and ordering a sandwich to go. Scenes like this have become more ordinary due to a growing number of workers and students, among others, using mobile technologies like cellphones, laptops, or smartphones to do work or leisure-related activities in cafés, libraries, public spaces, parks, and even transports or waiting spaces like train stations and bus stops. In Québec metropolitan area, this growing trend is interesting, notably from a sociologist and urban planner standpoint. Not only does it divert significantly from the usual commuting of workers and students between home and the workplace/school, it could also mark a certain revitalization of public and semi-public spaces as they become interesting spots for working and studying for mobile technology users (Doyle 2011).

These spaces of socialization and activity are often called *third places* (Doyle 2011) for workers and students, as they often constitute intermediate activity spaces between what is considered the first place, the home, and the second, the workplace or the school. Third places include common categories of spaces like public buildings (ex: libraries) or commercial places (ex: cafés, restaurants), but also more uncommon ones like transport vehicles (ex: buses, trains) or transit spaces (ex: bus stops, airports), which can nonetheless be high points of activity with mobile technology.

While working or studying in third places is nothing new, doing it with mobile technology appears to attract workers and students who wouldn't have done it otherwise. Furthermore, many studies (Alexander, Ettema, and Dijst 2010; Lee-Gosselin and Miranda-Moreno 2009; Lenz and Nobis 2007; Line, Jain, and Lyons 2012; Kesselring 2006; Taipale 2014) already highlight how some workers and students use the perceived flexibility to work 'on the move' with mobile technology to reorganize their daily mobility around multiple work or study locations in third places. Some even organize their lifestyles around it! (Kesselring 2006; Line, Jain and Lyons 2011). These studies, especially the qualitative ones, have pointed out how the use of mobile technology is part of intricate lifestyles, where the newfound possibilities opened by these devices (like working on the move) are envisioned by the filter of habits and what is deemed possible according to the personal situation. However, few quantitative studies take into account at the same time the socioeconomic, technological, and spatial logics that could help explore these lifestyles with mobile technology on a larger scale.

With these questions in mind, I wanted to better understand, using quantitative data, who are the users of mobile technology in Québec metropolitan area and what are the characteristics of individuals who use these technologies to work or study on the move. Based on a statistical and cartographic study I will present and elaborate the terms 'parked students' and 'surfing workers' to show a glimpse of the variety of time strategies and lifestyles observed regarding mobile technology use in third places among students and workers of Québec City. Beside the fact that the use of mobile technology in third places is skill based and generational, my study shows that it also is a matter of social contexts allowing both the geographic and temporal flexibility to do so.

A Statistical and Cartographic Study of Mobile Technology Users and Their Lifestyles

As part of a master's thesis (Després 2014, in French), I did research in 2011 on a non-probabilistic sample of 2338 residents of Québec metropolitan area. The Internet survey used for the research, administered as part of a research project by the Interdisciplinary Research Group on Suburbs (GIRBa), collected answers to a large range of topics, including the socioeconomic profile of respondents, their travel behaviors, and their use of mobile technologies like cellphones, laptops, and smartphones. The 992 respondents, frequent mobile technology users, were selected as a final sample. The survey respondents, well distributed across the Québec metropolitan area, counted 370 students, mainly from college and university, and 622 workers, mainly from the four biggest work sectors in Québec: public administration, the health sector, professional and research sectors, and the teaching sector. While non-representative of the Québec general population,[1] the sample offers a good perspective of those who are often called 'early adopters' and trendsetters in regards to practices with mobile technology. It is also worthy of note that, in 2011, smartphone users were few and the first iPad was just introduced. Still, results showed nearly one half of these students, and about a third of workers, report using cellphones, smartphones, or laptops for work or study purposes in one or many kinds of third places. While the percentages don't necessarily reflect the variety of mobile technology users that can be seen in the general Québec population (especially today, in 2017, where their use is much more widespread), further analysis nevertheless showed interesting findings regarding the lifestyles of mobile technology users in Québec.

70   *Michel Després*

One interesting finding showed significant differences in the way various profiles of workers and students inhabit space with mobile technology when they work on the move. Like the student presented in the first paragraph, the students tend to use space in a more *'parked'* way whenever they want to study elsewhere than home or school. Being more frequent users of laptop computers than the workers of the sample, these students sit down and usually stay a good while (mean time 2h09) in the places they visit, usually public libraries or cafés. Workers, on the other end (especially those between 18 and 34 years old), appear to *'surf'* from Wi-Fi hotspots to another while they work on the move, staying in one place only for short periods of time (around 20 minutes). We can imagine these workers, like the businesswoman above, being generally more frequent users of smartphones than the students in the sample, using their devices to quickly check their e-mails while on a sandwich break, to read in the bus, or to check social media while at the bus stop.

Who Is a 'Surfing Worker' or a 'Parked Student'?

When is someone a parked student or a surfing worker? What is different in the lifestyles of students and workers who work with mobile technology in third places compared to those who do not?

The not-so short answer: Working or studying in third places with mobile technology is most used by individuals whose social situation offers incentives to work on the move, encourages a certain flexibility concerning the places and time where they choose to work, and also because they appear to have an easy access to suitable third places in their daily travels. For instance, for many reasons university students show higher probabilities to park themselves in third places to study than college students. In part, in my view, because these university students' courses or theses cause them to do academic work more intensively and more often than college students. This is shown in our analysis of various regression statistics models taking into account socioeconomic variables and digital activities done frequently (ex: check e-mails, work offline, etc.).[2] But also because university students, as shown by a quick look at their localization on a map of Québec, tend to live closer to the city center, where cafés, libraries, and public spaces with Wi-Fi are plentiful, compared to other college[3] students, who tend to live farther out in the suburbs, many of whom with their parents.

Taking a look at workers of the same age in the study, the main difference between those using mobile technology in third places and those who didn't was much more straightforward: The presence of a young child at home. For many early-career workers, the moment when they decide to have children often follows the moment they get a steady full-time job. In this regard, for young workers, being a surfing worker was much more frequent among couples without children, single individuals, and especially among people with roommates rather than parents. In my view, this is due to the fact that most of these workers living with roommates, like university students, live near the city center where Wi-Fi hotspots are plenty, and that their situation offers both the time flexibility and sometimes the incentives to get some air outside and work elsewhere than home (you know, when one of your roommates plays music too loud or when one suddenly invites friends while you need to focus . . .).

Concluding Remarks

Whether it be students parking themselves with their laptop in places like cafés or libraries for longer time periods, or young workers surfing from one place to another with their phones for shorter time periods, the results presented here show only a glimpse of the variety of time strategies and lifestyles observed regarding mobile technology use in third places among students and workers of Québec City. A study like the one we did in 2011 can only present a quick snapshot (hell, a 'snapchat'!) of the various uses of mobile technology for work or study purposes, given the speed at which technologies evolve. However, they do show that the divides regarding the use of mobile technology in third places are not only skill based or generational, but also a matter of social contexts allowing both the geographic and temporal flexibility to do so. This, just as theorists inspired by the *new mobility paradigm* (Sheller and Urry 2006) have long argued, reaffirms the importance of considering the physical and virtual mobility of people, just like the mobilities of objects, ideas, and information, as interdependent instead of separate issues (see Urry and Büsher 2009 or Urry 2007, among so many others). On this point, while discussing the statistic and cartographic work done in my study would be too much for this article, simply spatializing data like the home and workplace locations of respondents after our statistical analysis helped to see results in a new light and showed new patterns. As pointed out by Sheller (2014), the new mobility paradigm was as much a social and cultural turn as it was a geographical one (in the way we do research on mobilities), and I couldn't agree more on the importance of spatializing data after realizing how much I would have missed without this very simple cartographic work in my research.

In *Mobile Technologies of the City* (2012), Sheller and Urry called for the importance of better understanding how various profiles of individuals use mobile technology on-the-move (depending on their age, gender, social status, etc.). While the study of Québec mobile technology users presented here shows a lot of limits (notably in regards to the use of mobile technology among workers of technical sectors), I believe it shows the importance of developing mobile methods that could follow individuals in space and time. More research is needed to better account for how different social contexts affect the way activities with mobile technology are maintained, reconfigured, or changed according to circumstances throughout various moments in the life cycle.

72 *Michel Després*

Notes

1. The sample presents respondents who are generally younger and with higher levels of education compared to the Québec general population. The sample also underestimates workers in technical sectors.
2. The full regression models include also the type of mobile technology used (cellphone, smartphones, laptops, or a mix of two) and type of transportation most often used as independent variables. Dependent variables (as dummy binary indicators) included the number of third places visited, type of third places visited, and day periods where mobile technologies are used.
3. In the Québec education system, 'college' refers to an education level between high school and university levels.

References

Alexander, Bayarma, Dick Ettema and Martin Dijst. 2010. "Fragmentation of Work Activity as a Multi-Dimensional Construct and Its Association with ICT, Employment and Sociodemographic Characteristics." *Journal of Transport Geography* 18: 55–64.

Després, Michel. 2014. "En temps et lieux: l'utilisation de technologies mobiles par différents profils de citoyens à Québec." Master's thesis in Sociology, Laval University.

Doyle, Michael R. 2011. "Designing for Mobile Activities: WiFi Hotspots and Users in Quebec City." Master's thesis in Architecture & Urban Design, Laval University.

Kesselring, Sven. 2006. "Pioneering Mobilities: New Patterns of Movement and Motility in a Mobile World." *Environment and Planning—Part A* 38: 269–279.

Lee-Gosselin, Martin and Luis F. Miranda-Moreno. 2009. "What Is Different About Urban Activities of Those with Access to ICTs? Some Early Evidence from Québec, Canada." *Journal of Transport Geography* 17: 104–114.

Lenz, Barbara and Claudia Nobis. 2007. "The Changing Allocation of Activities in Space and Time by the Use of ICT—"Fragmentation" as a New Concept and Empirical Results." *Transportation Research Part A: Policy and Practice* 41: 190–204.

Line, Tilly, Juliet Jain and Glen Lyons. 2011. "The Role of ICTS in Everyday Mobile Lives." *Journal of Transport Geography* 19: 1490–1499.

Sheller, Mimi. 2014. "The New Mobilities Paradigm for a Live Sociology." *Current sociology Review* 62 (6): 789–811.

Sheller, Mimi and John Urry. 2006. "The New Mobilities Paradigm." *Environment and Planning A* 38 (2): 207–226.

Sheller, Mimi and John Urry. 2012. *Mobile Technologies of the City*. London: Routledge.

Taipale, Sakari. 2014. "The Dimensions of Mobilities: The Spatial Relationships Between Corporeal and Digital Mobilities." *Social Science Research* 43: 157–167.

Urry, John. 2007. *Mobilities*. Cambridge: Polity Press.

Urry, John and Monika Büscher. 2009. "Mobile Methods and the Empirical." *European Journal of Social Theory* 12: 99–116.

13 Urban Borderlands of Mobility
Ethnographic Fieldwork Amongst Unconventional Elderly City People

Jon Dag Rasmussen

This chapter is based on a long-term[1] ethnographic fieldwork that explores the spidery and entangled social lives and relations of elderly people on the margins of society in the city of Copenhagen, Denmark. Building on unexplored leads emerging during prior research (Rasmussen 2012), the ambition has been to create knowledge about the intricate lives of a heterogeneous group of people living highly unnoticed lives in the *backyards of modernity* (Ehn and Löfgren 2010, 207–216). My work rests on an intense and insistent application of *participant observation* and was conducted in movement through the cityscape with informants and in contexts as e.g. street corners, shelters, park sites, bars, charitable organizations, and private homes. The research unveils a world of 'indigenous' *social infrastructure* (Simone 2004) not discernible by the ordinary big city dweller, and the aim of this chapter is to address how this world is constituted and maintained through mobility—how the ability to move is significant in the lives of my informants. In this regard I subscribe to the currents of the *new mobilities paradigm* (e.g. Cresswell and Merriman 2011) focusing on everyday life movement as embodied practice with an emphasis on the cultural and social organization of this mobility (Löfgren 2015).

The article supports a micro perspective on *networked urban mobilities* and hereby also the accentuation of an unnoticed and often shunned phenomenon: the pivotal relation between small-scale mobile practices, sociality, and the everyday lives of unconventional elderly city people.

Overture

The dim basement presents itself, at least by the first encounters, as an untamed and opaque wilderness. Literal piles of old artifacts; pottery, aged books, vinyls and electronics, garments, shoes, and an abundance of material curiosities cover the floor, the walls, and block out most of the daylight that meets the low and dirty windows facing the street. A narrow path leads from the door through this material plenitude, and ends at a solid wooden table at the far end of the tattered room. Here, five downward steps and some short-distance path finding from a heavily trafficked main artery in the city, a community of older persons unfold. The shop is owned by 86-year-old Hans, or Master, the moniker most regulars address him by, and who has occupied the small adjoining rooms for several decades. Regulars coming to the shop are people that share the experience of unconventional everyday lives on the margins of society and, in various ways, inhabit a metaphorical borderland of the city. The wooden table (seen in Figure 13.1) attracts an ensemble of persons that feed on the tales of past days, on the loose gossip and vicious rumors concerning each other, and on the mutual existential and practical support residing in the shop. Beer and wine, as well as the more occasional liquor and soft drinks, are flushed down while narratives are shared, contested and argued, repeated, and reconstructed in what seems like ever evolving circles. The people seeking a social life in the basement are elderly, above 65, with the exception of Erik, a homeless man in his late forties who spends most of his nights on the worn-out couch below the window, calm and by low lighting as carefully instructed by Master.

Flows

Frank is a regular in the shop. He stops by a couple of times a week to enjoy the chattering tone and the orange soda the shopkeeper usually retrieves from a drawer on the first notice of Frank's arrival. He sits quietly on his habitual side of the couch, sipping the beverage from his habitual glass,

Figure 13.1 Master's basement
Source: Jon Dag Rasmussen.

only to participate verbally in a minimum of the discussions. Alice visits the store once a week. She lives in the periphery of the city but takes the bus to reach the center. She usually brings a carton of red wine and cigarettes, and she has an open and talkative attitude appreciated by the others at the table. On most of her hour-long visits she purchases a couple of items found in the shop to take home. Erik, the homeless man sleeping in the store, returns from running errands in the neighborhood, and brings a bag of budget priced beers that Master is always covering. An old woman living in a nearby building, Ulla, is also paying a visit. This day she is asking for help carrying down a broken TV set from her third-story apartment. In the afternoon Carl enters the shop. The atmosphere changes upon his arrival. He has not been round the basement for months due to a suicide attempt and the subsequent hospitalization in a psychiatric unit. The embarrassment, and his awareness of the narrative processing of the incident taking place around the table, has kept him at a distance after the release. Carl knows that Master's daughter, Susanne, is visiting the shop on most Tuesdays. The two hold a close relationship, and the hope that she is present this afternoon makes him dare an infrequent call.

The people moving down the short flight of stairs at Master's and further into the basement, both changing and reaffirming the narrow trail between piles of old stuff, have (of course) other ends to attend to in their lives. All of these lived lines cling, entwine, and interweave in an Ingoldian *meshwork* (e.g. Ingold 2011, 2015) that spans the city. Like the boots, pottery, paintings, and other artifacts that inhabit the store, bearing a physical witness of past relations to the outside world, these beings circulate, they enmesh and correspond with the people and places of their surroundings. Most of the informants possess conventional homes, often very small apartments, but spend their waking time on the move. Frank, who received a brief attention above, lives in a crammed two-room apartment in the central part of Nørrebro,[2] Copenhagen. He has a long history of walking the city and leaves the home early in the morning, on most days to return late in the night. Throughout the day he is found circulating the city on foot, engaging in activities and ongoing self-defined projects, sitting on benches chatting to loose acquaintances and closer friends, or consulting different charitable organizations that serve free or cheap meals. I establish my connection with him in Master's shop and start following him around on his walks. The initial day-long explorations take on a character of guided tours through somewhat exotic *flipsides* of the city. As Rebecca Solnit writes, we all contain myriads of personal and social maps, and these maps are tickets to actual territory in the space of an *infinite city* (2010, 8–9). Frank walks (and talks) me deep into the unknowns of an environment I already inhabit, but in this regard only know by surface. He exposes me to the *geographies of the unnoticed* (see Rasmussen 2017). Over a period of months we develop a close and friendly relationship. The co-exploration of Frank's *small-scale mobility* (see Winther 2015) enables me to gain a first-hand experience

76 Jon Dag Rasmussen

of the odd paths of cohesion and the alternative social logics related to marginal elderly lives beyond the grasp of an outsider. Tales of mystifying lives and deaths, unexplained disappearances, and unconventional social patterns are made manifest through the puzzling friend- and companionships we meet along the way. It all seems to emerge in his company, like voices reverberating from the lines of footprints we carve into the surface of the world. Through this movement I get to acknowledge the changeable ties between curious and continuous mobile practices and the use of particular places of utmost importance in the city sphere. Phillip Vannini states that "the most quintessential expression of life, movement . . . marks what it means to be alive" (2012, 11). Frank, like all of my informants in varying degrees and modes, is dependent on this ability to move. His entire life is anchored in an intimate and embodied relation to the cityscape, its buildings, streets, vegetation, animals, stories, and people. For more than 30 years the asphalt has been the primary foundation of his everyday life, making passageway to uncanny and multiple experiences and relationships. In the process he has grown into the city to the extent that he is no longer separable from it. Drawing on my ethnographic work, it is empirically fair to assert that Frank's life *is* movement, and by this taking Vannini, as well as Tim Ingold (2011, 2015), very literally. But he is no special case. The same goes for all of my informants. They all escape small apartments to engage in different asphalt-routines,[3] to practice their *unnoticed geographies*, to indulge in circulation between the crucial street corners, shelters, bars, park sites, city benches, kiosks, and second-hand stores. The personal maps they continually re-articulate by movement, the tread lines that weave and knot in the landscape, form a socio-material infrastructure, or an intricate *meshwork*, that not only serves basic social needs, but also constitutes channels for the exchange of e.g. illegal substances and prescription drugs, a variety of goods, broad existential support, and information in regard to the acquisition of cheap food or other general necessities.

Concluding Remarks

My work reveals the existence of a non-transparent world of micro-mobility amongst marginal elderly city dwellers. With a foothold in one of numerous explored contexts, this chapter describes how a broad and extensive group is entangled in an existentially significant *circulation* in the cityscape; how beings are knotted together in the mesh of a socio-material infrastructure that span the urban world. And how this *circulation* is maintained by ceaseless flows of people, artifacts, and information that cover the distances between different metaphorical pockets and cracks in the sidewalks, places like Master's basement, shelters, and park sites; places of entanglement. My hope is that the writing reflects the quirky, beautiful, and harsh poetics experienced through ethnographic fieldwork in the borderlands of urban mobility.

Notes

1. The material I draw on is produced between September 2011 and June 2015.
2. A district of the city; historically a working-class quarter.
3. As Billy Ehn and Orvar Löfgren point out, *routine* is a diminutive of *route*, a small path (2010: 81).

References

Cresswell, Tim and Peter Merriman. 2011. "Introduction: Geographies of Mobilities—Practices, Spaces, Subjects." In *Geographies of Mobilities: Practices, Spaces, Subjects*, edited by Tim Cresswell and Peter Merriman, 1–18. Burlington: Ashgate.

Ehn, Billy and Orvar Löfgren. 2010. *The Secret World of Doing Nothing*. Berkeley: University of California Press.

Ingold, Tim. 2011. *Being Alive: Essays on Movement, Knowledge and Description*. New York: Routledge.

Ingold, Tim. 2015. *The Life of Lines*. New York: Routledge.

Löfgren, Orvar. 2015. "Modes and Moods of Mobility: Tourists and Commuters." *Culture Unbound: Journal of Current Cultural Research* 7 (2): 175–195.

Rasmussen, Jon D. 2012. *Steder at være for socialt udsatte ældre: Antropologisk studie af multihuset på Nørrebro*. København: Ensomme Gamles Værn.

Rasmussen, Jon D. 2017. "En upåagtet verden af bevægelse: Et etnografisk studie af hverdagsliv blandt usædvanlige ældre mennesker i storbyen." PhD diss., Aalborg University.

Simone, Abdoumaliq. 2004. "People as Infrastructure: Intersecting Fragments in Johannesburg." *Public Culture* 16 (3): 407–429.

Solnit, Rebecca. 2010. *Infinite City: A San Francisco Atlas*. Berkeley: University of California Press.

Vannini, Phillip. 2012. *Ferry Tales: Mobility, Place, and Time on Canada's West Coast* (Innovative Ethnographies). New York: Routledge.

Winther, Ida W. 2015. "To Practice Mobility—On a Small Scale." *Culture Unbound: Journal of Current Cultural Research* 7 (2): 215–231.

14 Understanding Everyday Mobilities Through the Lens of Disruption

Karolina Doughty and Lesley Murray

Along with existing scholarship on everyday mobilities, our research has aimed to elaborate on the ways in which movement, and the lack of it or its disruption, is socially, culturally, and materially contingent (Doughty and Murray 2016; Doughty 2013; Murray and Doughty 2016; Murray 2008, 2009). We suggest that the individualized approaches to mobility that dominate the policy debate need to be challenged by seeking to understand the many ways that mobilities are interdependent and culturally embedded. In the Research Council UK Energy Programme–funded project, 'Disruption: Unlocking Low Carbon Travel,' we examined the opportunities for changes to everyday mobility practices through moments when mobilities become 'disrupted' in some way (for a full report see Cass et al. 2015). The ethnographic element of this project, carried out in Brighton between 2011 and 2014, let participants themselves define what disruption means, and it reveals that rather than seeing disruption as a departure from 'normality,' it is best understood as an inherent aspect of interdependent mobile lives. Our data shows that disruption to mobilities should not be assumed to relate exclusively to breakdowns in transport infrastructure; it is more often triggered by an array of non-transport-related events, such as relationship breakdowns and illness, and nor is it always experienced as negative. We argue that understanding how people define, experience, and deal with disruption reveals the great complexity and uneven terrain of mobilities (see also Murray and Doughty 2016).

Methodology

The methodology used in this research allowed us to permeate the range of social connections upon which mobilities are generated, as well as reveal the situatedness of mobilities. In reflecting the importance of relationships in mobile lives, the research focused on 'families' rather than households, with 23 families and 42 individuals in Brighton participating in the study. In seeking to understanding the myriad interdependencies of daily movement, we adopted a critical approach to the concept of family, encompassing all key people in participants' lives that they identified

Understanding Everyday Mobilities 79

as 'family,' including parents and children, single parents, single people, non-cohabiting couples, intergenerational families living in the same house, and a range of social characteristics that reflect the diversity of the city of Brighton. Working with families was particularly useful in understanding networks of support and interdependencies in coping with disruption. We adopted mixed and negotiated methods of data collection including: narrative interviews, participant-generated data using a 'toolkit' of methods (such as photography, video, scrapbooking, writing, blogging, and posting on Facebook/Twitter), and mobile interviews or go-alongs. This generated a set of rich data on everyday mobilities and their disruptions, which illustrate that how disruptions are responded to is largely dependent on social and material contexts and constraints, often embedded within caring relationships.

Meanings and Experiences of Disruption

Inspired by a mobility cultures perspective that incorporates understandings of experiential movement and its meanings, the social and cultural production of mobilities and the political contexts in which these take place (Urry 2008; Cresswell 2006), we understand disruption to be similarly produced and situated, and result from complex interdependencies between different aspects of meaningful movements and the circumstances that sometime constrain them. As we discuss in further depth elsewhere (Murray and Doughty 2016), disruption has often problematically been understood as a departure from 'normality,' indeed much of transport policy involves interventions that rely on 'normality' as a baseline. However, our data illustrates (see Table 14.1) that disruption is an inherent and expected part of 'normal' everyday life, as others in the mobilities field have also argued (e.g. Graham 2010; Graham and Thrift 2007). Furthermore, as Table 14.1 shows, most examples of disruptions are not transport system related (cf. Vollmer 2013),

Table 14.1 Definitions of disruption by research participants

Transport related	Traffic jam, transport delays, roadworks, car breakdown, car not starting, traffic accidents, floods, changing seasons affecting numbers on the bus
Related to social and caring relationships	Illness of people you care for, injuring yourself, break in chain of picking up and taking children to activities, knock-on effects of traffic delays, end of a relationship, personal life events, family problems, messy room, tooth filling coming out, crowd trouble after football match, running out of money, being relocated at work, unwanted phone calls
Positive aspects to disruption	Breaking routines that are stuck, experiencing something new, creative process, stopping to do something disliked, recognizing need to change arrangements that appear difficult to change

80 *Karolina Doughty and Lesley Murray*

which points to the need to move beyond transport in understanding the intricacies of relational mobilities.

Responses to disruption are not always deviations from aspects of 'normal' life such as norms or routines, but on the contrary may involve following another established set of practices (Jensen 2011) to produce mobilities in ways that are socially and culturally acceptable. At an everyday level, there is much variability in 'normality':

> Well, as I say, there's no kind of normal day. At least, there are two kinds of normal day; there's a kind of day in the office and a day out of the office.
>
> (Nigel)

As Graham and Thrift (2007) point out, disruptions are only really noteworthy when they result in 'catastrophe,' and most minor disruptions are absorbed into the fracas of daily life:

> Tuesday was just a normal work day (Dad picked up the kids from Zumba), although Mum was the one who took me to the station, because Dad had trashed his car by putting water in the oil tank instead of the windscreen washer bottle.
>
> (Eleanor)

Nigel and Eleanor illustrate the changeability of normality and how it can be incorporated into their complex mobility practices, which are both dependent on and productive of mobility infrastructures, transport routes, and family. These dependencies are rooted in unevenness.

Different people have different capacities and opportunities to deal with a disruption to their personal mobility. In this way, we can understand disruption as defined by difference. Successfully navigating disruption often depends on social support networks, while caring for others or the breakdown of relationships can also be the cause of significant disruption in people's lives. Crucially, negotiating difference can mean needing to use more carbon-emitting modes of travel, for instance due to disabilities:

> Getting somebody around in a wheelchair by transport is no joke. Because my mum was in a wheelchair, and that really showed me up quite a few flaws in the system generally . . . I did get very, very cross about the whole thing, shops were inaccessible, you know, general things were inaccessible.
>
> (Mary)

Hence disruption is framed within everyday mobility practices but also dependent on broader socio-spatial contexts. For example, mobility is gendered (Uteng and Cresswell 2008), and this was reflected in narratives around 'good parenting' and the difficulty when caring routines get disrupted. In our research, in line with previous studies (Murray 2008), this is more significant for women. The complex routines associated with 'good parenting' often are responses to social contexts and involve a range of interconnecting mobile trajectories. So when one set of practices change, the interdependent practices and relations also change. This has implications for lowering carbon in that for many of our participants, the car was not just a metaphor for freedom but an embodied mobility practice that enabled freedoms, especially for those encumbered with the gendered responsibilities of life in the modern family.

Concluding Remarks

We have discussed some aspects of situated everyday mobility that become revealed through disruption. For us, a conceptualization of disruption concerned with micro socialities and spatialities allowed a framing of disruptive events and their impacts on mobility decision-making at this everyday level (Jensen 2011). We found that it is important not to underplay the inherent flux that we observed in the mobility practices of our participants. Hence people are constantly negotiating mobility practices as they deal with varying scales of disruption. These negotiations are based on mobilities that are shared, contingent, and situated, rather than individualized (Manderscheid 2014), and disruption is therefore characterized by a range of interdependencies. Given the embeddedness of mobility in everyday life, and the array of factors that determine experiences and effects of disruption, transport policy alone can never help us understand this complexity, and transport interventions can never be the whole solution. Mobility studies are an important way forward to helping move emphasis away from transport modes and choices towards the entanglement of travel practices with the daily activities and relations that produce and shape them.

References

Cass, Noel, Karolina Doughty, James Faulconbridge and Lesley Murray. 2015. "Ethnographies of Mobilities and Disruptions." Project report, University of Brighton/University of Lancaster. doi:10.13140/2.1.2179.4086

Cresswell, Tim. 2006. *On the Move: Mobility in the Modern Western World*. London: Routledge.

Doughty, Karolina. 2013. "Walking Together: The Embodied and Mobile Production of a Therapeutic Landscape." *Health & Place* 24: 140–146.

Doughty, Karolina and Lesley Murray. 2016. "Discourses of Mobility: Institutions, Everyday Lives and Embodiment." *Mobilities* 11: 303–322.

Graham, Stephen. 2010. "When Infrastructures Fail." In *Disrupted Cities: When Infrastructure Fails*, edited by Stephen Graham, 1–26. London: Routledge.

Graham, Stephen and Nigel Thrift. 2007. "Out of Order." *Theory, Culture & Society* 24: 1–25.

82 Karolina Doughty and Lesley Murray

Jensen, Anne. 2011. "Mobility, Space and Power: On the Multiplicities of Seeing Mobility." *Mobilities* 6: 255–271.

Manderscheid, Katharina. 2014. "Criticising the Solitary Mobile Subject: Researching Relational Mobilities and Reflecting on Mobile Methods." *Mobilities* 9: 188–219.

Murray, Lesley. 2008. "Motherhood, Risk and Everyday mobilities." In *Gendered Mobilities*, edited by Tanu Priya Uteng and Tim Cresswell, 47–64. Aldershot: Ashgate.

Murray, Lesley. 2009. "Making the Journey to School: The Gendered and Generational Aspects of Risk in Constructing Everyday Mobility." *Health, Risk & Society* 11: 471–486.

Murray, Lesley and Karolina Doughty. 2016. "Interdependent and Embodied Mobilities: Disruptions in 'Normality', 'Habit' and 'Routine'." *Journal of Transport Geography* 55: 72–82.

Urry, John. 2008. "Moving on the Mobility Turn." In *Tracing mobilities: Towards a Cosmopolitan Perspective*, edited by Weert Canzler, Vincent Kaufmann and Sven Kesselring, 13–24. Aldershot and Burlington: Ashgate.

Uteng, Tanu Priya and Tim Cresswell, eds. 2008. *Gendered Mobilities*. Aldershot: Ashgate.

Vollmer, Hendrik. 2013. *The Sociology of Disruption, Disaster and Social Change Punctuated Cooperation*. Cambridge: Cambridge University Press.

15 Experiences of Mobile Belonging

Mia Arp Fallov and Anja Jørgensen

In this chapter, we want to argue that mobility and local belonging are not mutually exclusive, but constitute each other in the performance of everyday life. Mobility is often portrayed as an antithesis to belonging (Fallov, Jørgensen, and Knudsen 2013), but there seem to be a much more complex and networked interconnection between these concepts (Jørgensen 2010). We have drawn on cases from a qualitative study of the relations between local belonging, mobility, and local community in Aalborg, North Jutland, Denmark,[1] in order to relay two interrelated stories about the interrelations between everyday experiences of mobility and feelings of belonging (Jørgensen, Fallov, and Knudsen 2011). The study is based on a mixed-method approach combining quantitative analysis of register data on population development and socioeconomic status with qualitative interview material. The interviewees in this study were selected from areas representing variations in demographic change (increase/decrease/stagnation/turbulence) or stability that via Geographical Information System (GIS) have been mapped onto a map of the municipality of Aalborg. Furthermore, the selection of interviewees was based on representing different urban-rural locations, with a distribution of 14 interviews in the countryside, villages, or small hinterland towns and 36 in the city of Aalborg.

The first is a narrative of how a mobile everyday life becomes dependent on different forms of anchoring (Urry 2007; Adey 2010), not only as socio-material infrastructures, but also as infrastructures of attachments. The second is a narrative of how local attachment is formed not only by variations in rhythms of mobility, but also by mobile infrastructures, and thus of the importance of researching local neighborhood-specific varieties. Underlying these narratives is a perspective on local belonging developed in Fallov, Jørgensen, and Knudsen (2013), where we view mobility as one of the dimensions of belonging in, alongside the dimensions of people and place. This is a view of local belonging that takes the temporal, spatial, and material dimensions of belonging seriously, and which view mobility not as the antithesis of either immobility or local attachment. Rather the dimensions of people, place, and mobility influence on the reciprocal process of 'home' and 'reaching out' (Buttimer 1980) and, therefore, a perspective on belonging that emphasizes its processual character and the importance of

84   *Mia Arp Fallov and Anja Jørgensen*

everyday movement (Seamon 1980), and potential for movement (motility) (Kaufmann, Bergman, and Joye 2004).

So what are the implications of this perspective on the interrelations between mobility and belonging in everyday experiences with mobility? In the following we draw out an example, which emphasizes that a highly mobile working life for many necessitates a strong attachment to home. For Paul, having his home and family anchored in village life makes it possible for him to sustain a mobile working life, which entails being away from home in long periods working in the off-shore oil industry.

> That is . . . because you are away from your family and your base, so coming back . . . your base means something. And it is important that it provides safety for my family and me and that there are others nearby who can take over, when I am not here, if needs be. . . . Because when you are away like that, and travel like that, you are often together many people in the same place and there is only work, and when you return home, then you need inclusiveness, a garden and light, so yes, absolutely. Silence, in my case silence.

Belonging to a local community provides Paul in this case with a sense of security that his family is safe, and with a space in which to recover after the strains of the mobile practices. When asked what this sense of belonging entails, Paul elaborates that is a question of familiarity and that his mundane everyday engagements with a web of social relations can occur without questioning their intent. A mobile working life depends on and is intertwined with immobility and the qualities associated with immobility such as bodily recuperation, silence, calmness, and mundane practices around the home. Therefore, local belonging cannot be seen as the antithesis of high mobility. Rather, they are mutually imbricated, as Massey writes: "For the truth is that you can never simply 'go back', to home or to anywhere else. When you get 'there' the place will have moved on just as you yourself will have changed" (2005, 124–125). Home is an anchoring point and as such is intertwined with mobility as a meeting point in the constant trajectories that form our lives. As such it does not simply coordinate paths and refresh the travelers, but also changes the meaning attached to being away and coming back.

The importance of mobility for everyday life is not simply a question of frequency or the familiarity and regularity of place-specific social networks anchoring everyday life to places, but also about the character of everyday mundane mobility practices. In Paul's case he emphasizes how the infrastructure of the village invites particular bodily practices of pedestrians and mobility considerations of people in cars:

> Previously, you drove your car in through the farm houses to get through the village and that is the funny part of it. This structure has been kept and that suits me fine. It all invites a bit to wellies and clogs [laughter] and that is also part of it [living here] that you can be as you like out here.

Lacking sidewalks and paved streets induce particular forms of behavior and clothing that are associated by this interviewee with greater tolerance and less snobbishness. Other interviewees emphasize in a similar manner the importance of the sensory interactions with place (Edensor 2010) in terms of noise from roads, disturbances from airplanes, etc. Together this points to how the interconnection between belonging and mobility is not simply a feeling or question of memory but also about our bodily performances and bodily orientations around the neighborhoods in which we reside, and the way human and more-than-human interactions co-constitute our belonging to places (Wright 2015). Lene is a case in point here, as she emphasizes how having the bike as the preferred means of transport changes the identity articulated in relation to place. Having the possibility of velomobility has for this interviewee meant that everything has come into close proximity. Her description of her neighborhood is articulated in relation to how she negotiates her routes on a bike, and in contrast with the interviewees that either practice or are dependent on automobility, she does not simply phrase her everyday practice in terms of time or access to main routes, but also in terms of weather, wind, and lighting. She expresses how moving back to Aalborg and to a residence where she can commute by bike has increased her sense of local belonging:

> I felt no attachment to where I lived on Seeland. . . . It irritated me [having to commute by train] since I was used to either being able to walk or bike to work. All of a sudden I had to spend such a long time that I gained a different social attachment to either the place I lived or to anyone when I had time off. You could say that it created a lot of irritation compared to biking over the bridge [in the strong westerly wind] which is not really a source of irritation.

Similarly, other of our informants who either commute by bike or use velomobility as main spare time activity articulate the importance of cycle paths and bike bridges as important to their sense of belonging. Moreover, Lene expresses, similar to others, that the possibility and ease of moving around on the bike provides them with bodily pleasure. Infrastructures of mobility and practices of different forms of mobility shape bodily experiences of neighborhoods—in this instance because their mobility to and from home is associated with physical exertion, as well as different forms of exposure to and visible perception of place. The way that their mobility practices shape their sense of place is overlaid with a different sensory performance than what characterizes the more dominant automobility (Pesses 2010; Urry 2006; Jensen 2006).

Concluding Remarks

To investigate the everyday experiences of mobile belonging as represented in the above selected case stories necessitates methods that are sensitive to variations across neighborhoods and which, at the same time, disclose variations in mobility resources across socioeconomic groups. Thus, in addition to ethnographic methods gaining access to how people relay experiences with and meanings attached to their everyday mobility practices, we need methods that enable us to connect these symbolic layers to motility, understood as the combination of access to mobility, mobility competencies, and mobility capital (Kaufmann, Bergman, and Joye 2004; Fallov et al. 2013). Mapping methods were introduced by the early Chicago-school sociologists and such techniques have been a role model in this study as a way to engage with research questions concerning relations between social life and the spatial/geographical surroundings. Using mapping techniques illuminates the geographical variation of the objects of the study and makes it possible to make strategic choices of locations for qualitative ethnographic field studies. Individual everyday experiences are, in this way, contextualized by a general socio-spatial picture of the distribution of important socioeconomic and demographic variables.

The present study's contribution to the field of mobility research stems primarily from its insistence on a perspective on mobility as intertwined with place-attachment, rather than considering belonging as the antithesis of mobility. It is obvious that mobility impacts greatly on contemporary everyday life, but empirical detailed studies are necessary in order to judge the scope, character, and scale of its impact. Contemporary societies are mobile, but it is the interconnections between fluidity and solidity that give the most interesting and the most accurate picture of modern everyday life. Further research must therefore be conducted in order to clarify how fluidity and solidity act and interrelate in different contexts.

Note

1. The material is sampled from the 50 qualitative interviews conducted in relation to the project 'Belonging, Local Community and Mobility' financed by a grant from The Danish Council for Independent Research | Social Sciences.

References

Adey, Peter. 2010. *Mobility*. London: Routledge.

Buttimer, Anne. 1980. "Home, Reach and the Sense of Place." In *The Human Experience of Space and Place*, edited by Anne Buttimer and David Seamon, 166–187. New York: St. Martin's Press.

Edensor, Tim, ed. 2010. *Geographies of Rhythm: Nature, Place, Mobilities and Bodies*. Farnham: Ashgate.

Fallov, Mia, Anja Jørgensen and Lisbeth B. Knudsen. 2013. "Mobile Forms of Belonging." *Mobilities* 8 (4): 467–486.

Jensen, Ole B. 2006. " 'Facework', Flow and the City: Simmel, Goffman, and Mobility in the Contemporary City." *Mobilities* 1 (2): 143.

Jørgensen, Anja. 2010. "The Sense of Belonging in New Urban Zones in Transition." *Current Sociology* 58 (3): 3–23.

Jørgensen, Anja, Mia Arp Fallov and Lisbeth Knudsen. 2011. "Local Community, Mobility and Belonging." *Danish Journal of Geoinformatics and Land Management* 46 (1): 22–35.

Kaufmann, Vincent, Manfred Max Bergman and Dominique Joye. 2004. "Motility: Mobility as Capital." *International Journal of Urban and Regional Research* 28 (4): 745–756.

Massey, Doreen. 2005. *For Space*. London: Sage.

Pesses, Michael W. 2010. "Automobility, Vélomobility, American Mobility: An Exploration of the Bicycle Tour." *Mobilities* 5 (1): 1–24.

Seamon, David. 1980. "Body-Subject, Time-Space Routines, and Place-Ballets." In *The Human Experience of Space and Place*, edited by Anne Buttimer and David Seamon, 148–165. New York: St. Martin's Press.

Urry, John. 2006. "Inhabiting the Car." *The Sociological Review* 54: 17–31.

Urry, John. 2007. *Mobilities*. Cambridge: Polity Press.

Wright, Sarah. 2015. "More-than-Human, Emergent Belongings: A Weak Theory Approach." *Progress in Human Geography* 39 (4): 391–411.

16 The Spaces, Mobilities, and Soundings of Coding

Sung-Yueh Perng

The mobilities of people, buildings, technologies, resources, and waste that constitute urban spaces are enacted and governed by complex, diverse, and often hidden paths, rules, and regulations (Urry 2007, 2014). Increasingly, the interconnectedness of these mobilities is enhanced by computational intelligence to monitor, measure, and preempt these flows at fine levels, creating new hopes, monsters, and fears when engineering networked cities (Büscher et al. 2016). In this process, software and its data processing capabilities have become pervasively embedded in urban sociotechnical systems, which generate insights about cities from knowledge practices that are shifting as a result of the 'data revolution' (Kitchin 2014) and preconfigures our experiences of living, working, and traveling in coded space, without conscious reflection and sometimes creating new uncertainties (Graham 2005; Kitchin and Dodge 2011; Perng and Büscher 2015). Despite its influences on urban spaces, software has largely remained a black-box for critical inspection, comprising specialist knowledge and reasoning and guarded against closer examination through compilation into executable files and by legal and intellectual property rights. The practices of compiling code often escape the public (and academic) gaze because the spaces where coding takes place are behind the badge-protected gates of corporate buildings. Alternatively, these spaces can be distributed online, or located in programmers' private rooms, and are difficult to access. This chapter opens up the black-box of coding by exploring how everyday experiences are translated into software code. It unpacks the complexity of code writing and indicates further complications when mobilizing code for civic purposes.

From Coded Spaces to Spaces of Coding

There has been an energetic mobilization of code writing beyond these legal, commercial, professional, and knowledge confines. The mobilization of software code for civic purposes, or civic hacking, has emerged as important everyday urban experiences. Regular events are organized by voluntary organizations such as Code for Ireland and Code for Boston, where people with programming skills can meet with community members or government officials to find out how their skills of building mobile phone applications (or apps), creating websites, or generating insights from open data can be appropriated to address local issues, such as estimating wait time at an immigration office in Dublin (https://myq.ie) or alarming delays of public transportation services in Boston (https://twitter.com/mbta_alerts).

Opening up the black-box of software writing, however, leads to more issues that require further examination. At civic hacking events, the articulations and discussions about local problems can influence the design and focus of the apps or websites to be built. The knowledge and experiences that the participants at these events have about urban living can engender immediate effects on how the problems are perceived and analyzed when considering whether any solution can be developed for them. With these issues surfacing when coding processes become more open and accessible than they used to be, 'spaces of coding' also require critical attention to analyze the social, spatial, and technical processes through which different kinds of urban experiences and knowledge become related to and translated into software solutions (for example, Lodato and DiSalvo 2016; Maalsen and Perng 2016). To do so, the chapter focuses on the fundamental process of software writing: transforming everyday experiences into sequences of code by observing the social and sonic activities happening at a workshop where participants were learning a new programming language. The focus on the introductory workshop also sheds light on the complexity and difficulty of interacting with software code that were already there at this early stage of the interaction. Accordingly, future research has to attend to much wider, and complicated, social, embodied, and collaborative practices that reshape the relationships between code, spaces of coding, civic hacking, and future cities.

'Code-Alongs,' Coding, and Soundscape

The chapter draws on my research method of 'code-alongs': participation in coding sessions to learn how to code or contribute to civic hacking initiatives, during 2014 and 2015 in Dublin. The discussion focuses on an introductory workshop organized by Coding Grace (https://codinggrace. com/) on 'Processing,' a programming language for the visual arts, in which I participated as a programming beginner. At the workshop, I followed the tutor to write code to create canvases and simple shapes before adventuring into the visualization and animation of 2D and 3D objects.

These coding sessions, including the civic hacking events I attended, can be quiet. At the workshop, the tutor explained the way Processing works, reasons, and acts, and the participants replicated the tutor's code as projected onto the screen at the front of the room. Particularly in the morning sessions, the delivery of these instructions dominated the space. While the tutor was experienced and confirmed with participants if his pace was appropriate, the responses were short. Instead, the prevailing sound coming from the participants was the typing at varying speeds for code writing and note taking. Participants did ask questions, but in a careful manner, fearful of disrupting other participants and the flow of tuition.

The tutor adopted live coding during the workshop, which created a mixture of wonder and fear. Participants were amazed when experiencing the immediate effect that these codes produced. But to live code well, the tutor had to have new lines of code keep appearing on the screen, while simultaneously providing enough context to understand and appreciate them (see Figure 16.1). He needed to explain the structure of the code, but more importantly the reasoning and appropriate amount of knowledge behind it, while avoiding delving in too deep to confuse tutees. The success of a living coding session also required considerable effort from the participants, because keeping up with the pace is no less a demanding task. Participants

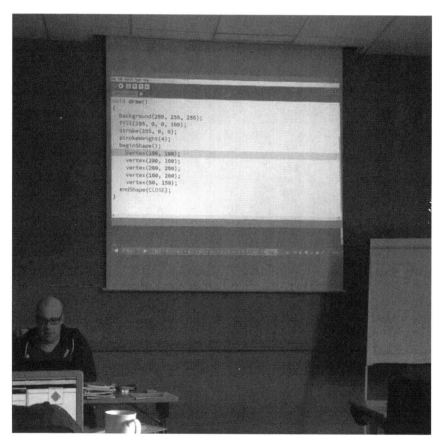

Figure 16.1 Live coding: writing and explaining code simultaneously
Source: Sung-Yueh Perng.

had to follow the code exactly as the tutor types on the screen and with a high degree of precision, otherwise they would be returned with nothing but error messages. Furthermore, neither the tutor nor the participants wanted the workshop to be a copy and paste exercise, and both aimed at becoming acquainted with the way in which this particular language reasons, acts, and often times confuses its users.

To do so, the tutor pointed out the difference between our normal day-to-day expressions and reasoning and how programming languages work. This meant for the participants that, when writing code, they were also laboring at converting everyday life experiences into highly stylized, regulated ways of expression. In the example below, when drawing a rotating diamond, the participants had to translate the mental image of the object into particular statements and numeric expressions of the position of the image on the screen ('rectMode(CENTER)'), the size of the image and the colors of the rectangle and the borders ('size(200,200; fill(0, 255, 0); stroke(0,0,25)'), the size of the diamond ('translate(width/2, height/2)'), and the amount it rotates each time ('(rotate(rotateAmount))' and 'rotateAmount = rotate-Amount + 1'), according to the specific order and style required by Processing.[1] All the participants got a revolving diamond on the screen, even with different colors and light effects. But it was after the hard work of refashioning human experiences and reasoning according to that of the machine. Accordingly, in the process, concentration was paramount and chatter had to wait until the final successful run of the code excited acclamation.

```
float rotateAmount = 0;
void setup()
{
size(200, 200);
fill(0, 255, 0);
stroke(0, 0, 25);
rectMode(CENTER);
}
void draw()
{
background(255, 255, 255);
translate(width/2, height/2);
rotate(radians(rotateAmount));
rect(0, 0, width / 2, height / 2);
rotateAmount = rotateAmount + 1;
}
```

Discussions and Reflections

Sound-making is only one mechanism through which different forms of knowledge, reasoning, and practices become engaged in collaboration or

92 Sung-Yueh Perng

contestation, and wider explorations on all possible mechanisms of creating spaces of coding can provide more insights into and the potentials for making alternative future cities. By describing the interconnectedness between the sounds and activities happening at the coding workshop, I begin to depict participants' difficult encounters with software. The lack of interaction observed in the workshop was not a symptom of the format of the tutoring. Instead, it was caused by the constant oscillation between familiar and highly formalized streams of reasoning, and the associated systems of knowledge, styles of articulation, and coding practices. When participants concentrated on repeating the tutor's code and using it for subsequent exercises, they were also rehearsing how they could reformulate their understanding of an object from their everyday experiences and points of view into series of expressions about the object according to the view of the software. Furthermore, for beginners and experienced programmers alike, little slips can put carefully compiled code out of action because of different naming conventions and syntax requirements when switching between similar programming languages or frameworks. That is, programmers also have to acquire highly specific, language-dependent and contingent ways of articulating the relationships between themselves, the object they create, and the context to situate the object. If a coding workshop quiets down as it goes on, it is because such reconfiguration of reasoning and articulation is complex and demanding, and participants were all committed to working through these difficulties for themselves.

Concluding Remarks

At a coding workshop, the scope of a project, the goal, the exercises, and the programming language to use are all preconceived, and participants have step-by-step instructions planned by the tutor to learn. However, these parameters are often more dynamic, fluid, and contingent, and have to be negotiated when a project is pursued under the context of civic hacking. Added complexities emerge from having to define affected communities, the project's intended benefits and costs, required hardware and software skills and resources, and possible solutions; and negotiations occur among individuals, governmental agencies, and civic organizations of differing motivations and concerns (Perng and Kitchin 2016). As a result, the quiet and peaceful coding time has to be reconsidered and situated in the wider embodied and sociotechnical interactions that bring in contact different forms of reasoning, articulations, rules, regulations, knowledge, and everyday practices. These interactions often unfold in situ, in short or sustained conversations to draw plans and sociotechnical imaginaries about urban futures, and in contestation when different motivations and interpretations about these futures confront one another. Accordingly, the ways the interactions cast shadow on code writing and solution development can change constantly and it remains uncertain how the hopes for more open and transparent spaces of coding can be materialized. To create better networked urban experiences and futures, continued research is thus required to make explicit the tricky processes of opening up the spaces of coding and the unanticipated problems emerging from them.

Acknowledgements

The research for this paper was conducted under the Programmable City project, funded by a European Research Council Advanced Investigator award (ERC-2012-AdG-323636-SOFTCITY). I am grateful for those who endeavor to make coding more accessible and diversify coding population and cultures, and Vicky in particular for her work for Coding Grace and PyLadies Dublin, as well as facilitating the research.

Note

1. Extracted from the organizer's workshop notes, available at https://hackpad.com/Introduction-to-Processing-YKTwteQ7PrV (1 September 2015).

References

Büscher Monika, Xaroula Kerasidou, Michael Liegl et al. 2016. "Digital Urbanism in Crises." In *Code and the City*, edited by Rob Kitchin and Sung-Yueh Perng, 163–177. London: Routledge.

Graham, Stephen D.N. 2005. "Software-Sorted Geographies." *Progress in Human Geography* 29 (5): 562–580.

Kitchin, Rob. 2014. *The Data Revolution: Big Data, Open Data, Data Infrastructures and Their Consequences*. London: Sage.

Kitchin, Rob and Martin Dodge. 2011. *Code/Space: Software and Everyday Life*. Cambridge: MIT Press.

Lodato, Thomas James and Carl DiSalvo. 2016. "Issue-Oriented Hackathons as Material Participation." *New Media & Society* 18 (4): 539–557. doi:10.1177/1461444816629467

Maalsen, Sophia and Sung-Yueh Perng. 2016. "Encountering the City at Hacking Events." In *Code and the City*, edited by Rob Kitchin and Sung-Yueh Perng, 190–199. London: Routledge.

Perng, Sung-Yueh and Monika Büscher. 2015. "Uncertainty and Transparency: Augmenting Modelling and Prediction for Crisis Response." In *Proceedings of the 12th International Conference on Information Systems for Crisis Response and Management*, edited by Leysia Palen, Monika Büscher, Tina Comes and Amanda Hughes, 1–7. Kristiansand, Norway.

Perng, Sung-Yueh and Rob Kitchin. 2016. "Solutions and Frictions in Civic Hacking: Collaboratively Designing and Predicting Wait Time for an Immigration Office." *Social & Cultural Geography*, Online First. doi:10.1080/14649365.2016.1247193

Urry, John. 2007. *Mobilities*. Cambridge: Polity Press.

Urry, John. 2014. *Offshoring*. Cambridge: Polity Press.

17 Mobility, Media, and the Experiences of Airbnb's Aesthetic Regime

Paula Bialski

Experiencing networked urban mobilities includes sensing—smelling, seeing, touching, hearing—things, events, people, media that are strange or uncanny. This approach of experiencing networked urban mobilities will discuss the way in which home-stays, hospitality networks, and short-term rental websites can foster uncanny experiences. What I want to enhance is how such platforms' aesthetic regimes set an agenda for this uncanny tourist experience, and more broadly, how 'the digital' has become central to the mobilities discourse.

Sensory Uncanny

It was a sunny August afternoon at Airbnb headquarters near San Francisco's Mission Bay, and I was walking slowly through the building's hallways, entirely in awe. The grandiose, sun-lit main lobby felt as if it floated me up towards their open 72,000-square-foot workspace that spanned a few floors. Hundreds of little details overwhelmed my senses—coffee machines, scribbles on the walls, hammocks, micro gardens, video game consoles, and nobody over the age of 30. After the first 15 minutes of sensory overload, my eyes slowly focused on one specific detail—a conference room. I looked inside its glass walls and pressed my palms up to get a better look. My gaze stopped at a bed covered in a bright duvet, accentuated by a bold-colored shelf filled with used books lining the wall. Next to the door near my hands, a photo hung above the standard boardroom sign-up sheet. I focused in and saw 'Milan' labeled across the door, with a small 5x3 photo of the bedroom inside hanging above it. I turned around and looked at my host. He smiled. "Our boardrooms are modeled after real listings." I looked back inside. I suddenly started imagining the couple in Milan who shared that bed. I was with them during their morning coffee, and overhearing their pillow talk at night. It was this Silicon Valley 'unicorn'—Airbnb—that helped bring millions of people into the bedrooms of other strangers, and they were indirectly underlining the power of this process as they appropriated one of these bedrooms for their staff meeting room.

One way in which we experience networked, urban mobilities is through the sensory uncanny—strange juxtapositions that borrow from one place and are found in another, leaving the one who is experiencing surprised, confused, or having to re-negotiate what they once knew before. Airbnb is one such example, and its San Francisco headquarters is just a reflection of the juxtapositions this type of tourism offers—where the private sphere is made public, and objects (the bed, a lamp) and places (the Milan bedroom) are transported to other dimensions (a boardroom in another city).

Digital Aesthetic Regimes and Tourist Experience

My interest in hospitality networks and short-term rental websites started when working with Couchsurfing.org, a year after they launched in 2006. Soon after the onset of the sharing economy, I caught wind of Airbnb, which I found was a monetized and smartphone-friendly version of the Couchsurfing service, and an empirical goldmine for mobilities and media cultures research. Yet this story of the way in which we experience mobilities will not be solely about the experience of Airbnb. What I want to underline is how such a platform's aesthetic regime sets an agenda for the tourist experience, and more broadly, how digital media became central to enabling this type of mobility.

Designed like a social networking website with a profile of each user, a friendship list, and a review system, the so-called 'community marketplace' of Airbnb allows the user to offer accommodation for a certain price to anybody who is willing to pay the given amount. The exchange differs from a hotel booking, as the host has to first accept the guest's request. Any host can deny the rental of their space, without giving a reason to the user requesting the space. The exchange is not purely about hospitality—the host-guest exchange is usually based on an economic imperative—where the host relies on the income of the guest, thus more often than not accepting the guest's request. While such new platforms undoubtedly impact the way tourism is 'done' (Germann Molz and Gibson 2007; Bialski 2012), such peer-to-peer websites cannot be fully understood without looking into the role of the platforms themselves in creating the tourist experience.

Unpacking 'Sharing' and Illusions of Authenticity

An apartment or room that is advertised on Airbnb is not available in an older media format—it is not a text message or video that is being shared, but rather space, time, the feeling of home, safety, rest, and coziness. What is being shared is an experience of home. How are such 'experiences' being communicated? Moving back to the Airbnb headquarters—I believe that the experiences of home and coziness are communicated to and from the travelers, the hosts, the coders, the designers, and platform creators, through a

96   *Paula Bialski*

constant feedback loop—running deep within the crochet bedding in the boardrooms, through the images on the website, back into the bedrooms of Milan.

As was mentioned in a previous paragraph, Airbnb is unlike other non-monetary, access-based sharing platform because of its monetary, competitive, market-based logic. While many peer-providers within the sharing economy have a primary money-based imperative to share their possessions, their practices are still cloaked in the illusion of being something good, world changing, and utopian. While Airbnb involves a monetary exchange, there still seems to be something sharing-like within Airbnb, and this is linked to the authenticity that is necessary when being a host. Participating in the sharing economy comes with an unwritten, yet quite specific 'how-to' guide of how to act as a host—and authenticity, or maintaining an illusion of authenticity, is very much part of the practice, and success, of sharing. When entering an economy of home atmospheres, authenticity is even more important. "Private life is the realm in which we attempt to behave in an authentic manner, to be 'true' to ourselves" (Sennett 2003, 7). The concept of 'the home' has particular resonances for the 'authentic' emotional self (Lupton 1998).

Aesthetics and Atmosphere

Airbnb, through the way in which their website is designed, is producing an aesthetic regime for and by a media-savvy, mobile class—and this class is not only sharing spaces but experiences and atmospheres. As atmosphere is an inherent aspect of the sense of home (Pennartz 2006), avid hosts start to abandon their aesthetic sense of what 'home' looks and feels like, and curates his or her apartment in such a way to convey an atmosphere which follows a certain aesthetic regime, fed back to them through the images and messages found on the website.

Hosts use adjectives that connote familiarity and a sense of home. Words like 'cozy,' 'relaxing,' 'elegant,' or 'pleasant' are often used to describe a listing. When placing a search for accommodation, some of the first listings carry slogans like 'Romantic Room in Artistic Flat,' 'Beautiful & Cozy Rooftop Room,' or even 'Dream Home with Bikes and Love.' Images of the space are also used to convey a sense of atmosphere. Some apartments might have warm colors, cozy pillows, candles, rustic bookshelves; others show photos of clean white walls, minimal expensive furniture, and tasteful artwork. Images are used to convey a sort of atmosphere appealing to the potential guest. Each listing also features a feedback section—a feature of the profile's interface where previous guests are expected to 'review' the listing based on accuracy, cleanliness, check-in experience, communication, location, and value, providing a written description of their experience. The success of any listing relies on 'positive' reviews, but these reviews not only convey a sense of trust but also help convey (to other guests) an atmosphere of a certain space.

In one way or another, this illusion of authenticity, and the illusion that sharing does take place, is inherently part of this form of mobility. This authenticity is made visible through the medium—or Airbnb's interface—through images and listing reviews. Advertising a listing as 'home,' rather than just an apartment, room, or space, already connotes that the peer user will gain an experience of a certain atmosphere—in this case, a sense of 'home.' This 'economy of atmospheres'—where what is being exchange is in fact a feeling, a 'dream,' a specific atmosphere—is intrinsic in the logic of the sharing economy, where what is 'shared' is also the non-tangible.

"Transport requires a basis, a medium," explained Knies, an early German economist who wrote about the telegraph, "on which it can operate, and an instrument, a force, that carries out this movement" (Knies 1857, 244, my translation). What I want to more generally underline around the theme of mobility and experience is that the question of how people operate upon media thus has to be complemented by the equally important question of how media operate upon people (Horn 2008, 7). Thus the way in which we experience mobility using a website like Airbnb is also a result of the constant people-medium feedback. As Eva Horn stated, the notion of 'medium' reduces to a fragile and even ephemeral state of 'in-between-ness,' as much a moment (let alone an object) of separation as of mediation, a moment taken by virtually becoming an actuality, a moment of structuring and encoding and thus of the creation of order, but also the source of disruption and 'noise' (Horn 2008, 7).

Concluding Remarks

While the digital platform of Airbnb can be seen as a form of mobilization that constitutes the basis for our mobility, it also informs our experience, promises us an experience of a place-to-come. These places-to-come are not public spaces such as parks, museums, or waterfalls, but private, intimate bedrooms and living rooms of strangers—purveying an instant experience of home, closeness, and intimacy. In looking at the case of Airbnb, we can see how certain platforms, the media, and the infrastructures they employ communicate a specific experience. Engaging in this experience can help us radically rethink the relation between bodies, movement, and space, as well as how a specific aesthetic regime of intimacy engages the three.

References

Bialski, Paula. 2012. *Becoming Intimately Mobile*. Frankfurt am Main: Peter Lang.
Germann Molz, Jennie and Sarah Gibson, eds. 2007. *Mobilizing Hospitality: The Ethics of Social Relations in a Mobile World*. Aldershot: Ashgate.

98 *Paula Bialski*

Horn, Eva. 2008. "Editor's Introduction: There Are No Media." *Grey Room*. 29 (Winter): 6–13.

Knies, Karl. 1857. *Der Telegraph als Verkehrsmittel*. Tübingen: Laupp.

Lupton, Deborah. 1998. *The Emotional Self: A Sociocultural Exploration*. London: Sage.

Pennartz, Paul J.J. 2006. "Home: The Experience of Atmosphere." In *At Home: An Anthropology of Domestic Space*, edited by Irene Cieraad, 95–106. Syracuse: Syracuse University Press.

Sennett, Richard. 2003. *The Fall of the Public Man*. New York: Penguin.

Part III
Modes and Emotions

18 Senses Matter

A Sensory Ethnography of Urban Cycling

Peter Cox

In recent research I have been considering the question, '*How* do people ride in the city, when bicycling is a mundane phenomenon?'[1] The core of this investigation builds on a discussion between the contributors to *Cycling Cultures* (Cox 2015) seeking to understand everyday practices and to evaluate appropriate methods for doing so. I wanted to explore in particular how important the physical spaces in which people ride are for the ways in which people ride. As sensory beings, our sensory experiences should have an important impact upon our choices and behaviors at a collective as well as individual level. My working hypothesis was that they are very important but problematic to measure in any meaningful way.

Thinking About Research Methods

To investigate and to try and make sense of how people move around, it is first necessary to observe. Spinney (2011) and Brown and Spinney (2010) used head-mounted video cameras and a 'ride-along' to investigate cycle commuters' practices and experiences. They found video elicitation, where a journey is filmed and then discussed, a successful means by which to understand people's thoughts about riding. Yet they also argue that much of the action they are investigating takes place at a pre-rational, pre-verbal level. When subject to rationalization and reason a significant and problematic gap is opened between the event and the language of description: "many of the experiences that make cycling meaningful are fleeting, ephemeral and corporeal in nature, and do not lend themselves to apprehension by language alone" (Brown and Spinney 2010, 134). Video recordings of journeys made and those journeying with fields notes recorded 'on the fly,' as a means to gather research data, appeared an obvious starting point: They provided a 'thick' data source for analysis.

Aware of the need to consider the corporeal and experiential, my study of urban mobility took a more deeply anthropological line. Everyday cycling takes place in a sensory landscape, a sense-scape, of urban life and form. The turn towards greater consciousness of the sensory world in ethnographic work is now well established (Pink 2009). Consideration of sensoriality has

102   *Peter Cox*

proceeded simultaneously with, and is frequently connected to the growth of mobilities studies (Urry and Larsen 2011). Responding to the modalities of mobility, new methods (including extensive use of digital media) have been extensively explored (Fincham et al. 2010; Büscher, Urry, and Witchger 2010). There is proper debate about the deployment and utility of novel methods on mobilities research: Do they provide a privileged understanding or are they simply another tool through which to see and understand? (Merriman 2014). While I would agree that many conventional methods of social scientific study are problematically geared towards considering society through a lens of stasis—where the units of investigation are constructed as (relatively) stable phenomena—I would only go as far as arguing that new methods augment understanding, rather than 'better' understanding. For this investigation, the use of digital techniques made available observations that might not otherwise have been so. However, their use and resulting data also raise significant ethical questions over their deployment.

Returning to the intersection of mobilities, methods, and visual and sensory ethnographies, it is notable that studies of cycling (e.g. Brown and Spinney 2010) have been integral to the development of these intertwined threads of inquiry. The field of cycling studies, while still relatively new, is also sufficiently established over the past decade for patterns of scholarship to be discernible, and key among these are ethnographic approaches (Jungnickel and Aldred 2013) and an interest in kinaesthetics as a focal point (Spinney 2007). These also connect to more established fields of social scientific work on the body and embodiment (Schilling 2014). There is, in short, no dearth of theoretical or practical perspectives from which to draw in the study of the cycling body.

Methodological Concerns

If this richness was not enough, underlying theoretical concerns also fed into the study. From one perspective, using video as a more direct method of data capture might suggest an exclusive interest in a new empiricism, seeking a realist ontology. Indeed, much of the background upon which this draws comes from an academic tradition peculiarly obsessed with empiricism. However, these connections were strongly tempered by engagement with non-representative theory. Following Thrift (2008), my work seeks to move from the cognitive towards a more performative methodology, where divisions between subject and investigator are questioned. This is especially important in conditions where "kinetic empathy . . . is both the means by which the body experiences itself kinaesthetically and also the means by which it apprehends other bodies" (Thrift 2008, 237).

Given that the original subject of my study was mundane behavior in public spaces, it was considered that filming journeys made, for the purposes of research only, and within the confines of the research context, would be justified as a legitimate means to investigate these practices. Ian

Walker's (2010) discussion of the ethics of recording and reporting road-use behavior provides a very clear starting point for consideration of the problems of using video investigation. Using video for data gathering and note taking poses a number of questions: One colleague suggested in jest that it might be described in other contexts as a form of stalking. While I was not deliberately tracking individuals, or even aiming to do so, the comments made me re-evaluate the research processes.

To move the focus away from an obsessive covert surveillance of others, the journey recording was re-evaluated reflexively. Rapidly, I realized that what was revealed in the film was not the actions and the world of others' behaviors as much as my own processes of learning to ride in a new and unfamiliar urban space. The study was reversed from a voyeuristic investigation of 'others' to a reflexive engagement with the self as traveling subject. Auto-ethnography allows the researcher to engage with lived experience as it is lived, within a spatial context, but avoiding the voyeuristic gaze. Ingold's (2014, 387) powerfully phrased argument, that "knowledge grows from the crucible of lives lived with others," insists on the reinvigoration of participant observation and the constant interactions of the social self. To investigate the sensory world in this manner is neither to identify a clearer picture of a singular reality, nor to produce new data sources as a further contribution to an ever stronger realism. Similarly, to consider and embrace the autobiographic or auto-ethnographic is not to reveal an essence of being in an identitarian register. Rather, it is to engage with, and become implicit in, a set of ongoing performances of selves and others in a constant process of encounter.

Findings

Reviewing films of the same journey repeated over a number of months, coupled with the verbal notes made en route, I saw how I responded differently to changing conditions. External factors from the condition and type of infrastructure, to changes in weather and season, altered the way I, and my fellow commuters, moved through the city. While I have previously argued strongly for the agency of landscape in the formation of cycling experiences, the more forceful engagements of this perspective in the built environment forced me to reconsider not simply the sensory experiences as the (agentic) body absorbs and processes information coming in, but also the emotional responses provoked by those outer conditions. For example, weather conditions present not just physically changing circumstances but also inputs that shape emotional changes.

Mauthner and Doucet (2003) highlight how the mechanics of the research process and sense of self interact for the situated researcher. Six months was sufficiently long to allow for an absorption every day of what initially had been new and unfamiliar into the mundane and unremarkable. It slowly became clear that my existing perceptions of fluency in the body language

104 *Peter Cox*

and performance of the cycle commuter were wholly inadequate for the realties encountered. While I have been riding bicycles for nearly 40 years and journeying to the same workplace for over a decade, this research was taking place in a city new to me.

Concluding Remarks

I realized how the experience of riding within the specific confines of Munich had altered the way I ride. Experiencing the spaces and routes had subtly reshaped my riding. Even though I have written on the disciplining of the riding subject through discourses of physical infrastructure and imagery (Bonham and Cox 2010), it was remarkable to see these processes in my own experience. Field notes made in the early weeks, read back five months later, revealed not simply the details of journeys made, but demonstrated changing points of significance and also of my understandings of place and space. What had been initially unfamiliar and strange—very 'other'—was slowly being absorbed into a sense of home, and belonging.

Above all, what I came to understand was that senses matter. The city shapes how cycle commuters ride, both positively and negatively. The way we respond to urban design is emotional and pre-rational, existing in sensory perception that goes beyond conventional categories. Spaces shape feelings and feelings change the actions we take. Understanding and being able to measure these dimensions prompts a number of areas of further research, most notable in designing evaluation tools to measure the experiential impacts of infrastructural investments.

Note

1. This work was enabled by a Leverhulme International Academic Fellowship (IAF-2014–2016) entitled 'Developing Cross-Disciplinary Research into Bicycling and the Environment,' undertaken at the Rachel Carson Center for Society and Environment in Munich, 2014/15.

References

Bonham, Jennifer and Peter Cox. 2010. "The Disruptive Traveller? A Foucauldian Analysis of Cycleways." *Road and Transport Research* 19 (2): 42–53.
Brown, Katrina and Justin Spinney. 2010. "Catching a Glimpse: The Value of Video in Evoking, Understanding and Representing the Practice of Cycling." In *Mobile Methodologies*, edited by Ben Fincham, Mark McGuiness and Lesley Murray, 130–151. Basingstoke: Palgrave Macmillan.
Büscher, Monika, John Urry and Katian Witchger, eds. 2010. *Mobile Methods*. London: Routledge.
Cox, Peter, ed. 2015. *Cycling Cultures*. Chester: University of Chester Press.
Fincham, Ben, Mark McGuiness and Lesley Murray, eds. 2010. *Mobile Methodologies*. Basingstoke: Palgrave Macmillan.

Ingold, Tim. 2014. "That's Enough About Ethnography!" *Hau: Journal of Ethnographic theory* 4 (1): 383–395. http://dx.doi.org/10.14318/hau4.1.021

Jungnickel, Katrina and Rachel Aldred. 2013. "Sensory Strategies: How Cyclists Mediate Their Exposure to the Urban Environment." *Mobilities* 9 (1): 238–255.

Mauthner, Natasha S. and Andrea Doucet. 2003. "Reflexive Accounts and Accounts of Reflexivity in Qualitative Data Analysis." *Sociology* 37 (3): 413–431.

Merriman, Peter. 2014. "Rethinking Mobile Methods." *Mobilities* 9 (2): 167–187.

Pink, Sarah. 2009. *Doing Sensory Ethnography*. London: Sage.

Schilling, Chris. 2014. *The Body and Social Theory* (3rd ed.). London: Sage.

Spinney, Justin. 2007. "Cycling the City: Non-Place and the Sensory Construction of Meaning in a Mobile Practice." In *Cycling and Society*, edited by Dave Horton, Paul Rosen and Peter Cox, 25–46. Aldershot: Ashgate.

Spinney, Justin. 2011. "A Chance to Catch a Breath: Using Mobile Video Ethnography in Cycling Research." *Mobilities* 6 (2): 161–182.

Thrift, Nigel. 2008. *Non-Representational Theory: Space/Politics/Affect*. London: Routledge.

Urry, John and Jonas Larsen. 2011. *The Tourist Gaze 3.0*. London: Sage.

Walker, Ian. 2010. "In-vivo Sampling of Naive Drivers: Benefits, Practicalities and Ethical Considerations." In *Mobile Methodologies*, edited by Ben Fincham, Mark McGuinness and Leslie Murray, 43–52. London: Palgrave Macmillan.

19 Feeling Community
Emotional Geographies on Cycling Infrastructure

Njogu Morgan

Cycling has been linked with personal and group identities (Popan 2014; Stoffers 2012; Fincham 2007; Ebert 2004; Carstensen and Ebert 2012; Edwards and Leonard 2009; Skinner and Rosen 2007). Skinner and Rosen (2007, 86) suggest that "identity [should be considered] as intrinsic to people's transport choices." They offer three models to think about the relationship between identities and transport. In the first model, identities shaped by social contexts sway transport choices. In the second, travel experiences generate collective identities that influence transport mode choice. In the third, the first two interact, such that transport choices are shaped by identities and in turn travel experiences shape identities.

In this chapter I explore their second model of how experiences in travel generate identities that inform transport choice. I am interested in this model because it is less abstract than other processes through which existing or emergent identities shape transport behavior. Cycling is a deeply embodied practice that draws connections amongst sensory bodies, bicycles, landscapes, infrastructures, and other road users. Mobilities scholars have shown how experiences derived in movement generate meanings which in turn influence transport choice. Here the journey itself is an important site of inquiry (Sheller and Urry 2006; Jensen 2009; Spinney 2009).

Following these lines of research, I will explore how emergent emotions while cycling can create a sense of community. Drawing on auto ethnographic research while conducting fieldwork in Chicago, I argue that 'street-level moments of assembly,' when cyclists meet as they wait to proceed onwards at a traffic light, can create feelings of mutuality. Such feelings can encourage everyday cycling. However, these micro moments must be understood in a wider context. My broader doctoral research (Morgan forthcoming) sheds light on how other macro processes including economic changes, grassroots activities to promote everyday cycling, and consumer logics underpin these feelings of community.

Methodological Approach

This essay is drawn from personal experiences of cycling in Chicago as part of a doctoral study exploring changes in the symbolic meanings of utility cycling from a historical comparative perspective. Chicago was chosen because it has demonstrated a high rate of growth in everyday cycling albeit from a low base (League of American Bicyclists 2013). Moreover, since I lived in the city for about a decade, I had some prior knowledge that would ease the research process.

One element of the data collection approach in the doctoral study involves direct participation: cycling. As Larsen (2014, 60) notes, "in autoethnography, the researcher's own embodied participation makes up the empirical material and features as the main protagonist in the text." This approach enabled me to deepen my understanding of the contemporary experiences of cycling in Chicago, the spatial and demographic variations in cycling practices, and patterns of interactions with different modes of transport. It also allowed me to observe different kinds of bicycle use. Over two research visits conducted in the summer of 2014 and spring of 2015, I rode a bike in various parts of the city during the morning and evening rush hours when I could observe the highest volumes of commuter cycling.

Many scholars have used auto-ethnographic approaches in studying symbolic and affective dimensions of travel and made broader social claims (Jones 2005; Edensor 2003). Is this justified? Manderscheid (2016, 10) argues that one weakness of approaches in some mobilities research is that focus on the "micro level of experiences, practices and motives . . . [is the lack of] systematic consideration of their positionality in space, time and the social." D'Andrea, Ciolfi, and Gray (2011, 158) have similar concerns. Therefore, while focusing on the personal experience of cycling, I was aware that the micro moment arises from and reproduces macro arrangements.

In studying how emotions connect individuals to social groups, I draw on Randall Collins' (2004) theory of interaction rituals. The theory of interaction rituals offers a model of how social solidarities are created in situations of togetherness where more than two people are physically copresent. I will elaborate on the theory as I illustrate its operations in my bicycling experiences in Chicago.

Into the Trees: Emotions, Community, and Everyday Practice

I am riding my bike on Milwaukee Avenue in Chicago, a street which has some of the highest bike traffic in the city (Crandell 2014; Resman 2014). It is known as the 'hipster highway' to refer to the social identity of people who ride bikes on it (Page et al. 2009). I am now behind a group of everyday cyclists. We approach an intersection as the traffic signal turns red. My sense of expectation grows as I approach since this is my first immersion in Chicago's bicycle traffic; this is what Collins (2004) describes as a baseline mood or emotion. When I get to the light, I meet others already waiting. I do not look back to count or see who is around us. However, I can sense there are at least three others behind me. Ahead of me there are four more. *We* wait for the traffic light to change. The wait feels long. I am now aware

108 *Njogu Morgan*

that I am in a group of commuter cyclists because, as Collins (2004) would have it, we are all engaged in a common activity.

The length of the wait provides time for emotions to build up. This is *us*! I am overjoyed. I want to embrace these anonymous people. To Collins this is the first key outcome of a successful moment of assembly: a feeling of group membership. Here individuals step, as it were, out of themselves into the collective. It is difficult to describe such a fleeting though powerful emotion. This is not something I had been expecting. In fact, when I attempt to consciously relive it later, I cannot, which emphasizes the role of the non-rational in travel as many mobilities scholars have observed. In this light Collins argues that participants of a successful interaction ritual develop proxy methods to recall the grand moment of inter-subjectivity. These might include symbols and shared practices after the ritual is over. Furthermore, they will act to protect the collective—this imagined community (Anderson 2006).

A successful interaction ritual is also one where there occurs a high degree of emotional energy in individual participants expressed through such feelings as "confidence, strength, enthusiasm" and most critically "*initiative in taking action*" (Collins 2004, 48). As a result of my immersion in the moment of assembly, I felt motivated to continue cycling. When I was away from the 'hipster highway' I yearned to return for the joy of riding together; for that feeling of mutuality here revealing why the theory of interaction rituals is also known as "the mutual-focus/emotional entrainment mechanism" (Collins 2004, xi). Participants of successful rituals like me will seek out opportunities to re-experience the emotional high. When I found my moments of assembly, I was loath to leave other participants, so I kept riding on even when it took me away from my intended destinations. Thus, street-level moments of assembly can be key micro sites for building solidarities, where the bicycle is a signifier of group belonging and an enabler of continuing practice.

Seeing Both the Woods and the Trees

But we need to exit the street level to see how this micro moment is produced by macro processes. My doctoral research into the resurgence of cycling in Chicago since the late 1990s reveals a range of factors that led to the concentration of cyclists I encountered on Milwaukee Avenue (Morgan forthcoming). Firstly, Milwaukee Avenue connects a range of neighborhoods that in the early 1990s offered cheaper rents and proximity to the city center where there are employment, entertainment, and educational opportunities. Artists, film-makers, musicians, writers, students, and others with moderate incomes were attracted to these neighborhoods (Page et al. 2009; Perry 2006).

In the early phase of everyday cycling resurgence, these neighborhoods also benefited from dense grassroots activities that sought to change the public image of biking and provide practical cycling skills (Herlihy and Barnes 2015; Lane 2015; Kaminecki 2001; Winkle 2015; Redd 1998). Moreover, later on they were also some of the areas where the bicycle industry, real estate developers, and neighborhood associations deliberately associated bicycle use with fashionable urbane lifestyles (Salvatore 2014; Huebner 1994) as urban gentrification processes were unfolding (Lloyd 2002; Page et al. 2009). These processes recruited a new class of bicycle users—'hipsters'—who found affinity with the social distinction value being offered by the aforementioned actors within a context of socioeconomic difference. Therefore, while the feelings of community that I experienced can be understood as emergent in practice, they also could not have occurred without macro processes.

Concluding Remarks

Mobilities scholars have opened up important research lines into the role of travel experience in shaping transport mode choice. In such studies Manderscheid (2016) has rightly cautioned against a tendency to focus on what she calls the 'solitary mobile subject.' This chapter suggests a way of bridging this problem through an auto-ethnographic approach that connects micro moments to the social. I was therefore able to argue that emotions generated in street-level moments of assembly may weave feelings of mutuality amongst strangers on bicycles and engender continuing practice. While there is reasonable theoretical and empirical basis for this claim, more work is needed to explore findings in different contexts and from a wider sample.

References

Anderson, Benedict. 2006. *Imagined Communities: Reflections on the Origin and Spread of Nationalism* (Revised ed.). London and New York: Verso.

Carstensen, Trine Agervig and Anne-Katrin Ebert. 2012. "Chapter 2 Cycling Cultures in Northern Europe: From 'Golden Age' to 'Renaissance.' " *Cycling and Sustainability* 1: 23–58. Transport and Sustainability 1. Emerald Group Publishing Limited. www.emeraldinsight.com/doi/abs/10.1108/S2044-9941%282012%2900000 01004

Collins, Randall. 2004. *Interaction Ritual Chains*. Princeton: Princeton University Press.

Crandell, Lee. 2014. Personal Interview. Interview by Njogu Morgan.

D'Andrea, Anthony, Luigina Ciolfi and Breda Gray. 2011. "Methodological Challenges and Innovations in Mobilities Research." *Mobilities* 6 (2): 149–160. doi: 10.1080/17450101.2011.552769

Ebert, Anne-Katrin. 2004. "Cycling Towards the Nation: The Use of the Bicycle in Germany and the Netherlands, 1880–1940." *European Review of History* 11 (3): 347–364. doi:10.1080/1350748042000313751

Edwards, Andrew and Max Leonard. 2009. *Fixed: Global Fixed-Gear Bike Culture*. London: Laurence King Publishing.

110 Njogu Morgan

Edensor, Tim. 2003. "Defamiliarizing the Mundane Roadscape." *Space and Culture* 6 (2): 151–168. doi:10.1177/1206331203251257

Fincham, Ben. 2007. "Bicycle Messengers: Image, Identity and Community." In *Cycling and Society: Transport and Society*, edited by Dave Horton, Paul Rosen and Peter Cox, 179–195. Aldershot, Ashgate.

Herlihy, Tim and Maria Barnes. 2015. Personal Interview. Interview by Njogu Morgan.

Huebner, Jeff. 1994. "The Panic in Wicker Park | Feature | Chicago." August 25. www.chicagoreader.com/chicago/the-panic-in-wicker-park/Content?oid=885350.

Jensen, Ole B. 2009. "Flows of Meaning, Cultures of Movements—Urban Mobility as Meaningful Everyday Life Practice." *Mobilities* 4 (1): 139–158. doi:10.1080/17450100802658002

Jones, Phil. 2005. "Performing the City: A Body and a Bicycle Take on Birmingham, UK." *Social & Cultural Geography* 6 (6): 813–830. doi:10.1080/14649360500353046

Kaminecki, Matt. 2001. "The Ride of Many Names." *Old Critical Mass Website*. April 27. http://old.chicagocriticalmass.org/ridereports/april01writeup.html.

Lane, Steve. 2015. Personal Interview. Interview by Njogu Morgan.

Larsen, Jonas. 2014. "(Auto)Ethnography and Cycling." *International Journal of Social Research Methodology* 17 (1): 59–71. doi:10.1080/13645579.2014.854015

League of American Bicyclists. 2013. "Where We Ride: An Analysis of Bicycling in American Cities." http://bikeleague.org/WhereWeRide.

Lloyd, Richard Douglas. 2002. "Neo-Bohemia: Culture and Capital in Postindustrial Chicago." PhD diss., The University of Chicago. http://0-search.proquest.com.innopac.wits.ac.za/pqdthss/docview/305469269/abstract/191AF84EEC284FCDPQ/1?accountid=15083.

Manderscheid, Katharina. 2016. "Who Does the Move? Affirmation or De-Construction of the Solitary Mobile Subject." In *The Mobilities Paradigm: Discourses and Ideologies*, edited by Marcel Endres, Katharina Manderscheid and Christophe Mincke, 91–113. Abingdon: Routledge.

Morgan, Njogu. Forthcoming. *An Inquiry into Changes in Everyday Bicycling Cultures: The Case of Johannesburg in Conversation with Amsterdam, Beijing and Chicago*. Johannesburg, South Africa: University of the Witwatersrand.

Page, Scott, Mindy Watts, Leah Murphy, Todd Fagen, Mark de la Vergne, Matt Cunningham and Dan Houston. 2009. "Wicker Park Bucktown Master Plan." Chicago, IL, United States: Wicker Park Bucktown SSA. http://wickerparkbucktown.org/projects/master-plan/.

Perry, Forrest. 2006. "Why Hipsters Aren't All That Hip." *Monthly Review*, September 4. http://monthlyreview.org/2006/09/01/why-hipsters-arent-all-that-hip/.

Popan, Cosmin. 2014. "Cycling, Togetherness and the Creation of Meaning." In *Newcastle Upon Tyne*, UK. http://newcycling.org/events/20131130/cycling-society-annual-symposium-2014.

Redd, Jim. 1998. "Critical Mass April 1998 Ride." *Old Critical Mass Website*, April. http://old.chicagocriticalmass.org/ridereports/cmridap8.html.

Resman, Rebecca. 2014. Personal Interview. Interview by Njogu Morgan.

Salvatore, Michael. 2014. Personal Interview. Interview by Njogu Morgan.

Sheller, Mimi and John Urry. 2006. "The New Mobilities Paradigm." *Environment and Planning A* 38 (2): 207–226. doi:10.1068/a37268

Skinner, Dave and Paul Rosen. 2007. "Hell Is Other Cyclists: Rethinking Transport and Identity." In *Cycling and Society*, edited by Dave Horton, Paul Rosen, and Peter Cox, 83–96. Aldershot: Ashgate.

Spinney, Justin. 2009. "Cycling the City: Movement, Meaning and Method." *Geography Compass* 3 (2): 817–835. doi:10.1111/j.1749–8198.2008.00211.x

Stoffers, Manuel. 2012. "Cycling as Heritage: Representing the History of Cycling in the Netherlands." *The Journal of Transport History* 33 (1): 92–114. doi:10.7227/TJTH.33.1.7

Winkle, Hannah. 2015. "The Rides." *Chicago Critical Mass*, July 17. http://hannahwinkle.com/ccm/ride.htm.

20 Urban Velomobility and the Spatial Problems of Cycling

Till Koglin

Being on a bike and cycling through cities is a fascinating way of experiencing the urban surroundings and the everyday life of cities one lives in or visits. Cycling has garnered the attention of several research disciplines in recent decades, and much has been written about best-practice cases of cycling in European cities (e.g. Buehler and Pucher 2012; Pucher and Buehler 2008), velomobility, the marginalization of cyclists in urban space (e.g. Koglin 2013, 2015a; Koglin and Rye 2014; Furness 2007, 2010), and cycling safety (e.g. Minikel 2012; Jacobsen and Rutter 2012). However, this experience can differ greatly between different cities. Most research on urban cycling has been conducted in cities that could be described as 'bicycle hostile' and not known for their bicycle culture (see, for example, McCarthy 2011; Furness 2010; Aldred 2013; Aldred et al. 2016).

In this chapter, I discuss some issues and conflicts as perceived by cyclists in Copenhagen, Denmark, and compare them to those of cyclists in Stockholm, Sweden. Empirically the research consists in observations and a survey study conducted in both cities in 2010/2011. Quantitative studies are quite rare within the field of mobilities research; thus this approach offers a new dimension for analyzing cyclists' experiences. The analysis presented here is set in the theoretical framework of 'space wars' (see Bauman 1998, 1999) and takes a spatial perspective. Through the spatial lens, my analysis offers an explanation for how these issues are connected to the interpretation of space produced through transport planning. How cyclists perceive their situations might also affect whether they choose to continue cycling and thus the everyday mobilities in urban networks.

Space Wars in Motion—a Theoretical Foundation for Analyzing Mobility Conflicts

Cyclists in both Stockholm and Copenhagen seem to experience a fight over public space similar to what Bauman termed 'space wars' (Bauman 1998; Koglin 2013). According to Bauman, social space is not created from measurable and objective space, rather the objective space is developed from social space. It is in the social relations where Bauman sees the battles over

Urban Velomobility 113

space occurring (Bauman 1998, 1999). Bauman understands that cities work to push space into objectively measurable units to avoid local subjectivities when these local subjectivities might have different views on the meaning of space, particularly in urban contexts. The basis for space wars is thus an effect of the attempts to objectively measure space.

The interpretation of what space means changes over time. Therefore, space must be seen in terms of subjective social relations, and it is from these relations that conflict in urban areas arises. Cities and global actors attempt to objectify space in order to discourage the development of interpretations of space other than the neoliberal views of space and mobility (Bauman 1998). The priority given to motorized traffic as a modern way of moving within a city has marginalized bicycling and has fostered urban space wars between different modes of transport (Koglin and Rye 2014; Koglin 2013).

Societies are influenced by mobilities because the complex social relations in people's everyday lives are strongly connected to being mobile or immobile. Analyzing social and spatial relations from a mobilities viewpoint can offer new insights into power relations, spatial dimensions, and policies (Urry 2000, 2007). People experience this in their everyday movements in urban spaces, and thus they are important when analyzing and developing transport systems. Motorized modes of transport dominate urban spatial networks and this form of development leads cities to marginalize bicycling and thus create the power relations that develop into urban space wars. The theoretical concept of urban space wars offers deeper insights into the issues, challenges, and problems that cyclists experience in their movements within urban spatial networks.

Cycling in Stockholm and Copenhagen

Stockholm and Copenhagen show significant differences when it comes to cycling, and this can be seen, for example, in differences in the modal split (Table 20.1). Thus I wondered how cycling is experienced in the two Scandinavian cities. What do cyclists think about it, and how would I, myself, experience cycling in the two cities?

Table 20.1 Modal split in Stockholm and Copenhagen

	Stockholm	*Copenhagen*
Car trips	31.9%	33.3%
Bike trips	6.6%	26.9%
Walking	13.7%	21%
Public transport trips	46.9%	18.3%
Other	0.9%	0.5%
Total	100%	100 %

Source: National Travel Survey Data Sweden and Denmark 2011/2012.[1]

114 *Till Koglin*

I took my own bike on the train to Copenhagen and started cycling around in the city. I also cycled through Stockholm, but, unfortunately, I could not take my own bike with me and had to rent a bike in Stockholm. The experiences of cycling through Stockholm and Copenhagen were quite different. I was involved in many more conflicts with cars in Stockholm than in Copenhagen. Furthermore, the infrastructure was much less convenient in Stockholm than in Copenhagen.

The differences could be seen more or less directly on my first bike ride in either city. While cycling through Copenhagen and Stockholm, I observed better cycling infrastructure in Copenhagen compared to Stockholm. However, although Copenhagen is often seen as one of the best cycling cities, it still has more work to do to prevent the fight over urban street space. It seems that the cyclists in Copenhagen never really can escape car traffic, and fellow cyclists can make the cycling experience in Copenhagen unpleasant. Despite these issues, it seems that cycling in Copenhagen is quite highly prioritized in transport planning (Koglin 2015a; Koglin 2015b). The situation in Stockholm is quite different for cyclists and truly embodies the fight over urban street spaces. While in Copenhagen the cycling networks were occasionally interrupted, such networks in Stockholm either did not exist or were often interrupted and very confusing. The bicycle tracks not only end and lead cyclists onto streets, but they often end with barriers such as construction sites or walls.

Cyclists' Experiences in Stockholm and Copenhagen

In the survey study in Copenhagen and Stockholm, cyclists answered questionnaires about their experiences of cycling in their respective cities. Cyclists in Copenhagen reported that cycling is better in Copenhagen than in Stockholm. For example, 96% of the cyclists in Copenhagen think that it is efficient to ride a bike in the city compared to 88% in Stockholm. Also, in Copenhagen 76% of the cyclists feel that they are prioritized in traffic, whereas in Stockholm only 36% of the cyclists feel this way. When it comes to traffic safety, cyclists in Copenhagen feel safer (67%) than cyclists in Stockholm (42%). One aspect cyclists in both cities have in common is that they feel stressed in traffic (54% in Copenhagen and 52% in Stockholm).

These data show that cyclists in Copenhagen have a better experience while cycling than those in Stockholm. However, it does not seem that daily velomobility always works smoothly in either city, which is reflected in the stress the cyclists experience about their safety. In the same survey, the cyclists also had to reflect on which mode of transport created the most problems for them (Figure 20.1). This clearly showed that cars and fellow bicyclists are problematic in both cities. Despite feeling that bicycles are prioritized as a mode of transport, cyclists do not feel that the bicycle is prioritized when multiple traffic types are combined.

Cycling in both cities seems to be a fight over public space and over how it is prioritized. Different interpretations of space seem to be at the heart of the problem. Cyclists in both cities see the car and other cyclists as most problematic and not, for example, public transport. Much more space is allocated to motorized traffic, which seems to be the normal way of handling traffic space in modern transport planning (Koglin and Rye 2014; Brown 2006). Through this thinking, certain representations and interpretations of space are often connected to the view that street space is equal to car space, which excludes cycling from the streets.

Concluding Remarks

Cyclists in Stockholm and Copenhagen experience similar problems in their daily velomobility. They feel that cars and other cyclists create the most

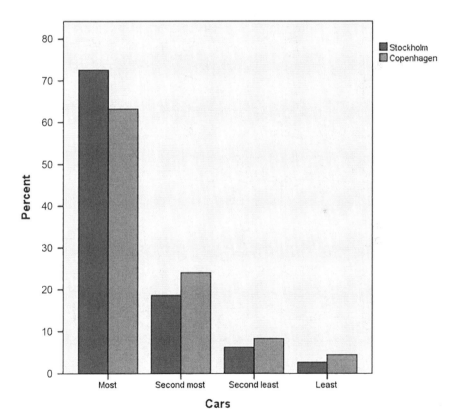

Figure 20.1 Comparison of Stockholm and Copenhagen. The histograms show the responses to the question, "Rank from 1 (most) to 4 (least) which categories of road user you think create the greatest problems in your city"[2]

Source: Lund University.

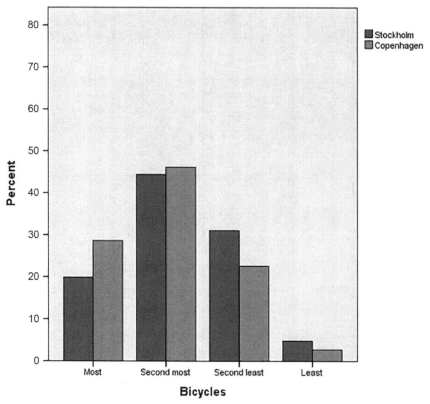

Figure 20.1 (Continued)

problems for them. Furthermore, it seems that cycling in the two cities is stressful, which might be related to this. In both cities, motorized traffic has more space and often more power over public space due to city planning and the interpretation of space. The interpretations are more in favor of car traffic, which marginalizes space for cycling, and this leads to space wars. Theories of mobilities and space wars can lead to a deeper understanding of the risks and issues cyclists experience as well as a deeper understanding of urban power relations.

Mobilities research seldom engages in quantitative methods. Nevertheless, much can be learned from conducting survey studies such as the one used here. The survey study generated a very different kind of data than the ethnographic research. The combination of two very different methods for data collection created a form of knowledge that is otherwise not obtainable. Not only have I experienced the state of velomobility in both cities first-hand and could observe conflicts, etc., I also have generalizable, quantitative data that tell a similar story of cyclists' experiences of their everyday velomobility in the two cities. Through the use of both ethnographic and quantitative methods, urban space wars can be illuminated.

Notes

1. The modal split is calculated as the share of modes for all trips that end or start in the city.
2. The bicyclists ranked four modes of transport, Cars, Bicyclists, Public Transport, and Pedestrians. I chose only to show the most problematic modes here, meaning cars and bicyclists, since those two really stick out in the analysis.

References

Aldred, Rachel. 2013. "Cycling and Society." *Journal of Transport Geography* 30: 180–182.

Aldred, Rachel, James Woodcock and Anna Goodman. 2016. "Does More Cycling Mean More Diversity in Cycling?" *Transport Reviews: A Transnational Transdisciplinary Journal* 36 (1): 28–44.

Bauman, Zygmund. 1998. *Globalization—The Human Consequences.* Cambridge: Polity Press.

Bauman, Zygmund. 1999. "Urban Space Wars: On Destructive Order and Creative Chaos." *Citizenship Studies* 3 (2): 173–185.

Brown, Jeffrey. 2006. "From Traffic Regulation to Limited Ways: The Effort to Build a Science of Transportation Planning." *Journal of Planning History* 5 (1): 3–34.

Buehler, Ralph and John Pucher. 2012. "International Overview: Cycling Trends in Western Europe, North America, and Australia." In *City Cycling*, edited by John Pucher and Ralph Buehler, 9–30. Cambridge: The MIT Press.

Furness, Zack. 2007. "Critical Mass, Vélomobility and Urban Space." *Mobilities* 2: 299–319.

Furness, Zack. 2010. *One Less Car—Bicycling and the Politics of Automobility.* Philadelphia: Temple University Press.

Jacobsen, L. Peter and Harry Rutter. 2012. "Cycling Safety." In *City Cycling*, edited by John Pucher and Ralph Buehler, 9–30. Cambridge: The MIT Press.

Koglin, Till. 2013. "Vélomobility—A Critical Analysis of Planning and Space." PhD diss., Lund University.

Koglin, Till. 2015a. "Vélomobility and the Politics of Transport Planning." *GeoJournal* 80: 569–586.

Koglin, Till. 2015b. "Organisation Does Matter—Planning for Cycling in Stockholm and Copenhagen." *Transport Policy* 39: 55–62.

Koglin, Till and Tom Rye. 2014. "The Marginalisation of Bicycling in Modernist Urban Transport Planning." *Journal of Transport and Health* 1 (4): 214–222.

McCarthy, Deborah. 2011. "'I'm a Normal Person': An Examination of How Utilitarian Cyclists in Charleston South Carolina Use an Insider/Outsider Framework to Make Sense of Risks." *Urban Studies* 48 (7): 1439–1455.

Minikel, Eric. 2012. "Cyclist Safety on Bicycle Boulevards and Parallel Arterial Routes in Berkeley, California." *Accident Analysis & Prevention* 45: 241–247.

118 *Till Koglin*

Pucher, John and Ralph Buehler. 2008. "Making Cycling Irresistible: Lessons from the Netherlands, Denmark and Germany." *Transport Reviews: A Transnational Transdisciplinary Journal* 28: 495–528.

Urry, John. 2000. *Sociology Beyond Societies: Mobilities for the Twenty-First Century*. London: Routledge.

Urry, John. 2007. *Mobilities*. Cambridge: Polity Press.

21 The Role of the Driver-Car Assemblage in the Practices of Long-Distance Aeromobility

Julie Cidell

In studying the connections between networked cities, we often focus on one mode: rail, plane, car, etc. In developing a richer understanding of these mobility systems, however, we also need to consider how they overlap and reinforce or contradict each other. In this chapter, I consider the extent to which the automobile is a part of journeys by plane, particularly for travelers who live some distance from a major airport. This is not just a question of how one gets to the airport, but how one's plans for the entire long-distance journey require consideration of the automobile. This example also serves to remind us of how the global air transportation system is grounded in local places and experiences of mobility.

Hybrid Long-Distance Travel

Automobility describes a system that ostensibly gives us the autonomy to go where we want when we want and with whom we want (although each of these assertions has been challenged (Adey et al. 2007; Dodge and Kitchin 2004; Hagman 2006). Aeromobility in many ways describes the reverse: We go when the airlines want us to go, and we travel beside strangers and through places in which we have no interest in going. Nevertheless, automobility and aeromobility are closely intertwined when we consider long-distance travel. Particularly for travelers coming from smaller airports, long-distance travel is often a combination of car and plane, including not only the usual factors of price and scheduling, but how to take advantage of the automobile's benefits and/or avoid its negatives. At the same time, aeromobility may inadvertently become automobility, not only from major events like September 11 or Eyjafyallajökull (Birtchnell and Büscher 2011), but from thunderstorms, snow, or mechanical failure. This unintentional modal shift, including the reassembly of a different driver-car hybrid, may in turn condition future travel decisions.

The car and the airplane have generally been treated as separate systems in work on the social and cultural aspects of mobility. There are obvious differences in vehicle ownership, travel distance, cost, and identity-shaping between these two systems which make it worthwhile to consider each one

120   *Julie Cidell*

independently. However, for travelers originating in smaller cities that are spokes in the North American hub-and-spoke network (what I term 'spoke travelers'), and who constitute about half of all air passengers in that region, the long-distance air journey involves the automobile. Aero-automobility is therefore a hybrid form of long-distance travel, combining the features of individual control and freedom of the car with the long-distance reach and highly structured nature of air travel (Cidell 2014).

Spoke Travelers in the American Midwest

This study originated not only in my own personal experience, but also that of my colleagues. The University of Illinois at Urbana-Champaign, about 200 kilometers south of Chicago, operates a commercial airport with regularly scheduled service to Chicago on a single airline. Since O'Hare International Airport is one of the most frequently delayed airports in the country, it is quite common to be delayed on the return flight home. This flight takes about half an hour, but is at a distance that could be driven within three hours. That last flight is frequently canceled as well. US Department of Transportation statistics show that Champaign's airport experiences 30% of its flights being delayed (with the average delay over an hour) compared to a 22% national average, and 5% of its flights being canceled compared to a 2% national average. In other words, out of every ten trips, it is likely that a flight will be canceled either coming or going. The question of whether to drive to O'Hare in the first place and thus avoid the troublesome air connection is one that we all face, and being a major research university, some of us travel very frequently. Based on stories I had heard from my colleagues, I set out to see how spoke travelers make choices about the mobility systems they use in their long-distance travel.

In my study of spoke travelers at four different universities within a half hour's flight from O'Hare, I found that these travelers have three options: 1) to leave from their small home airport and connect through O'Hare with a strong possibility of delay or cancelation; 2) to travel about three hours by car or bus to O'Hare, therefore reducing the likelihood of a missed connection; or 3) to travel by car or bus for one or two hours to an intermediate-sized airport such as Indianapolis or Milwaukee. The four research sites were all public universities: University of Illinois at Urbana-Champaign, Illinois State University in Bloomington-Normal, University of Wisconsin at Madison, and University of Wisconsin at Oshkosh. Research was conducted via semi-structured interviews with 51 university employees, both faculty and staff, at these four universities. All of these spoke cities are a two-and-a-half to three-hour drive to O'Hare; Urbana-Champaign and Bloomington-Normal have train service to Chicago but not to O'Hare; and all but Oshkosh have bus service to O'Hare. Across these four sites, travelers chose the first option (flying from the home airport) about 60% of the time, the second option (traveling by ground to O'Hare) about 15% of the time, and the third option (traveling by ground to an intermediate airport) about 20% of the time.

By Car and by Plane

While well-studied factors such as price and scheduling influenced the decision of how to travel, open coding of qualitative data from interviews led me to conclude that the automobile played a significant role as well. For some people, the freedom and flexibility afforded by the car or by a commercial bus were enough to make them travel first by ground and then by air. In particular, having ground travel available in case the final flight home was canceled was very attractive. This is something that travelers who originate from hub airports do not have to consider. The ability to visit friends or family in Chicago, or to carry out shopping trips while in the area, could also make the automobile a part of the long-distance air journey. Finally, travelers journeying with small children found the car-to-plane transfer easier than the plane-to-plane transfer, and would accordingly drive a greater distance to obtain a non-stop flight. For these people, incorporating multiple mobilities and the relationships involved in maintaining those mobilities are necessary to understanding long-distance travel.

For others, however, the automobile presented too much of a hassle to be included in long-distance air travel. This could be because of the unpleasantness of driving close to O'Hare, since these spoke travelers live in cities of 50,000 to 100,000 people and are not accustomed to congested urban traffic. Or it could be because their bodies would not be up to the task of driving for hours after a long international flight (in the North American context, 'international' almost always means 'trans-oceanic'). Alternatively, if the family automobile was kept in a distant parking lot for days or weeks, it would be unavailable to other drivers within the household. For these people, the negative aspects of automobility outweighed its inclusion as part of long-distance travel, even if cheaper fares or more convenient flying times could be accessed via car.

Concluding Remarks

While much of the work in aeromobilities has focused on the experience within the airport itself, it is important to remember that a network of social connections enables getting to and from the airport, and choosing which airport, in the first place. It is also important to remember that not everyone accesses the global airline network in the same way, and that 'spoke travelers' have a different set of possibilities because of their location within the network. Within the North American hub-and-spoke network, about half of the traffic at hubs originates in a spoke and involves a transfer. The sometimes precarious nature of air travel, particularly in a region where snowstorms and thunderstorms can cause delays or cancelations during

122 *Julie Cidell*

most months of the year, means that ground travel needs to be considered explicitly as a backup when making long-distance travel plans. In fact, since I began this research project, I myself have been twice stranded at O'Hare when the last flight home was canceled!

Beyond the need to consider aero-automobility as a hybrid system, this study also indicates the importance of geographic context in our studies of mobilities. Even a global system such as the air network needs to be considered within local and regional contexts, including the extent to which it intersects with other mobility systems. As Lin (2016) has argued, most work on aeromobilities has been done in Europe, where 'international' and 'long-distance' travel are synonymous, and where rail travel often substitutes for air. Not so in the United States, where border crossing is not a regular feature of long-distance travel—but the automobile is. As more work is done on the political and cultural aspects of air travel in Asia, Africa, and Latin America, as well as North America (e.g. Lassen and Galland 2014; Lin and Yeoh 2015), we will continue to find ways in which networked mobilities vary from region to region and within regions.

References

Adey, Peter, Lucy Budd and Phil Hubbard. 2007. "Flying Lessons: Exploring the Social and Cultural Geographies of Global Air Travel." *Progress in Human Geography* 31: 773–791.

Birtchnell, Thomas and Monika Büscher. 2011. "Stranded: An Eruption of Disruption." *Mobilities* 6: 1–9.

Cidell, Julie. 2014. "Spoke Airports, Intentional and Unintentional Ground Travel, and the Air Travel Decision-Making Process." *Transportation Research Part A* 69: 113–123.

Dodge, Martin and Rob Kitchin. 2004. "Flying Through Code/Space: The Real Virtuality of Air Travel." *Environment and Planning A* 36: 195–211.

Hagman, Olle. 2006. "Morning Queues and Parking Problems: On the Broken Promises of the Automobile." *Mobilities* 1: 63–74.

Lassen, Claus and Daniel Galland. 2014. "The Dark Side of Aeromobilities: Unplanned Airport Planning in Mexico City." *International Planning Studies* 19: 132–153.

Lin, Weiqiang. 2016. "Re-assembling (Aero)Mobilities: Perspectives Beyond the West." *Mobilities* 11: 49–65.

Lin, Weiqiang and Brenda Yeoh. 2015. "Moving in Relation to Asia: The Politics and Practices of Mobility." *Environment and Planning A* 48: 1004–1011.

22 U.Move 2.0

The Spatial and Virtual Mobility of Young People

Dirk Wittowsky and Marcel Hunecke

This chapter presents our findings from the research project U.Move 2.0, which focuses on young adults' use of mobile technology in relation to mobility in Germany. It is our intention to overcome the lack of reliable data on young adults' (age 14–24) behavior, examining the influence of information and communication technologies (ICT; e.g. social media) on activity patterns as well as the impact on daily mobility. We have developed a multi-method survey approach to validate the relationship (intensity and direction) between ICT and mobility—and even to conduct a small methodological experiment to test the validity of our survey design. We explored from different perspectives how ICT reshapes the temporal and spatial organization of daily travel behavior. Our specific approach is important to get a better understanding about causes and effects of the interactions between ICT and mobility. In addition to the new mobility paradigms, the significance of virtual mobility will become increasingly important—though not confirming the expectation that virtual mobility will substitute most young people's activities (Konrad and Wittowsky 2016a).

Digital Age and Physical Mobility

Digitalization is increasingly affecting our daily behavior in space and time and penetrating especially young adults' lives. The availability of smartphones and mobile Internet usage has increased dramatically. We now live in a world where we can search for anything online—from everywhere at any time—using more or less useful applications, constantly interacting and communicating with people via messenger services and making appointments more spontaneous. Furthermore, the digital age is characterized by a variety of innovative technologies and services. ICT are key drivers of innovative transport services and create the conditions to make better use of the existing transport system—perhaps boosting the transition of sustainable personal mobility. The digital natives represent the first generation to grow up with new technology, have moved into a world where their behavior changed radically: They receive information very fast and like to do parallel activities (Prensky 2001). Moreover, ICT are pervading modern lifestyle

124   Dirk Wittowsky and Marcel Hunecke

activities, whether at work or during our free time, whether shopping or socializing—including how they travel. ICT are key drivers of innovative transport services and have the power to make multimobility more attractive and feasible (precise information and real-time assessment of transport alternatives, using travel time for socializing, gaming, or working).

Currently, there are a vast number of studies that seek to explore and understand the relationship between ICT and physical mobility. Furthermore, there exist a variety of assumptions about the influence of ICT on daily life, but in terms of mobility behavior and transport use they are not empirically well documented so far. It's evident that ICT are influencing many aspects of daily life and the demand for mobility, whether physical or virtual. But the knowledge base is fragmentary and uncertainty is associated with the results. Nonetheless, there are many theoretical and empirical challenges to further research and discussions. Logically the question arises: How will ICT influence mobility in the future? '

ICT and Mobility

Many national and international studies have identified changes in the mobility behavior of young adults (e.g. ifmo 2013; Frontier Group 2012). In Western industrial countries young adults are increasingly using sustainable and alternative forms of mobilities such as bicycles, public transport, and car-sharing systems. Among this group it is significant that the use of private cars is no longer a dominant choice of transport mode. Instead, different forms of mobility and transport services are combined to spontaneously cover their complex activity patterns. For all intents and purposes, the whole population of young adults (regardless of country and social class) has easy and permanent access to information and social media (BITKOM 2013/2014; JIM 2013), with user-friendly applications at their fingertips for organizing activities and trips. Using devices like smartphones and tablets, it is easy for them to access real-time travel information, download and store a ticket, or unlock a shared vehicle belonging to a self-service system (e.g. a bicycle or car). And they use these devices as a personal assistant in all traffic situations. A number of research projects are studying ICT usage in relation to mobility patterns (Salomon 1986; Mokhtarian 1990; Wittowsky 2008; Lenz 2011; Lyons 2015; Pawlak et al. 2015). Among these researchers it is acknowledged that the influence of ICT in terms of mobility behavior and transport use is not as yet empirically substantiated. One reason for this is that measuring effects in a survey is perceived as difficult. However, this may become easier in the future through applications tracking mobility and ICT behavior.

Survey Approach

The multi-method survey approach was used on young adults ages 14 to 24. The survey involved three parts: a face-to-face personal theme-centered interview covering 40 items representing mobility-based attitudes; a paper-and-pencil trip diary kept over a period of three days (a weekend and one weekday); and an ICT diary (a paper-and-pencil protocol for the whole daily ICT usage) for the same period. The standard trip diary included the question, 'Was this trip affected by ICT use?' while the ICT diary included the reverse question: 'Did ICT use affect the conducted trips?' In addition, we used GPS loggers to validate the movements reported in the diary. In association with general questions about the link between ICT use and social media and recreational activities such as 'Does ICT usage lead to more/less meetings with friends or does it allow more spontaneous meetings?' we built a database to estimate the effects of such interactions. Based on the early works of Mokhtarian (1990), Salomon (1986), and Lyons (2015) the link and interaction between virtual and physical mobility were classified into three main categories: substitution, enhancement, and modification of the reported and planned trips. The sample covered 180 people from three different social milieus in the Rhine-Ruhr Area: cosmopolitan, middle class, and those living under precarious circumstances. To categorize the young adults in these three milieus, we adopted a simple approach, focusing on three variables: education, attitudes to ways of living, and budget. Additionally we made a bigger online survey with nearly 1000 participants who reported their trips and ICT activities in a diary. For further information on this read Konrad and Wittowsky (2016b).

Empirical Findings

Using this data as our basis, we described the virtual and physical mobility of young adults and analyzed the link between their physical mobility and ICT use. What we found is that young adults adopt an increasingly environmental attitude towards transport by prioritizing public transport and walking, accounting for significant shares of the modal split over private car ownership. While the proportion of car drivers (27.4%) is largest in the middle-class social milieu, those living in precarious circumstances do more than 40% of their trips by foot. A further important detail is that cosmopolitans make 4.6 trips each day and cover the largest daily distances. By contrast, those in precarious circumstances make fewer trips.

What characterizes today's digital natives? ICT play a major role in the everyday lives of young adults, as seen by the fact that they use such devices as smartphones or tablets nearly five hours a day—much more than on physical mobility. The main focus is on messaging (e.g. WhatsApp) and socializing (e.g. Facebook and Twitter). Over three-quarters of young adults plan or modify their trips and activities online, investing 11 minutes a day thereon—mainly for better information about different mobility modes. We found a significant correlation between the number of trips and the number of ICT activities. Young people with high ICT usage also featured an above-average number of trips. From our study it is also evident that both

126 *Dirk Wittowsky and Marcel Hunecke*

the number of trips and the number of ICT interactions are dependent on the milieu. Cosmopolitans make the highest number of trips as well as the number of ICT usage. On the other hand, young adults from the precariat are less active in number of trips and the use of ICT.

Our study also reflects and addresses the motivations and effects of young adults' mobility choices. It is therefore relevant to investigate whether people use ICT more intensely to pass commuting time during trips or do they make more trips as a consequence of new activities planned through social media and mobile technology? Our study show that young adults use their mobile devices on almost 44% of their reported trips, i.e. practically on every second trip using public transport. They thus actively make use of their mobility budget for other activities, e.g. ICT-based communication. This analysis underlines the concurrency of physical and virtual mobility and the importance of the latter for research. In the survey more respondents reported that ICT acted as an enhancement rather than a substitution—all with a moderate influence on their mobility behavior per se. But it seems that ICT fosters a higher level of physical mobility in young people and leads them to (re)organize and modify their daily activity and mobility patterns.

ICT facilitate inter- and multimodal travel—e.g. with a travel-plan smartphone application that combined different modes and their individual timetables. Users can choose the mode of travel best fitting the situation and their individual time and financial budgets. Given the penetration of ICT into all areas of private life as well as new forms of mobility (e.g. car-sharing and bike-sharing, carpooling or intermodal transport services), it is obviously that car use is becoming increasingly less attractive. There are many hypotheses why these changes have taken place (e.g. changes in transport infrastructure, use of ICT, or the reallocation of mobility budgets). Looking at the development of ICT over the last ten years and the link between mobility and ICT, another hypothesis is the young adults' attitudes toward public transit and biking, and their rejection of private car usage. For the older generation, owning a car symbolized adulthood. It would seem that today's technological innovations such as smartphones or other mobile devices are now replacing cars as symbols—or at least makes the other mobility choices more flexible and accessible. The impact of virtual mobility on physical mobility has a further dimension in the mobility turn that both time and space constraints will no longer play any great role (Konrad and Wittowsky 2016a). As a result, traditional behavior patterns and physical constraints will change and be transformed due to new forms of interaction and organization modifying and/or sometimes simplifying our mobile lives.

Concluding Remarks

However, our approach generates valuable indications for further empirical research. As one intermediate survey finding we found that the recruitment and supervision of participants as well as the accuracy and quality of the data—especially the travel diary and the ICT protocol—were significantly dependent on the milieus. Overall the quality and precision of our data is very good, but nevertheless our approach shows the limits to gathering physical and virtual mobility with paper and pencil. Additionally for this purpose an automatic data recording app would be indispensable.

Moreover, mobility-related attitudes—such as items for motives, preferences, and beliefs to use a specific transport mode—are increasingly favoring public transport and environmental responsibility. Furthermore our study shows that changes in the transport infrastructure and new mobility forms as well as the widespread use of season tickets are leading to increased public transport use. The ability to use ICT while traveling further fosters the attractiveness of public transport, biking, and walking. In summary, it can be stated that the link between virtual and physical mobility remains complex, requiring further research and proper survey methods. It might be that future research designs have to combine automatic data recording with in-depth or standardized interviews for smaller sample sizes. Obviously the short innovation cycles of increasing ICT require new data quality based on higher actuality.

The high volume of overlapping trips and ICT activities illustrates that virtual mobility is primarily an additional activity type now integrated into activity patterns. We expect ICT to give us—at least in theory—a greater scope to reorganize or optimize our daily lives, reacting more spontaneously than ever. It is no longer we who determine our movements in space and time, but increasingly precise real-time data and information. Yet, can technical devices in themselves hold the potential to optimize our individual mobility?

References

BITKOM. 2013. *Soziale Netzwerke 2013*. Berlin: BITKOM.

BITKOM. 2014. *Kinder und Jugend 3.0*. Berlin: BITKOM.

Frontier Group/US PIRG Education Fund. 2012. "Transportation and the New Generation: Why Young People Are Driving Less and What It Means for Transportation Policy." www.uspirg.org/sites/pirg/files/reports/Transportation%20%26%20the%20New%20Generation%20vUS_0.pdf. accessed April 4.

ifmo. 2013. "'Mobility Y'—The Emerging Travel Patterns of Generation Y." www.ifmo.de/tl_files/publications_content/2013/ifmo_2013_Mobility_Y_en.pdf. accessed May 23.

JIM. 2013. *Jugend, Information, (Multi-) Media. Basisstudie zum Medienumgang 12- bis 19-Jähriger in Deutschland*. Edited by Medienpädagogischer Forschungsverbund Südwest Geschäftsstelle: c/o Landesanstalt für Kommunikation Baden-Württemberg (LFK). Stuttgart, DE.

Konrad, Kathrin and Dirk Wittowsky. 2016a. "Digitalisierung der Lebenswelten junger Menschen—der Zusammenhang von virtueller und physischer Mobilität." *ILS-TRENDS* January 2016.

128 Dirk Wittowsky and Marcel Hunecke

Konrad, Kathrin and Dirk Wittowsky. 2016b. "Digital Natives mobil—Die virtuelle und räumliche Mobilität junger Menschen." *Internationales Verkehrswesen* 1: 56–58.

Lenz, Barbara. 2011. "Verkehrsrelevante Wechselwirkungen zwischen Mobilitätsverhalten und Nutzung von IuK-Technologien." *Informationen zur Raumnutzung* 10: 610–618.

Lyons, Glenn. 2015. "Transport's Digital Age Transition." *The Journal of Transport and Land Use* 8 (2): 1–19.

Mokhtarian, Patricia L. 1990. "A Typology of Relationships Between Telecommunications and Transportation." *Transportation Research A* 24 (3): 231–242.

Pawlak, Jacek, Scott Le Vine, John Polak, Aruna Sivakumar and Johanna Kopp. 2015. *ICT and Physical Mobility: State of Knowledge and Future Outlook.* London: Institute for Mobility Research (ifmo) and conducted by Imperical College London.

Prensky, Marc. 2001. "Digital Natives, Digital Immigrants." *On the Horizon* 9 (5): 1–6.

Salomon, Ilan. 1986. "Telecommunications and Travel Relationships: A Review." *Transportation Research A* 20A (3): 223–238.

Wittowsky, Dirk. 2008. "Dynamische Informationsdienste im ÖPNV—Nutzerakzeptanz und Modellierung." In *Schriftenreihe Institut für Verkehrswesen*, Karlsruher Institut für Technologie 68, edited by Dirk Zumkeller, 7–16 and 60–69. Karlsruhe: Institut für Verkehrswesen, Universität Karlsruhe (TH).

23 Inhabiting Infrastructures
The Case of Cycling in Copenhagen

Jonas Larsen and Oskar Funk

This chapter presents some of the *distinctive* everyday practices of cycling in pro-cycling Copenhagen. Here cycling is a 'strong regime' supported by a robust infrastructure and bike-friendly policies that normalize cycling as a legitimate everyday practice. The municipality has the overt ambition to be 'the best cycle city in the world' and extensive networks of curb-elevated bike lanes are the key material agent in this campaign. The city already has more kilometers of bike lanes than any other international city of roughly the same size. Bike lanes are said to encourage many to take up cycling, and these bike lanes are indeed inhabited: One in two Copenhageners, and 45% of those commuting *to* Copenhagen, travel by bike (City of Copenhagen 2015). In this chapter we discuss cycling practices in the infrastructural spaces of Copenhagen seen from an embodied user 'staging from below' perspective arguing that cycling practices are not completely pre-formed and there is always something 'more-than-designed' to people's practical engagement with the world.

Copenhagen Cycling and Staging From Below

Much cycling research has focused on cycling infrastructure (or lack of) and how it supposedly impacts upon the practices of cyclists. Less mobilities research has explored how everyday cyclists corporeally inhabit such infrastructures as part of their everyday routines. We believe it is crucial to address this paucity, as mobilities are not only staged 'from above' but also 'from below.' Jensen suggests that specific mobilities designs are always staged from above (by engineers, planners, and politicians) *and* "acted out, performed and lived from below, individually and especially in social interactions" (2014, 14), while Creswell (2010) has urged mobilities scholars to explore how different mobilities are corporeally performed and sensed. Degen and Rose (2012) investigate in a more generic sense how everyday, multi-sensuous experiences of, and within, designed places always exceed design logic. Such approaches are also seen in cycling research. Latham and Wood (2015, 301) explore how cyclists go about dwelling within, or inhabiting, the infrastructural spaces of London, while Jones (2012), Spinney

(2010), and Larsen (2014) use the notion of 'affective capacity' to draw attention to the corporeal resources required for inhabiting different cycling environments and for different riding styles. These studies have explored emerging cycling cities but similar studies of pro-cycling cities are still to be conducted (but see van Duppen and Spierings 2013). This absence in mobilities literature induced us to write this article.

Informed by such theories (and the mobilities paradigm more broadly), we discuss cycling practices in the infrastructural spaces of Copenhagen seen from an embodied user 'staging from below' perspective. By exploring some of the materials, meanings, and competences associated with cycling in this city, we hope to answer the question: How is everyday cycling in Copenhagen performed materially, culturally, and corporeally? In another, much larger article (which we draw upon in this paper), we also explore the staging of cycling in Copenhagen 'from above' (see Larsen 2017b; see also Larsen 2017a; Larsen and Christensen 2015). And we provide hyperlinks where some of the distinctive practices to which we refer are exemplified.

This chapter is part of a larger research project called Urban Bicycle Mobilities at Roskilde University, which has explored how, and why, cycling takes place in Copenhagen, as well as how it is designed and planned.[1] With regards to the user-perspective, we have conducted around 40 in-depth interviews and some 100 street-interviews as well as much street observation, 'ride-alongs,' and film-recordings, such as asking interviewees to wear head cameras while riding to work. Moreover, shorter studies in Amsterdam, London, and New York have enabled us to compare and evaluate cycling in Copenhagen with cycling in these other places.

Materials

Embodied 'inhabitation' of infrastructure is mediated by specific configurations of bikes and clothing. While the bike scene in Copenhagen is becoming increasingly diversified through expensive cargo bikes, cool vintage bikes, and state-of-the-art road racers, it is still the case that many Copenhageners ride fairly cronky and nondescript bikes, many of which are subject to much wear and tear and lack of maintenance. In Copenhagen, the bike is more of a mundane object than one of fetish (Larsen and Christensen 2015). Another key feature is that few adults use helmets and even fewer wear specialized clothing. The vast majority of people cycle in their work clothes; the city is the polar opposite of 'lycrafied London' (Larsen 2014, 2017b).

Copenhageners are supportive of bike lanes and they prefer to ride on them instead of the main road, as they feel safer here. When riding on roads without bike lanes, Copenhageners, in line with the law, 'hug the curb,' and, in doing so, they inadvertently elevate cars to the status of 'kings of the road' and themselves to subordinates. Yet sometimes some bike lanes are teeming with cyclists and they are so polyrhythmic they can be intimidating and annoying for all riders, whether slow or fast, experienced or inexperienced.

Our interviewees dismissed the public bike racks for being overcrowded and seldom 'at hand'; instead, Copenhageners have cultivated unique parking strategies from 'below.' Bikes are casually 'fly-parked' on the pavement with prop-stands or against a building (and inside communal courtyards and basements), and they are causally locked with a simple frame-fitted O-lock as few lock or 'moor' their bike against something solid with a U-lock, as is the norm in London, New York, and even Amsterdam. This ensures convenient, flexible, and fast parking (for more detail, see Larsen 2017a).

Meanings

This timesaving aspect is crucial as the interviews illustrate that people only cycle if it is faster or at least as fast and practical as driving and/or public transport. Moreover, unlike car-dominated societies (as in London; Steinbach et al. 2015), Copenhageners do not correlate cycling with environmental responsibility or an alternative lifestyle. Cycling is too common to serve such purposes (for more detail, see Larsen 2017b).

However, not all Copenhageners are keen cyclists. For instance, our observations in the most ethnically diverse neighborhood in Copenhagen revealed very few cyclists with 'dark skin': the bike lanes were populated by ethnic Danes while Black and Middle Eastern Copenhageners were seen walking, getting on the bus, and driving. The teenagers we interviewed (between 16 and 18 years of age) with parents of Middle Eastern origin are unenthusiastic about cycling despite being Copenhageners by birth and cyclists as children. They cannot wait to turn 18 so that they can start driving. In the meantime, they—and their friends—prefer public transport to 'strenuous' cycling.

Competencies

The competencies required for cycling in Copenhagen are much lower than in car-dominated cities such as London and New York. Here we were blown away by how intimidating and demanding cycling is, with cars and cyclists constantly mingling. And we observed, often in disbelief, how some cyclists ride assertively in the middle of the road and slalom around waiting cars (Larsen 2014, 2017c; see also Spinney 2010; Latham and Wood 2015). In Copenhagen there is little such mixing between cars and bikes. Moreover, given that most rides are only a few kilometers long and moderately paced, and the topography of Copenhagen is very flat, cycling in this city is rarely arduous, and there is "little heavy breathing or sweating bodies at red lights" (diary notes, 25 May 2015). It requires only basic fitness and stamina. However, inhabiting busy and sometimes chaotic bike lanes with close proximity between cyclists does necessitate some alertness, equanimity, and discipline to avoid perilous situations and crashes.

Often cycling in Copenhagen has more in common with walking than with driving. While novices and cautious Londoners also 'hug the curb' and walk their bikes (Latham and Wood 2015), these behaviors are widespread among Copenhageners. For instance, Copenhageners make turns like pedestrians by going from corner to corner (see Figure 23.1 and video: vimeo.com/137162683. Code: cosmo).

This 'Copenhagen left' slows down cyclists as it often involves two red lights instead of one. To avoid this, cyclists constantly make left turns through the pedestrian crossing (see video: vimeo.com/137162685. Code: cosmo). The irony is that the law permits cyclists to make a left turn in *one* movement. Once they have reached the other side they are allowed to make a left turn against a red light if the traffic allows it. Yet this rule is essentially unknown and the road design does not indicate that this is possible. Moreover, this type of turn seems intuitively wrong and dangerous for many Copenhageners.

Ironically, at the same time, cyclists routinely bend or break the rules to maintain their flow, especially at crossings. They make right turns against a red light, or cycle over the pedestrian crossings as just mentioned. We may call this competency 'gentle law breaking' as they rarely endanger others or cause road rage, as they are only 'committed' when it is considered safe and appropriate. The interviewees excuse their unlawfulness while cycling by the fact that it is the norm, harmless, and saves them much time. If they had to follow the rules then cycling would become slower and therefore less appealing and commonplace (for more detail, see Larsen 2017b).

Figure 23.1 'The Copenhagen left'
Source: Jonas Larsen and Oskar Funk.

Concluding Remarks

While cycling practices are always staged 'from above,' they are not completely pre-formed and there is always something 'more-than-designed' to people's practical engagement with the world. In the case of cycling in Copenhagen, we can see this in relation to a user-generated cycling culture of short cuts, gentle law breaking (sometimes by walking), ordinary clothing, informal parking, and casual locking. Without such 'staging from below' the numerous bike lanes would not have been built in the first place, or be so popular and established today. The development of a 'bicycle city' inextricably relies upon devoted everyday users as much as supportive planners and politicians. This article also highlights that future 'mobilities studies' must pay closer attention to the embodied everyday appropriation and re-appropriation of specific bike designs and other networked urban designs; their immediate and long-term success depends upon attracting loyal practitioners who reproduce the system by becoming both skillful users and vocal advocates (for more detail, see Larsen 2017b).

Note

1. http://rucforsk.ruc.dk/site/da/projects/urban-cycle-mobilities(15be6713-4a4d-4374-b993-36118d935307).html. This project is funded by the Danish Council for Independent Research | Social Sciences (FSE) [grant number 0602-02062B].

References

City of Copenhagen. 2015. *Copenhagen, City of Cyclists: Bicycle Account 2014*. Copenhagen: Municipality of Copenhagen.

Cresswell, Tim. 2010. "Towards a Politics of Mobility." *Environment and Planning D: Society and Space* 28 (1): 17–31.

Degen, Monica and Gillian Rose. 2012. "The Sensory Experiencing of Urban Design: The Role of Walking and Perceptual Memory." *Urban Studies* 49 (15): 3271–3287.

Jensen, Ole B. 2014. *Designing Mobilities*. Aalborg: Aalborg Universitets Forlag.

Jones, Peter. 2012. "Sensory Indiscipline and Affect: A Study of Commuter Cycling." *Social & Cultural Geography* 13: 645–658.

Larsen, Jonas. 2014. "(Auto)Ethnography and Cycling." *International Journal of Social Research Methodology* 17: 59–71.

Larsen, Jonas. 2017a. "Bicycle Parking and Locking: Ethnography of Designs and Practices." *Mobilities* 12 (1): 53–75.

Larsen, Jonas. 2017b. "The Making of a Pro-Cycling City: Social Practices and Bicycle Mobilities." *Environment and Planning A* 49 (4): 876–892.

Larsen, J. 2017c. "Leisure, Bicycle Mobilities and Cities." In *Tourism and Leisure Mobilities: Politics, Work and Play*, edited by Jillian Rickly, Kevin Hannam and Mary Mostafanezhad, 39–54. London: Routledge.

Larsen, Jonas and Mathilde Dissing Christensen. 2015. "The Unstable Lives of Bicycles: The 'Unbecoming' of Design Objects." *Environment and Planning A* 47 (4): 922–938.

134 *Jonas Larsen and Oskar Funk*

Latham, Alan and Peter R. H. Wood. 2015. "Inhabiting Infrastructure: Exploring the Interactional Spaces of Urban Cycling." *Environment and Planning A* 47 (2): 300–319.

Spinney, Justin. 2010. "Improvising Rhythms: Re-Reading Urban Time and Space Through Everyday Practices of Cycling." In *Geographies of Rhythm: Nature, Place, Mobilities and Bodies*, edited by Tim Edensor, 113–128. Aldershot: Ashgate.

Steinbach, Rebecca., Judith Green, Jessica Datta and Phil Edwards. 2011. "Cycling and the City: A Case Study of How Gendered, Ethnic and Class Identities Can Shape Healthy Transport Choices. *Social Science & Medicine* 72 (7): 1123–1130.

Van Duppen, Jan, and Bas Spierings. 2013. "Retracing Trajectories: The Embodied Experience of Cycling, Urban Sensescapes and the Commute Between 'Neighbourhood' and 'city' in Utrecht, NL." *Journal of Transport Geography* 30: 234–243.

24 Comparing and Learning From Each Other for a Better Cycling Future

Henk Lenting

Can two countries learn from one another about cycling when one of the countries in the comparison has significantly more cyclists than the other? The author is a researcher from the Netherlands who has worked in cycle planning, and is interested in how comparative perspectives might enable better understandings of cycling as a social practice and of the attitudes towards those practices. Working from the premise that this comparison can be fruitful, I found a lot of do's and don'ts for encouraging cycling in both countries. In the process, we have gained deeper understanding of why some people cycle and others don't (Lenting 2014). It is perhaps impossible to fully understand what truly distinguishes these two groups of people. However, by understanding their decisions better, we can learn a lot about sensible ways to encourage sustainable choices. Comparing the differences between two countries—and finding important lessons for both—can bring us a step closer to this goal.

The Netherlands and Denmark have been and are the Western world's leaders in cycling mode shares. This position has resulted in a lot of arrogance in the experts on cycling in 'our' countries. Based on personal observations and experience it seems that the general opinion among traffic planners in both countries is that 'our' approach to cycling is best. Furthermore, the belief is that these countries can only teach (not learn from) others. This arrogance has somewhat decreased over the last couple of years as the Netherlands and Denmark are learning from each other's strengths, but still the notion persists that we can only teach those places with lower mode shares of cyclists. A primary premise of my research was to compare two similarly sized cities (Chester, UK, and Leeuwarden, NL) to examine how both countries might learn something through the comparison. This premise was met by a lot of skepticism among Dutch colleagues and superiors. The end result of the research, however, proves that intelligently looking into differences in cycling cultures does enable us to learn from one another, even across widely differing cycle mode shares.

136 Henk Lenting

Approach

It is now widely understood that cycling in one form or another can be an essential element of low-carbon futures, contributing to solutions of ecological and spatial problems as well as economic inequality. When we identify cycling's increasing importance in our mobilities network this way, cycling research now becomes important for successful urban mobility in the future. In order to move toward higher cycle use, we want to be able to learn from each other internationally, but have found that copy-pasting is not the solution. In order to better understand the degree to which solutions cannot be universal, and how and why they need to be tailored to the local specificities, we need to analyze and compare at an individual case study level. As an exploration of possibilities, a comparison was made between Chester in the UK and Leeuwarden in the Netherlands, using the main research question: Where do intrinsic motivations for cycling in Chester (UK) differ from those motivations in a comparable Dutch town, how can these differences be explained, and how can they be used?

The two towns used are similar in demographics and spatial layout, making the comparison between them as promising as possible. Building on previous studies' identification of relevant factors (Heinen et al. 2010; Parkin, Ryley and Jones 2007; Vivanco 2013; Aldred 2010), questionnaires and interviews were used to elicit a series of responses concerning intrinsic motives for cycling. A total of 335 valid questionnaires were filled out, 150 in Chester and 185 in Leeuwarden; in each country six interviews were held to solidify data gained from the questionnaires. These revealed important differences between comparable selected population groups. Together with field observations, these results help explain differences in levels of cycling, and we can see what lessons can be learned from each other. A few downsides of the limited reach of this research are listed in the next paragraph.

The main downside of the approach used for this research is that I wasn't able to get a response that was representative for the entire city/area/country. The outcome of the comparison is still valid since the response groups in both countries were similar. Both response groups mainly consisted of students and cycling enthusiasts. These groups are not entirely representative of the population, but they are both very important in the system and they give a general idea about the rest of the population.

Social Sciences

Combining social sciences and mobility research in this project has made it possible to understand what we should or should not be doing on a more abstract level. By combining knowledge on how people make choices with what we know about cycling, we can encourage bicycle use more efficiently since this teaches us which improvements are most important to (potential) cyclists. The mobilities turn then has definitely inspired my work, and particularly this research project. With my background in traffic planning, a study of differences between the UK and the Netherlands in cycling would likely not have resulted in anything that could be interesting for the Netherlands without the influence of social sciences. The most interesting of these findings are set forth in the following section.

Findings

In this study, I have found that cycling has to be salient (it has to be in someone's mind as an option) before any other factors come into play. People have to start considering cycling first. You can build all the infrastructure you want, but it will not help unless potential users are considering biking. Some ways to achieve salience are:

- showing cycling as an option in travel plans
- making sure potential cyclists can see that other people are cycling too
- asking people to consider what steps they should take when using a bicycle for one of their regular trips (e.g. a trip to work or getting groceries)
- encouraging current cyclists to take a friend along

Even though this is not an exhaustive list, it does illustrate how knowledge from social sciences can be used to get one step closer to getting more people to use a bicycle as a mode of transport.

Once salience has been established, safety issues become important. In order to improve safety, cycling-specific infrastructure has to be built where needed and possible. Where this is not the case, drivers have to recognize that they can encounter a cyclist on their trip, know how to behave in traffic together with cyclists, and be willing to adjust to sharing the road.

When safety stops being an issue for cyclists, a number of factors increase in importance. This is at least the case for relaxation and for enjoyment of surroundings while cycling. Therefore, any efforts to improve how much people can enjoy a portion of their route is likely superfluous until they can ride safely from origin to destination. On the other hand, better safety or a better cycling network cannot improve one key element: the feeling of independence while riding a bicycle. This is present, even where basic requirements for cycling (by Dutch standards) aren't met.

Just as investing in attractiveness of a part of the cycling network is obsolete before the entire network is safe, there are a number of things that cities should not invest too much in at one time. A number of factors can discourage people from cycling, but never really encourage them to start cycling. Budgets can be spent more sensibly taking this into account. My research has found this to be the case for:

- type and quality of infrastructure
- attitudes towards cars, public transport, and walking

138   Henk Lenting

- having the skills and fitness required to cycle
- support from family or university

So while a lack of good infrastructure can deter people from cycling, amazing infrastructure will not encourage them to start doing so according to my research. Similarly, the fact that someone loves public transport may discourage him or her from starting to cycle, but hating public transport does not encourage him or her to start either.

Finally, a bike is a lifestyle for most cyclists in Britain (see also Aldred 2010) whereas it is an everyday tool for most cyclists in the Netherlands, as it is in Denmark. To improve cycling in both countries, the way people in the UK regard their bicycles can work as an inspiration to make cycling a lifestyle in the Netherlands, while the way Dutch people utilize their bikes can help people in the UK realize how a bicycle can be a useful mode of transport.

Concluding Remarks

This chapter has demonstrated that comparative studies, even across dissimilar patterns of cycling behaviors, can be fruitful. More importantly, it shows that using social sciences in transportation research by comparing cycling systems and attitudes towards cycling can help us learn about what makes some people cycle and what keeps others from doing the same. Furthermore, it shows that by using mobilities research we can reach further towards a common goal: creating a system with more sustainable transport for more sustainable futures.

References

Aldred, Rachel. 2010. "'On the Outside'? Constructing Cycling Citizenship." *Social and Cultural Geography* 11 (1): 35–52.

Heinen, Eva, Bert van Wee and Kees Maat. 2010. "Commuting by Bicycle: An Overview of the Literature, Transport Reviews." *A Transnational Transdisciplinary Journal* 30 (1): 59–96. Accessed February 17, 2014, doi:10.1080/01441640903187001

Lenting, Henk. 2014. "Comparison of Intrinsic Motivations for Cycling. Thesis research by H.K. Lenting." Bachelor thesis, NHL Hogeschool. http://goo.gl/eeTjun. accessed November 3, 2014.

Parkin, John, Tim Ryley and Tim Jones. 2007. "Barriers to Cycling: An Exploration of Quantitative Analyses." In *Cycling and Society*, edited by Dave Horton, Paul Rosen and Peter Cox, 67–82. Aldershot: Ashgate Publishing Limited.

Vivanco, Luis A. 2013. *Reconsidering the Bicycle: An Anthropological Perspective on a New (Old) Thing.* Abingdon: Routledge.

25 The Velomobilities Turn

Tim Jones

This chapter highlights how the 'velomobilities turn' (Horton et al. 2007) has paralleled the general mobilities turn (Sheller and Urry 2006) and how this inspired my personal journey in this rapidly evolving field and helped me to reflect on my approach to understanding cycling in society. First, I look back at the key turning point for researchers of cycling and how this has more recently become enmeshed within broader mobilities research that the Cosmobilities Network represents. Following this I will highlight two examples of studies that were inspired by the mobilities turn and enabled my research colleagues and I to think differently about velomobility, to conjoin quantitative and qualitative approaches, and to provide empirically grounded accounts of contemporary cycling the UK.

Combining Velomobility and Mobilities Research

The tenth anniversary conference of the Cosmobilities Network, Networked Urban Mobilities, in 2014 was timely in that it coincided with the tenth anniversary of the Cycling and Society Research Group (CSRG). The CSRG was an outcome of the inaugural Cycling and Society Symposium of social science research into cycling, which a small crowd of researchers and I attended in June 2004 at the Centre for Mobilities Research (CeMoRe), Lancaster University. The Symposium was successful in bringing together multiple disciplines to understand velomobility above and beyond the domain of transport studies and its heartland of mathematics, engineering, computing, IT, and economics. It sowed the seeds of velomobilities thinking in highlighting how—despite the ubiquity of cycles and cycling from a social science perspective—velomobility remained remarkably 'unthought.' This spawned the edited publication by Horton, Cox, and Rosen (2007), *Cycling and Society*. A pivotal publication, this represented a turn towards amplifying cycling's diversity and the need to understand cycling in relation to the society within which it exists "of lifeworlds, histories, structures and cultures" (Horton et al. 2007, 1).

In parallel with the velomobile turn, catalyzed by the now annual Cycling and Society Symposia, was the broader mobility turn and the growth in

140 Tim Jones

mobilities research. Early mobilities research, however, tended to focus on the omnipotent practice of car-driving and aeromobility while multifarious 'alternative ways of moving' were devoted less attention (Vannini 2009). Thankfully, this is changing and the 'Cycling Futures' session at the Cosmobilities conference Experiencing Networked Urban Mobilities in 2014 was an opportunity to (re)engage with velomobilities research. The session provided space for researchers from different disciplines to come together to focus on practices of cycling, intersections of meanings, technologies, and competencies and their place both in changing current urban milieu and in anticipating low-carbon futures.[1]

My journey started over a decade ago from 'moorings' in transport studies within the School of the Built Environment at Oxford Brookes University. Straddling the interstices of geography and urban planning and design, my early attention focused on the 'brute facts' of travel (notably walking and cycling) and the link between urban structure and individual attitudes and behavior through the lens of social psychology. Inspired by the aforementioned events, and taking inspiration from the (velo)mobilities turn (Horton et al. 2007), this shifted over time towards a broader understanding of mobility ('mobilities thinking') and the adoption of mobile methods (Büscher et al. 2010; Fincham et al. 2010). I became inspired by the notion of understandings of how movement is inscribed with meaning by those walking, and particularly cycling, in different geographical, social, and cultural circumstances. This has also involved focusing more on the performance and experience of the practice of cycling in all its diverse forms and settings and the influence of technology and assemblages of 'things' in mediating that experience.

That the CSRG has aligned itself within the broader field of mobilities studies has given renewed impetus for exploring 'velomobilities' in all its manifestations. From my personal perspective, mobilities thinking has enabled me to appreciate the multiplicity of theoretical and conceptual ways of engaging with mobilities research. It has also encouraged me to interact with researchers from multiple disciplines including sociology, geography, anthropology, and science and technology studies, and develop new areas of activity applying different concepts, methodological approaches, and techniques of analysis. Here I highlight two studies that I have been involved with that were inspired by the mobilities turn and shaped the approaches that were used.

Excavations of Contemporary Experiences With Movement and the Design of Them

The UK Engineering and Physical Sciences Research Council (EPSRC) *Understanding Walking and Cycling* (*UWAC*) study (2008–2011) was distinctive in that it utilized a multi-method approach (Jick 1979) integrating quantitative and qualitative methods rarely applied in studies of travel behavior. A major aspect of this was immersive ethnographic work that involved engaging in the lifeworld of participants by 'moving-with' them as they performed journeys on foot or by cycle in four English cities to better understand how mobility is done, or in other words, how people walk and cycle and how they feel when they walk and cycle. This mobilities-oriented approach focused on uncovering life as it is lived. It enabled excavation of the contemporary experience of movement on foot and by cycle in the English context and allowed much greater reflection on how to connect walking and cycling to wider society (see Pooley et al. 2013 for a full overview).

The subsequent *cycle BOOM* study[2] (2013–2016) aimed to develop a better understanding of how the design of towns and cities, along with bicycle technology, is shaping older people's experience of cycling. It investigated older people's willingness to engage with cycling and how this affects independent mobility, health, and wellbeing. The study paid particular attention to the effect of the physical and technological environment and the impact of social, economic, and technological changes that have taken place over time as well as how earlier life experiences may shape later life mobility practices. Like the *UWAC* study, the multi-method approach was inspired by the mobilities turn and used, among other techniques, biographical interviews, shadowing older people on routine cycle journeys to find out more about their day-to-day experience, documenting journeys using photography and video, and using diaries, GPS, and other sensor equipment to record physical and mental responses to different environmental conditions. It is my view that use of mobile methods as part of a mixed-methods approach used in both of these studies provided compelling evidence to decision makers of the situational context of how cycling is experienced and the implications for policy and practice. During the *cycle BOOM* study we hosted the workshop 'Velomobile Methods: Investigation | Interrogation | Interpretation' (11 May 2016) at Oxford Brookes University. This enabled researchers from a myriad of fields with an interest in cycling to come together to explore and critically reflect on their mobile methodological approaches and practices.[3]

Mobilities research and the adoption of mobile methods has involved developing the confidence to diverge from traditional thinking and methodological approaches in transport studies—i.e. by placing mobile practices and cultures, in this case velomobility, at the center of social processes and exploring mobile bodies in mobile contexts. Engaging in reviews of key literature in the mobilities field (Sheller and Urry 2006; Shaw and Hesse 2010; Vannini 2010) enabled me to appreciate of the plurality of approaches and subjects and to develop my own 'critical mobilities thinking' and to challenge taken-for-granted understanding of mobility (see for example, Jones 2010). Indeed, I am conscious that my approach to research is far from a passive act of collecting data waiting to be discovered. Both the *UWAC* and *cycle BOOM* studies involved extensive and immersive fieldwork and active forms of knowledge production with participants. They focused on the act

142 Tim Jones

of doing mobility and attended to velomobility as meaningful social action through 'unthought' routine movement through space. Moreover, my colleagues and I, through the *cycle BOOM* study, have attempted to extract the embodied sense of mobility—the feelings and sensations and emotional and affective dimensions that are both simultaneously representational and unrepresentational. There are of course challenges in making sense of multiple situations and practices within different geographical and social contexts and truly integrating multiple forms of data (e.g. text, photo, video, sensor, etc.). However, by engaging with mobile methods and by prioritizing 'being there' and engaging with the lifeworld of participants in coproducing knowledge, I believe we can begin to untangle the complexity of a world increasingly constituted by movement.

Concluding Remarks

Still, convincing academics, policymakers, and practitioners that the mobilities approach is relevant to the field of transport and built environment studies sometimes requires patience and effort and also acceptance that not everyone is inspired by similar thinking! There has been criticism that the mobilities turn has neglected planning and urban design despite what this could offer the field and vice versa (see Jensen 2013, 2014). New theoretical frameworks have emerged which are carving out a design for mobilities focus and may help bridge the gap between these disciplines (e.g. urban planning and sociology) and highlight the relevancy of critical mobilities thinking to urban planning and design (Jensen 2013, 2014). These are exciting times as the canon of research flourishes and researchers become inspired and emboldened to escape the traditional straight-jacket of their discipline and begin to explore different ways understanding and communicating, and potentially shaping, the world of movement around them.

Notes

1. See Oskar Funk, 'The Imaginaries of Velomobilities,' 2015, www.cosmobilities. net/2015/01/28/imaginaries-of-velomobilities/ for an overview.
2. See more at www.cycleboom.org.
3. See www.cycleboom.org/cycle-boom-blog/.

References

Büscher, Monika, John Urry and Katian Witchger. 2010. *Mobile Methods*. London: Routledge.
Fincham, Ben, Mark McGuiness and Lesley Murray. 2010. *Mobile Methodologies*. Hampshire UK: Palgrave Macmillan.
Horton, Dave, Paul Rosen and Peter Cox, ed. 2007. *Cycling and Society*. Surrey, UK: Ashgate.
Jensen, Ole B. 2013. *Staging Mobilities*. London: Routledge.

Jensen, Ole B. 2014. *Designing Mobilities*. Aalborg: Aalborg University.

Jick, Todd D. 1979. "Mixing Qualitative and Quantitative Methods: Triangulation in Action." *Administrative Science Quarterly* 24 (4): 602. doi:10.2307/2392366

Jones, Tim. 2010. "Book Review: The Cultures of Alternative Mobilities: Routes Less Travelled." *Transport Reviews* 31 (3): 419–420. doi:10.1080/01441647.20 10.520828

Pooley, Colin, Tim Jones, Miles Tight, Dave Horton, Griet Scheldeman, Caroline Mullen, Ann Jopson and Emanuele Strano. 2013. *Promoting Walking and Cycling: New Perspectives on Sustainable Travel*. Bristol: Policy Press.

Shaw, Jon and Markus Hesse. 2010. "Transport, Geography and the 'New' Mobilities." *Transactions of the Institute of British Geographers* 35 (3): 305–312. doi:10.1111/j.1475-5661.2010.00382.x

Sheller, Mimi and John Urry. 2006. "The New Mobilities Paradigm." *Environment and Planning A* 38 (2): 207–226. doi:10.1068/a37268

Vannini, Phillip. 2010. "Mobile Cultures: From the Sociology of Transportation to the Study of Mobilities." *Sociology Compass* 4: 111–121. doi:10.1111/j.1751-9020.2009.00268.x

Part IV
Sites and Strategies

26 Governing Everyday Mobilities
Policymaking and Its Realities

Chelsea Tschoerner

Whether physical, virtual, social, or ideational, mobility is gaining in complexity in cities and urban regions today. The mobilities paradigm moves beyond traditional understandings of everyday movement in urban areas to foster reflection on how such movement is experienced as well as how it is made meaningful by collectives (Cresswell 2006). Governing everyday mobilities thus has to do with more than the physical movement of individuals, goods, or modes of transport. As Miciukiewicz and Vigar argue, the social dimension of mobility can shed light on the "the diversity of socio-economic and cultural contexts where particular transport systems are in operation" (2012, 1948). For policymakers, this means that they need to consider these diverse mobilities, seen here as as the socially shared meanings of specific formations of mobility or 'mobility realities,' in their policy practices. Through deliberating and reflecting on such realities, policymakers can develop a better understanding of how everyday mobilities are governed as well as how they can govern such mobilities. This is especially true for those working to transform those embedded and taken-for-granted meanings related to everyday physical movement.

In policymaking, there is also a second dimension in which mobilities can be observed. Understanding and governing urban mobilities not only requires reflecting on the socially shared sets of meaning and practices concerning everyday movement. There are also ideational mobilities in processes of policymaking and planning. It's not only *what* policymakers frame as the issue, but also *how* they frame the issue. In policymaking, actors engage in argumentative practices and form narratives on specific social realities (Hajer 1995). These practices are structured by local and external forces, and actors call upon and bring in wider understandings as well as power relations to their definitional struggles (Healey 2006). Such practices frame what various mobilities come to be percieved as meaningful and how or even if they should be collectively governed. These 'policy mobilities' (Kesselring 2007; Wood 2015) are key to the social construction of what a policy is, or what it could be.

148   *Chelsea Tschoerner*

Mobilities in Policymaking and Mobilities of Policy

This chapter reflects on an approach for studying the governance of everyday mobilities in specific local contexts. I began to develop this to research and make sense of policymaking for sustainable mobility in the German city of Munich in Tschoerner (2016). In doing so, I drew strongly upon two fields of research. Firstly, I drew upon the growing field of critical policy studies, which is often referred to as the 'deliberative' or 'argumentative' turn in policy analysis (Fischer et al. 2015; Fischer and Forester 1993; Fischer and Gottweis 2012; Hajer and Wagenaar 2003). Critical policy studies stretch across a diverse number of fields of social science research and are rooted in the traditions of the policy sciences (Lasswell 1936; Dewey 1954) and in interpretive methods and ontologies of research (Rabinow and Sullivan 1987; Yanow and Schwartz-Shea 2014).

Interpretive approaches to policy argue first and foremost that policymaking and its analysis cannot be seen as neutral, as something "entirely uncommitted to and removed from interests and values" (Fischer et al. 2015, 1). Rather, policymaking is normatively driven by collectives of actors. The making and changing of policy takes places through these actors, who produce, reproduce, and transform socially shared sets of meaning by practicing and forming narratives on social realities (Hajer 1995). Having its roots in the policy sciences, though, critical policy studies further reflects a specific democratic and political unerstanding of social realities. "Political understanding," as Fischer et al. further argue, ". . . is by no means the exclusive province of experts; it belongs even more fundamentally to the domain of citizens" (2015, 2). Thus, in drawing from this field, I also take a normative slant on policymaking and argue that a key element of policy analysis in the transport sector is to better understand the power relations as well as embedded and dominant discourses on mobilities. These specific 'political understandings' of the world are often veiled by technocratic, expert discourse and the historically powerful field of transport engineering and economics. Interpretive approaches can contribute to balancing out this picture by developing knowledge on the dynamics and complexities of mobilities, seen here as meaningful movement, as well as the power relations of actors in governing everyday mobilities.

Secondly, in the process of my research, I also began to draw upon the new mobilities paradigm (Sheller and Urry 2006; Hannam, Sheller, and Urry 2006) in order to make sense of these various ideational and policy mobilities during analysis. Mobilities is approached here as both an analytical term and an ontological understanding of social and power relations. Researchers in the 'mobilities turn' propose that rather than focusing on the fixity of objects and meanings, one can rather consider their 'less mobile' or 'more immobile' state in the context of multiple, diverse, and networked mobilities (Sheller 2014). A 'sociology of mobilities' argues that the structure and fixity of concepts of social science analysis needs to be (re)conceptualized in

Governing Everyday Mobilities 149

terms of being more fluid and reflecting flow and movement in itself (Urry 2000; Vannini 2010). In this sense, mobilities can be seen as a metaphorical category for analyzing the movement of not only ourselves, but especially our social relations.

Urry wrote on traveling and movement that "object mobility as objects are constituted through mobilities and are as such mobile" (2000, 4). This quote particularly fits well to distinguishing and interconnecting mobility realities and policymaking practices as it highlights the presence of mobilities in the social construction of mobilities. Urry described that while we focus—also in policymaking—on mobility as object, and through this try to understand its dynamics through e.g. measuring, modeling, planning, and ordering it, we are also mobile in producing and reproducing these specific mobility realities. It is particularly these policy practices which then become interconnected with actors' production, reproduction, and transformation of specific mobility realities. Cresswell's (2006) understanding of mobility reflects these two dimensions well. He argues that it is not only the 'brute physicality' of mobility which is relevant for understanding the physically mobile world. Rather, such physical movement must be seen in relation to the ways through which mobility is represented (given meaning) as well as through which it is lived and experienced. It is particularly the practices through which actors make specific mobilities meaningful in the context of policy that can shape dominant or hegemonic mobility realities.

Local Policymaking and Mobility Realities

Considering this in the context of local policymaking, policy actors are just like everyday individuals in how they engage with urban systems and mobilities. It is their reflexivity of these processes, more than anything, which makes them adept at problematizing such routine practices. As Giddens wrote, "in many contexts of social life there occur processes of selective 'information filtering' whereby strategically placed actors seek reflexively to regulate the overall conditions of system reproduction either to keep things as they are or to change them" (1984, 27–28). In policymaking, their position as transport engineer, elected official, influential business owner, or loud group of activists provides them a platform to form coherent and convincing arguments on everyday mobilities. These policy actors engage in processes of 'sense-making' as they collectively attempt to define a specific, shared mobility reality. As Yanow (2000) described it, these processes of sense-making build key moments when specific mobilities (or other social realities) are made meaningful and politically relevant. Actors might (re) produce specific discourses, as those more 'immobile' structures of policy-making, in order to gain credibility or acceptance for their specific interests (Hajer 1995). These interests, though, are relatedly shaped by individuals' and collectives' larger cultural understandings and perceptions of everyday mobilities.

150 *Chelsea Tschoerner*

Concluding Remarks

Although ideas play an important role in policymaking, those practices through which such ideas are produced and made meaningful are equally as important. In my research, I found not one policymaking reality in analyzing cycling promotion and electric mobility promotion in Munich. In each case I found multiple interconnected policy and mobility realities. Over time, and in two distinct contexts and cases, I found constellations of actors struggling to define the institutional field and practices of public policy and to ultimately govern urban mobilities. Although I saw a strong and powerful technocratic discourse on engineering systems of transport, often described as a key element of systems of automobility (Urry 2004; Böhm et al. 2006; Manderscheid 2014), I also saw alternative discourses and thus alternative practices and narratives on mobility realities. What was exciting were those alternative mobility realities actors articulated in policymaking. In the face of a 'single' positivist rationality, which continues to drive planning paradigms and institutions globally, such reflexivity in policymaking is needed more than ever (Fischer 2009). Policymaking practices are highly interconnected with the mobility realities through which actors define and shape specific policies. Thus governing urban mobilities is not merely about reflexive policymaking for mobilities, but equally about reflecting on the mobilities of policymaking, i.e. the mobilities through which specific mobilities, as objects of policymaking, become objectified as such.

References

Böhm, Steffen, Campbell Jones, Chris Land and Mat Paterson. 2006. "Part One Conceptualizing Automobility: Introduction: Impossibilities of Automobility." *Sociological Review* 54: 1–16.

Cresswell, Tim. 2006. *On the Move: Mobility in the Modern Western World*. New York: Routledge.

Dewey, John. 1954. *The Public and Its Problems*. Athens, OH: Ohio University Press/Swallow Press.

Fischer, Frank. 2009. *Democracy and Expertise: Reorienting Policy Inquiry*. Oxford: Oxford University Press.

Fischer, Frank and John Forester. 1993. *The Argumentative Turn in Policy Analysis and Planning*. Durham, UK: Dukes University Press.

Fischer, Frank and Herbert Gottweis, eds. 2012. *The Argumentative Turn Revisited: Public Policy as Communicative Practice*. Durham: Duke University Press.

Fischer, Frank, Douglas Torgerson, Anna Durnová and Michael Orsini. 2015. *Handbook of Critical Policy Studies*. Cheltenham, UK: 'Edward Elgar Publishing, Inc.

Giddens, Anthony. 1984. *The Constitution of Society: Introduction of the Theory of Structuration*. Los Angeles: University of California Press.

Hajer, Maarten. 1995. *The Politics of Environmental Discourse: Ecological Modernization and the Policy Process*. Oxford: Oxford University Press.

Hajer, Maarten and Hendrik Wagenaar, eds. 2003. *Deliberative Policy Analysis: Understanding Governance in the Network Society*. Cambridge: Cambridge University Press.

Hannam, Kevin, Mimi Sheller and John Urry. 2006. "Editorial: Mobilities, Immobilities and Moorings." *Mobilities* 1: 1–22.

Healey, Patsy. 2006. "Transforming Governance: Challenges of Institutional Adaptation and a New Politics of Space1." *European Planning Studies* 14: 299–320. doi:10.1080/09654310500420792

Kesselring, Sven. 2007. "Mobile Politics in Munich: Learning from Deliberation Under the Conditions of Reflexive Modernization." 4S/EASST conference, August 25–29 2004, Paris, 2007.

Lasswell, Harold D. 1936. *Politics: Who Gets What, When, How.* Whittlesey house: McGraw-Hill book Company, Incorporated.

Manderscheid, Katharina. 2014. "The Movement Problem, the Car and Future Mobility Regimes: Automobility as Dispositif and Mode of Regulation." *Mobilities* 9: 604–626.

Miciukiewicz, Konrad and Geoff Vigar. 2012. "Mobility and Social Cohesion in the Splintered City: Challenging Technocentric Transport Research and Policy-makingPractices."*UrbanStudies*49:1941–1957.doi:10.1177/0042098012444886

Rabinow, Paul and William M. Sullivan, eds. 1987. *Interpretive Social Science: A Second Look.* Berkeley: University of California Press.

Sheller, Mimi. 2014. "The New Mobilities Paradigm for a Live Sociology." *Current Sociology* 62: 789–811. doi:10.1177/0011392114533211

Sheller, Mimi and John Urry. 2006. "The New Mobilities Paradigm." *Environment and Planning A* 38: 207–226.

Tschoerner, Chelsea. 2016. "Sustainable Mobility in Munich: Exploring the Role of Discourse in Policy Change." PhD diss., University of Freiburg.

Urry, John. 2000. *Sociology Beyond Societies: Mobilities for the Twenty-First Century*, International Library of Sociology. London and New York: Routledge.

Urry, John. 2004. "The 'System' of Automobility." *Theory, Culture & Society* 21: 25–39.

Vannini, Phillip. 2010. "Mobile Cultures: From the Sociology of Transportation to the Study of Mobilities." *Sociology Compass* 4: 111–121. doi:10.1111/j.1751–9020.2009.00268.x

Wood, Astrid. 2015. "The Politics of Policy Circulation: Unpacking the Relationship Between South African and South American Cities in the Adoption of Bus Rapid Transit." *Antipode* 47 (4): 1062–1079.

Yanow, Dvora. 2000. *Conducting Interpretative Policy Analysis.* London: Sage.

Yanow, Dvora and Peregrine Schwartz-Shea, eds. 2014. *Interpretation and Method: Empirical Research Methods and the Interpretive Turn* (2nd ed.). Armonk, NY: M.E. Sharp, Inc.

27 Planning for Sustainable Mobilities

Creating New Futures *or* Doing What Is Possible?

Nina Moesby Bennetsen and Julie Overgaard Magelund

Future sustainable mobilities are topics of interest not only to the authors behind this chapter, but to researchers, politicians, and planners around the world. The main question is what mobilities of tomorrow will look like in this anthropogenic era (Steffen et al. 2011; Sheller and Urry 2016). The question is no longer if humans play a role in climate change, but rather how changes in societies can minimize carbon emissions and use of fossil fuels (Urry 2011; Steffen et al. 2011; Klein 2014). Based on the Cycle Super Highways project in the Greater Copenhagen area, we examined how planners work with, and talk about, sustainable mobilities. We investigated how the initiative influenced their daily practices—how visions were transformed from glossy paper to physical infrastructural designs.

When looking at change in society, the city is an interesting object of study; it represents a melting pot of social, political, economic, technical, and digital mobilities bound together in complex networks (Graham and Marvin 2001). In an urbanized society, this understanding makes it essential to look at the infrastructural systems in order to find and understand potential cracks (Nielsen 2005) for future sustainable mobilities (Sheller and Urry 2016). Mobilities and the infrastructural systems making physical and virtual mobilities possible are fundamental for society and for understanding everyday life today (Urry 2007; Freudendal-Pedersen 2009). It is necessary to understand the complex connections between infrastructure and everyday life practices as it is made possible with the new mobilities paradigm (Sheller and Urry 2006; Sheller and Urry 2016).

An Alternative Commute

The Cycle Super Highways project aims to create alternatives to car-based commuting in and out of Copenhagen through fast, comfortable, and safe highways for cyclists (Cycle Super Highways 2015). It is a cross-municipal project funded by 20 municipalities and the Capital Region of Denmark, which started in 2012 with the first track between Copenhagen and the suburban town Albertslund—a 17.5-kilometer track to create better facilities

Planning for Sustainable Mobilities 153

for commuters on bicycles (Cycle Super Highways 2015). In Copenhagen, the bicycle and bicycle tracks play a vital part in the city's infrastructural system and hence the everyday life of the city's inhabitants (Freudendal-Pedersen 2015a, 2015b). Throughout the year, Copenhageners ride their bicycle as part of their everyday mobilities. The extended network of bicycle tracks serves not only Copenhagen, but also longer distance commutes in surrounding suburban municipalities and aims to create an attractive alternative to car-based commuting. The design, quality, and sheer amount of bicycle tracks have been emphasized as an important motivation for cycling as part of everyday life mobilities (Andrade et al. 2011; Freudendal-Pedersen 2015a), which is why we find the Cycle Super Highways to be of relevance for research on future sustainable mobilities.

To gain insight into how this project developed from vision to result, we investigated the first established track. The Cycle Super Highways project proposed great visions for future sustainable mobilities. What we found, however—through interviewing five planners involved in the project—was that they have difficulties meeting the visions when implementing solutions that work in a local context as well (Magelund and Bennetsen 2014). The planners tended to create the best possible solution at the time, instead of creating solutions that met the visions behind the Cycle Super Highways. We see this pragmatic planning as the art of the possible, rather than planning for the best possible solution (Magelund and Bennetsen 2014).

The first highway is not a new plan or construction, but consists primarily of improved bicycle tracks that existed before the Cycle Super Highways project. The infrastructural system in the Greater Copenhagen area is influenced by the urban development plan known as The Finger Plan (Illeris 2010) and the new bicycle highways are developed as a suggestion of infrastructures of future sustainable mobilities within this existing infrastructure. Cycle Super Highways are not lines on a blank map, but contributions to existing infrastructure and a way to fill in the missing links (Magelund and Bennetsen 2014).

Our Theoretical and Methodological Approach

To have the courage and vision to imagine new futures is essential in order to create sustainable cities, sustainable societies, and not least sustainable mobilities (Pinder 2002; Dennis and Urry 2009). Sustainability must be a part of social sciences and of understanding cities because of the consequences of human behavior, such as climate change (Urry 2011; Steffen et al. 2015; Sheller and Urry 2016). We find the notion of cracks (Nielsen 2005) to be an interesting approach to changing mobilities structures and practices through policies and planning initiatives towards sustainable alternatives. Mobilities and movement are cornerstones in today's society, which must be understood through the new mobilities paradigm (Urry 2007; Sheller and Urry 2006; Freudendal-Pedersen 2009). We combine the mobilities turn (Sheller and Urry 2006) with the acknowledgement of human influence on climate change, termed the 'resource turn' (Urry 2011), or what can be understood as an emerging sustainability paradigm in the social sciences (Bennetsen and Magelund 2015). The acknowledgement that human behavior has a huge impact on both the climate and the planet leads to discussions about how humans can behave differently, and on how planners can work with sustainable mobilities. Through qualitative interviews, we asked planners how they worked with the Cycle Super Highways project in order to analyze the differences between the visions and the result of the first established highway.

Sustainable Commuting in the Greater Copenhagen Area

With still more people commuting longer distances everyday, the question of sustainable mobilities does not only concern urban mobilities, but also commutes between cities and surrounding suburbs. The average commuting distance in the Capital Region of Denmark was 20.1 kilometers per day in 2013 (Statistics Denmark 2015). In Copenhagen the bicycle and the extended network of tracks that make cycling possible are an important part of everyday life for many inhabitants.

To promote sustainable mobilities, municipalities and companies in the Greater Copenhagen Area have created initiatives aimed at making commuting by bicycle easier on longer distances. Among these are the Cycle Super Highways. This collaboration is founded by many different interests from the municipalities and the region such as branding, health, tourism, reducing congestion, and decreasing CO_2 emissions, but the common tool for reaching different goals is the same: increasing the use of the bicycle as a mode of transport for everyday commuting (Region Hovedstaden 2014).

A New Future for Sustainable Mobilities?

A bicycle lane for commuters with a promise of the same high standard from A to B, even across administrative, municipal borders: This is the description of a Cycle Super Highway (Cycle Super Highways 2015). The grand vision can, however, be difficult to see in the implemented solutions, and the project has been target of debate because of the minor changes made along the first track as well as the design of the tracks (Bradtberg and Larsen 2014). Investigating these differences, it became clear to us that for the planners, the project had become a matter of the art of the possible rather than trying to achieve the best possible solution (Magelund and Bennetsen 2014). When the planners talked about their work with Cycle Super Highways, they described it in a different way than the vision describes the project. They did not mention the project with a different approach than their other work tasks, even though the Cycle Super Highways project is a cross-municipal project envisioned as a greater initiative.

Planning for Sustainable Mobilities   155

One planner found that the vision of the project "promotes another level than the municipalities do" (Magelund and Bennetsen 2014, 42). When describing the approach to establishing the new Cycle Super Highway in the municipality, she said, "When we established the track, we thought: 'Well . . . we already had existing bicycle tracks close by and they are staying. We are not changing them!'" (Magelund and Bennetsen 2014, 42). Instead of creating a new track, the bicycle highway was mostly made up of tracks that existed long before anyone thought to create a Cycle Super Highway. It is difficult to imagine the same approach to planning a new road for car-based mobilities. Following this example, a new major highway intended for cars would merely be an upgrade of the design and some missing links on an already existing minor road, which was close to the intended placement of the new highway. This example shows how bicycle-based mobilities still do not exist in an integrated system such as the car. It becomes clear how planning for sustainable mobilities becomes the art of the possible and not the best possible solution either—a scenario which is rarely seen when planning for car-based mobilities. Even though the bicycle is prioritized as a mode of mobility in Copenhagen, the car is still the starting point when planning mobilities (Freudendal-Pedersen 2015a).

One of the visions behind the Cycle Super Highways is that it should be easy to combine the bicycle with other modes of transport. However, the first highway is in some places situated about 3 kilometers from the train stations along the track. This might not sound like a long distance, but it can be for a busy bicycle commuter. Combining the bicycle with the train is not the easy solution if it involves a 3-kilometre detour from your normal route. We find this to be an example of pragmatic planning; already existing bicycle tracks were implemented as part of the Cycle Super Highway instead of establishing new tracks wherever it would be most beneficial for the route. Existing tracks were used because there was a possibility to upgrade, instead of just building new tracks (Magelund and Bennetsen 2014). As a result, 3 kilometers was not deemed far enough to prioritize the establishment of a new bicycle track.

Concluding Remarks

The Cycle Super Highways project is created to give commuters an alternative to commuting by car. The project seeks to show what future mobilities can be, and to show a way for the bicycle to become a natural and easy choice for everyday life mobilities. We find that the project supports visionary ideas and the courage needed to imagine new futures. However, courage and vision is not enough. Courage must be present when planning, and vision should be involved during planning practices. The way planning is organized in municipalities, and how sustainable mobilities initiatives are dealt with at the desk of the planner, are of great importance to how new futures turn out. When planning becomes the art of the possible, and

156 Moesby Bennetsen and Overgaard Magelund

planners find pragmatic solutions, the vision behind a project is not always apparent in the implemented solutions. The interviewed planners expressed problems combining the visions with their daily planning practices, and that they did not feel they had the tools to change these practices—here, visions and courage to imagine new futures did not impact the local planning practices; it only served as a grand vision (Magelund and Bennetsen 2014).

A way of changing this could be a holistic approach to planning, one that emphasizes the visions behind sustainable mobilities initiatives. Planning for future sustainable mobilities becomes not only a matter of changing the physical infrastructures, but a cultural change in planning practices to a holistic approach (Magelund and Bennetsen 2014). Mobility management is a beneficial approach in order to focus on intermodality (Magelund and Bennetsen 2014; EPOMM 2013). In addition, to create sustainable mobilities we need not only to think of what could be done within the current planning system, but also to look at how to change the system (Egmose 2015) in order to give planners the courage to imagine new futures and to work to implement visionary sustainable mobilities initiatives. As concluded elsewhere, there is great value for planners in creating spaces from the daily work routine when working with future mobilities in order to give room for new ways of thinking (Kjærulff 2015). In this chapter, we have emphasized the importance of viewing planning in a holistic manner if planning for sustainable mobilities is to become more than the art of the possible.

References

Andrade, Victor, Ole B. Jensen, Henrik Harder and Jens C. O. Madsen. 2011. "Bike Infrastructures and Design Qualities: Enhancing Cycling." *Danish Journal of Geoinformatics and Land Management* 46 (1): 65–80.

Bennetsen, Nina Moesby and Julie Overgaard Magelund. 2015. "Hverdagshåndteringer—En undersøgelse af bæredygtighed og mobilitet i hverdagslivet." Master's thesis, Department of Environmental, Social and Spatial Change, Roskilde University.

Bradtberg, Nils Eigil and Jonas Larsen. 2014. "Et designkritisk blik på Cykelsuperstierne." *Trafik & Veje*, January 1, 2014. http://asp.vejtid.dk/Artikler/2014/01/6781.pdf.

Cycle Super Highways. 2015. www.supercykelstier.dk.

Dennis, Kingsley and John Urry. 2009. *After the Car*. Cambridge, UK: Polity Press.

Egmose, Jonas. 2015. *Action Research for Sustainability: Social Imagination Between Citizens and Scientists*. Surrey: Ashgate.

EPOMM. 2013. *Mobility Management: The Smart Way to Sustainable Mobility in European Countries, Regions and Cities*. Bruxelles: EPOMM—European Platform on Mobility Management. http://epomm.eu/docs/file/epomm_book_2013_web.pdf.

Freudendal-Pedersen, Malene. 2009. *Mobility in Daily Life: Between Freedom and Unfreedom*. Surrey: Ashgate.

Freudendal-Pedersen, Malene. 2015a. "Cyclists as Part of the City's Organism: Structural Stories on Cycling in Copenhagen." *City & Society* 27 (1): 30–50.

Planning for Sustainable Mobilities 157

Freudendal-Pedersen, Malene. 2015b. "Whose Commons are Mobilities Spaces?—The Case of Copenhagen's Cyclists." *ACME: An International E-Journal for Critical Geographies* 14 (2): 598–621.

Graham, Stephen and Simon Marvin. 2001. *Splintering Urbanism: Networked Infrastructures*. Abingdon: Routledge.

Illeris, Sven. 2010. *Regional udvikling—Regionplanlægning og regionalpolitik i Danmark og Europa*. Nykøbing Sjælland, Denmark: Bogværket.

Kjærulff, Aslak Aamot. 2015. "Mobiliteter i planlægning—Eksperimenter i Formel M med organisering af relationer og etiske værdier." PhD diss., Department of Environmental, Social and Spatial Change, Roskilde University.

Klein, Naomi. 2014. *This Changes Everything: Capitalism vs. the Climate*. New York: Simon & Schuster Paperbacks.

Magelund, Julie Overgaard and Nina Moesby Bennetsen. 2014. *Cykelsuperstier som værktøj til at skabe omstilling til bæredygtig mobilitet?—En undersøgelse af Albertslundruten*. Department of Environmental, Social and Spatial Change, Roskilde University.

Nielsen, Lise Drewes. 2005. "Reflexive Mobility—A Critical and Action Oriented Perspective on Transport Research." In *Social Perspectives on Mobility*, edited by Thyra Uth Thomsen, Lise Drewes Nielsen and Henrik Gudmundsson. Aldershot: Ashgate.

Pinder, David. 2002. "In Defence of Utopian Urbanism: Imagining Cities After the 'End of Utopia'" *Geografiske Annaler* 84 B (3–4): 299–241.

Region Hovedstaden. 2014. *Regionalt cykelregnskab*. Hillerød, Denmark: Koncern Regional Udvikling. www.regionh.dk/til-fagfolk/trafik/Analyser-og-rapporter-om-trafik/cykler/Documents/17751Cykelregnskab_WEB_2.pdf.

Sheller, Mimi and John Urry. 2006. "The New Mobilities Paradigm." *Environment and Planning A* 38: 207–226.

Sheller, Mimi and John Urry. 2016. "Mobilizing the New Mobilities Paradigm." *Applied Mobilities*, 1 (1): 10–25.

Statistics Denmark. 2015. www.statistikbanken.dk/statbank5a/SelectVarVal/Define.asp?MainTable=AFSTA2&PLanguage=0&PXSId=0&wsid=cftree.

Steffen, Will, Wendy Broadgate, Lisa Deutsch, Owen Gaffney and Cornelia Ludwig. 2015. "The Trajectory of the Anthropocene: The Great Acceleration." *The Anthropocene Review* 2 (1): 81–98.

Steffen, Will, Åsa Persson, Lisa Deutsch, Jan Zalasiewicz, Mark Williams, Katherine Richardson, Carole Crumley, Paul Crutzen, Carl Folke, Line Gordon, Mario Molina, Veerabhadran Ramanathan, Johan Rockström, Marten Scheffer, Hans Joachim Schnellnhuber and Uno Svedin. 2011. "The Anthropocene: From Global Change to Planetary Stewardship." *AMBIO* 40 (Springer 7): 739–761.

Urry, John. 2007. *Mobilities*. Cambridge: Polity Press.

Urry, John. 2011. *Climate Change & Society*. Cambridge: Polity Press.

28 Let People Move!

The New Planning Paradigm of 'Shared Spaces'

Enza Lissandrello

In recent years, the idea of shared spaces, as introduced by a Dutch traffic planner in the early 1990s, has spread across Europe and the world and has become widely interpreted and contextualized. The original idea was that traffic engineering devices in urbanized areas, such as signs, traffic lights, and crosswalks, when placed for safety reasons, increase instead of reduce the risk of accidents. Since then, the shared space idea has become more than just an issue of traffic safety—its relevance has been applied to the urban space that might emerge when traffic devices largely disappear from the urban scene. Shared spaces have been defined as one of the many approaches developed in response to the dominance of the automobile and the realization of the adverse environmental and social impacts from decades of planning and design primarily focused on the priority of motor vehicles (Karndacharuk et al. 2014). Many of these recent discussions and debates have been developed in relation to urban design and walkability, but little attention has been paid to the planning dimension of shared spaces. This chapter explores the specific issue of planning for shared spaces as infrastructures of urban social life and metaphors of the radical change that mobilities (Sheller and Urry 2006) require in urban planning. Shared spaces are here interpreted as the 'meetingness' of mobility patterns and as a manifestation of the shift to a post-car era in which the complexity of urban movements, different mobility patterns, and contingent ordering (Urry 2007, 9) are questioned. This issue is approached from the perspective of how planners understand and conceive shared spaces in the context of a changing paradigm in which stasis, structure, and social order have been transformed.

For a long time, the goal of urban planning was the search for order in segregated, predefined infrastructures regulated by signs of surveillance, e.g. traffic devices, that guaranteed the 'right to movement' and 'regulated' voyagers to protect them from unpredictable, chaotic, and risky consequences. In his study *Flesh and Stone*, Richard Sennett maintains that urban space enslaves powers of motion. With regard to motorized mobility, urban space is understood as "a means to end pure motion" (Sennett 1996, 17): The driver can drive safely only with a minimum of idiosyncratic distractions; to drive well requires standard signs and dividers as well as streets that are emptied of life. Thus, navigating the geography of modern urban society requires very little physical and sensorial effort; hence, engagement in it results in a lack of contact (Sennet 1996, 18). Sennett compares the highway engineer to the television director and frames their work as a freedom from resistance. As the engineer designs ways to move without obstruction, effort, and engagement, so too does the television director when designing ways for people to look at something without becoming too uncomfortable. Urban planners have long pursued the same idea by ordering and regulating urban space to minimize conflicts and contact and simplify the urban complexities with ideas such as zoning and the segregation of urban and traffic functions. These motions now seem to be challenged by a radical, diverse, and emerging urban planning paradigm in which functional areas and mobility patterns are changing from segregated to integrated. This chapter discusses this shifting paradigm in urban planning through the idea of shared spaces: Spaces where 'control' is replaced by diverse motion because traffic control devices are no longer viewed as indispensable. Instead, the flow of mobilities, e.g. motorized public and private vehicles, cycles, and pedestrians, becomes increasingly viewed as potentially spontaneously self-regulated through social interaction, eye contact, and individuals negotiating conflict. Shared spaces reinforce users' ability to improvise and negotiate their power of movement and their space-time differently—as pedestrians and/or drivers through contingent networked urban mobilities. An important aspect that this chapter elaborates on is therefore the following question: What type of planning paradigm do shared spaces represent for planners when breaking the certainty and control over physical mobilities and the ways in which such 'spaces' are planned?

The theoretical value of this article, in addition to the mobilities paradigm, is grounded in the relationship between discourses and space (Flyvbjerg and Richardson 2002) and on the idea that "the organization of space may come to gradually mirror dominant discourses" (Richardson and Jensen 2003, 357) and vice versa. The article attempts to identify the dominant discourses on shared spaces in planning for a better understanding about what shared spaces represent in relation to an ongoing urban planning paradigm that transforms the issues of the control and segregation of patterns of mobility and emphasizes the everyday flows of improvised social relations. It argues that these elements contribute to an understanding of the networked urban mobilities that shape contemporary ideas in urban planning. The analysis of discourses surrounding 'shared spaces' is here derived from analyses of 'practice stories' from first-hand interviews led by the author with professionals engaged in planning for shared spaces in diverse urban areas in the Netherlands, the UK, Italy, and Denmark. The study utilizes the 'practice stories' of planning practitioners through conversational interviews (Forester 2012; Laws and Forester 2015) as a mobile method (Urry 2007, 409) that can be understood as *talking with* and exploring a form of reflexive engagement within the planners' worldviews (inspired by Forester 1999) (Lissandrello et al. 2016).

160   *Enza Lissandrello*

Dominant Discourses About Shared Spaces in Urban Planning

Many 'practice stories' related to changes in planning *for* shared spaces require the relation and integration of diverse mobility patterns or changes to the existing mobility patterns and their segregation. The dominant discourses about shared spaces can be synthesized as 1) the use of space, 2) the prioritization of mobilities, 3) governance and regulations, and 4) safety.

The Use of Space

Various urban planners have discussed shared spaces as spaces for networked mobilities and as parts of urban life. A shared space is a space where diverse mobilities and immobilities co-exist, which raises the issue of whether re-evaluating the sensations of the urban space is a means to improve social interaction. Within a shared space, both the driver and the pedestrian cannot travel safely unless their passage and space are based on eye contact with other travelers within the complexity of street life. Thus, navigating the geography of shared spaces requires both physical and sensorial effort, i.e. engagement, and that contact is mandatory. The planner for a shared space must think of the multiple ways that mobilities and immobilities will interact in this space, and that will require negotiations of passage, conflicts, effort, and engagement, such that an individual who perceives a sense of risk will become comfortable when engaged in and surrounded by urban life.

The Prioritization of Mobilities

Many conversations with the planners shifted almost immediately to the prioritization of certain mobilities over others within the urban space. The planners argue that car passage reduction is one of the goals and strategies of planning for shared spaces. To be realistic, a careful analysis of the context of existing mobility patterns is required. In the Netherlands, shared spaces are not understood as anti-car infrastructures per se, and an analysis of the diverse spatial scales that planning for mobilities currently requires in urban areas becomes most relevant: Fast networks support shared spaces. Thus, a careful analysis of the diverse spatial scales such as cities and regions and the localization of shared spaces among slow suburban networks is required.

Governance and Regulations

Other issues that emerged from these stories of planning for shared spaces were related to governance and regulations. Shared spaces presuppose an unpredictability of regulations that is based on improvisation among self-governed individuals, i.e. pedestrians, cyclists, and drivers of motorized vehicles. The role of human interaction and communication among individuals thus becomes crucial, but the learning experience of the practical users is also important. In Denmark, shared spaces still rely on predictability based on experience and trial and error and on the planners' role, which is important because shared spaces work well when they are 'well planned.' Planners usually refer to the fact that a minimum number of clear signals on the road is still an important factor. In some cases, especially in the Netherlands, the practice of the individuals in appropriating space and practicing mobility by negotiating and finding their way through social interactions is a form of educating individuals on responsibility and including risks as part of their urban social life.

Safety

The safety issue is also part of the dominant discourses on shared spaces. In the Netherlands, safety in shared spaces is considered an individual responsibility. This approach has become a topic for debate for many citizens, from children to old, blind, and handicapped people. However, from conversations with the planners, the issue is learning from experience and accepting that risks are part of human nature and that no one can guarantee safety. This approach is itself a mind-shift that shared spaces have brought about in contemporary urban planning. In Denmark as well as Italy and the UK, such an approach is not so radical. The public planner seems to feel responsible for people's safety when he sees that the number of accidents has decreased; it is often considered "the number one factor" defining whether the shared space that "we planned was a good one" (interview with Aalborg's municipal planner, September 2015).

Concluding Remarks

Planners see shared spaces as shaped and reshaped in relation to how people construct their everyday flows, perceive their risks, frame their physical and sensorial engagement with other people as drivers or pedestrians, form their power of mobility in multiple space-time dimensions, and address conflicts through eye contact. Shared spaces represent the metaphor of a new paradigm emerging in urban planning for further research in this area: a shift from the idea of space 'as a means to the end of pure motion' when prioritizing motorized mobility to the idea of space shaped by multiple spatial scales of multiple motions—networked urban mobilities. Shared spaces refer to a 'flickering' space that is itself stimulating, risky, exciting, and surrounded by the complexity of urban life.

References

Flyvbjerg, Bent and Tim Richardson. 2002. "Planning and Foucault: In Search of the Dark Side of Planning Theory." In *Planning Futures: New Directions for Planning*

162 *Enza Lissandrello*

Theory, edited by Philip Allmendinger and Mark Tewdwr-Jones, 44–62. London and New York: Routledge.

Forester, John. 1999. *The Deliberative Practitioner: Encouraging Participatory Planning Processes*. Cambridge, MA: MIT Press.

Forester, John. 2012. "Learning to Improve Practice: Lessons from Practice Stories and Practitioners' Own Discourse Analyses (or Why Only the Loons Show Up)." *Planning Theory & Practice* 13 (1): 11–26.

Karndacharuk, Auttapone, Douglas J. Wilson and Roger Dunn. 2014. "A Review of the Evolution of Shared (Street) Space Concepts in Urban Environments." *Transport Reviews* 34 (2): 190–220.

Laws, David and John Forester. 2015. *Conflict, Improvisation, Governance: Street Level Practices for Urban Democracy*. New York: Routledge.

Lissandrello, Enza, Robert Hrelja, Aud Tennøy and Tim Richardson. 2016. "Three *Performativities* of Innovation in Public Transport Planning." *International Planning Studies*. http://dx.doi.org/10.1080/13563475.2016.1196579.

Richardson, Tim and Ole B. Jensen. 2003. "Linking Discourse and Space: Towards a Cultural Sociology of Space in Analysing Spatial Policy Discourses." *Urban Studies* 40 (1): 7–22.

Sennett, Richard. 1996. *Flesh and Stone: The Body and the City in Western Civilization*. New York and London: W. W. Norton & Company.

Sheller, Mimi and John Urry. 2006. "The New Mobilities Paradigm." *Environment and Planning A* 38 (2): 207–226.

Urry, John. 2007. *Mobilities*. Cambridge: Polity Press.

29 Travels, Typing, and Tales

Emmy Laura Perez Fjalland

> All I had heard about them was how poor they were, so that it had become impossible for me to see them as anything else but poor. Their poverty was my single story of them. . . . Stories matter. Many stories matter. Stories have been used to dispossess and to malign, but stories can also be used to empower and to humanize. Stories can break the dignity of a people, but stories can also repair that broken dignity.
>
> (Adichie 2009, 3:43 and 17:36)

Narratives surround us in everyday life; in planning, politics, media coverage, research, and among children. But as mobilities and planning researchers we do not seem to fully connect the practice with storytelling, academic writing, or representation. Due to the more poetic, fabulous (from 'fable'), and narrative language, stories can 'voice' humans' shambles of ambiguousness, delightfulness, and quirkiness, and our ongoing rationalization to try and make life meaningful. This knowledge can help us understand the assembly of modern urban environments and societies, and expose sense-making in urban societies in the perpetual construction of cities. My contribution is based on my negotiations with myself on how to communicate and represent my fieldwork and studies of the urban development of the Colombian capital, Bogotá. It is about performing urban consultancy and being transnational. The main argument is to highlight the power of stories, both as method and representation, and to show how stories can 'shake' path dependencies that are part of reproducing urban challenges such as 'sustain-ability,'[1] inequality, and discrimination. These kind of stories are not about moving readers to tears, or about navel-gazing, but to demonstrate that those who 'write culture' suggest how 'reality' could be different, and this in itself can endorse a mobilization of the sociological imagination (Denzin 2001; Sandercock 2004; Sandercock 2003).

Traveling: Embodied Mobilities

> Yet how could there be places, I wondered, if people did not come and go? . . . Life is lived, I reasoned, along paths, not just in places. . . . It is along

164   *Emmy Laura Perez Fjalland*

> paths, too, that people grow into a knowledge of the world around them, and describe this world in the story they tell.
>
> (Ingold 2007, 2)

As a *Colombodanesa* (my father's definition of my ethnicity—a Columbian and Danish combination), Bogotá captured my interest years ago; both as a personal desire to know my father's culture and country better, and as a Copenhagen-based academic's and professional's interest in the notable urban development of Bogotá between 1994–2003. This period stands out as a provocative, highly innovative, and game-changing way of governing cities and practicing urban and mobilities planning (Berney 2008; Silva 2009). Antanas Mockus and Enrique Peñalosa, the two mayors who led the development, explicitly placed co-existence, civic culture, and morality on the public political agenda by changing the stories *about* and *for* Bogotanos (Caballero 2007; Mockus 2002; Peñalosa 2007).

I had been to Colombia and Bogotá several times before, but in November 2012 I went to Bogotá again on a field trip with a colleague from the Danish Architecture Centre. We were meant to study, communicate, and present what had happened in Bogotá ten years after the before-mentioned period. During our ten days there we conducted 12 interviews and participated in three artistic-activism events. For two days the former mayor of Bogotá, Enrique Peñalosa, showed us the city, primarily areas with low-income families. Amid all this, we collected impressions by staying, strolling, biking, and driving through the city spaces. Based on our impressions and gathered knowledge, we published 11 blog posts on the website of the International Federation for Housing & Planning. Furthermore, I also used this fieldwork in an academic research project I was working on at the time.

The conflicting interests and roles may already be clear. While I was in Bogotá, I was totally confused. At first, I thought I was giddy due to the thin Andes air and jetlag, but soon found that I worked my brain off trying to find out how to navigate in-between places, languages, time zones, roles, and emotions. The fieldwork turned out to include auto-ethnographic studies of *being in motion*, of embodied experiences with the networked urban mobile. As with much fieldwork, it was a matter of distance and involvement; giving oneself entirely without being absorbed. Storytelling helped me deal with these ambivalences (Hartmann-Petersen 2009) in an academic manner, and it became my way into the mobilities research.

Typing: Writing Mobilities

> We have told our tales from the field. Today we understand that we write culture, and that the writing is not an innocent practice. . . . It belongs to a moral community. . . . The meanings of lived experience are inscribed and made visible in these performances.
>
> (Denzin 2001, 23, 24, 26)

Writing about embodied mobilities—committing something flowing and moving to paper—seems contradictory. It challenges how we can communicate the currently mobile. Inspired by Vannini (2012), Ingold (2007), Van Maanen (1988), Sheller (2014), and Denzin (2001), written materials of mobilities become time-space fixities as they capture moments of flows and condense complexities, experiences, emotions, and time in a concrete, linear fashion. "Writing is linear" (Ingold 2007, 120), but our experiences are ephemeral and often not so straightforward. Writing about experienced mobilities helped me to understand what the fieldwork was about and what to bring home from it.

While staying in Bogotá, I took field notes, wrote blog entries, Facebook and Twitter updates, e-mails and SMSs with family, friends, and colleagues, describing my experiences. When I came back to Copenhagen, I started writing tales—short evocative pieces that tried to capture fleeting moments of mobilities. To do this, I chose a combination of Van Maanen's two method writing styles—the confessional and the impressionist tale—in order to combine a reflexive ethnography (Pink 2006) of my role as researcher in the field, and to incorporate and communicate my experiences and observations. To get started, I used different versions of popular creative writing based on situations I had been in. Some tales were pages long; some were short notes and sentences; some were lists; some were impulsive. After the first month of production, I chose 13 tales that I wanted to continue working on. Each tale presented something important and new in relation to the urban mobile context. I wrote them in Danish, so the one I chose for this chapter ('Waking Up in Bogotá'), is an English translation. (N.B. my original texts were in both Danish and Spanish—as this is how I tend to think).

Waking Up in Bogotá

It is Saturday and 4am. Can't sleep any more due to jetlag and excitement. Feeling giddy, almost like I suffer from vertigo. But I am 2600 above sea level. Finally I am here. Sitting up in my bed looking out the hotel room window. Lovely view from this Chapinero modern, classy hotel with a vertical garden. Heavy dark, crisp blue shadows from las montañas. Madrugada. Click! I take my first picture. Where is he going to take us today? What am I about to see today? I take a shower and start getting dressed. I change four times before finding something suitable and comfortable. We are going to visit slum areas and attend a cocktail party later in the evening. Doña. Hungry and impatient I go to the lobby even though there is one hour until I have to meet my colleague for breakfast. I sit at a table with my laptop, and a man pours me a cup of coffee. Gluk, gluk, gluk. My first Juan Valdez. Black and dense, sweet and round. Señor: puedo pedir huevos

> revueltos con tomate y cebolla, pan tostado, una ensalada de papaya, limón, banano y granadilla, y un jugo de lulo? My favorite breakfast with fruits that I cannot get in Denmark. As other business people in the hotel restaurant I start checking e-mails, Facebook, Instagram, Twitter—Wow! Joe Peach is only in Bogotá. Must get in contact with him. Look out the window. Next to a big four-wheel-drive with tinted windows walks a man with his donkey and wagon with piles of trash. He is one of Bogotá's famous civil trash collectors. Here comes my colleague. Godmorgen, har du sovet godt?

'Waking Up in Bogotá' made the mobilities of our emotional bodily practice clear by representing the balancing act between time zones, borders, identities, ethnicity, and languages. When I had to translate and juggle between Danish, English, and Spanish, I felt like I had to perform some kind of linguistic dance. I experienced how language reflected body and identity when my colleague said that my body, voice, and character changed significantly when shifting between languages. Subsequently, I had to ask myself, who am I? as well as all other nerve-wracking existential questions. The tale presents my practical ethical conflicts of being a privileged, highly educated traveler, interfacing a networked global society across old borders, consuming societies and communities, both physically and digitally. Of being a *Colombodanesa* both returning home and being a foreigner at the same time, and in this sense embodying the detachment of identity and place (Massey 1994), finding identity *in motion* (Ingold 2007). It made me understand how motion and emotion is "kinaesthetically intertwined and produced together through a conjunction of bodies, technologies, and cultural practices" (Sheller 2004, 227). Based on a relational ontology, it co-constituted my whole idea of subjects, spaces, and meanings, and the significance of connections in-between (Vannini 2012).

Tales: A Simulacrum of Networked Urban Mobilities

'Waking Up in Bogotá' and other tales showed me how storytelling can enable and illuminate concrete actions, the gamut of emotions, conflicting rationalities, and the whole sensory apparatus by which we engage with our surroundings and construct meaning (Simonsen 2007; Sheller 2004; Sayer 2011). The semantics we use in tales allows us to reflect pre-meaningful, dark, ambiguous thoughts, and in this way, tales can represent semiotics: production, movement, reception, interpretation, reaction, and storing of sense-making based on signaling—spoken, written, and non-verbal communication (Fairclough, Jessop, and Sayer 2002)—and our interaction with materialities and technologies (Sheller 2014).

Practice of language and our ability to construct are two aspects that define humanity (Leth and Willerslev 2016). Languages make it possible for humans to relate to others, and make it possible for humans to negotiate and overcome alienation[2] to some degree. Communicating and storytelling foster our essential abilities to construct the city; to negotiate plans and find out who will do what. Within 'the walls' we create a life that we define as urban, and what kinds of lives are possible are inherent in the communication behind urban planning and policymaking. Perceiving urban planning, not only as a physical process but also as a societal, social, cultural, *and* physical activity of transformation, tells us to take into account what defines this complex context—and what is about to be transformed and reproduced (Graham and Marvin 2001; Sheller and Urry 2006; Amin and Thrift 2002; Harvey 2000). Storytelling and tales can help clarify these processes of ongoing construction of urban realities and built environments.

> Stories are central to planning practice: to the knowledge it draws on from the social sciences and humanities; to the knowledge it produces about the city; and to ways of acting in the city. Planning is performed through story, in a myriad of ways.
>
> (Sandercock 2003, 12)

The power of tales lies in their inherent ability to produce, reproduce, and cement certain normalization and justification of realities—social, cultural, and economic orders. Therefore, at the same time they also hold the potential to question these realities. Due to urban planning's transformative character, there seems to be an inherent ideological and normative goal within planning practice and theory to find out how the urban life can be 'better' for its citizens. Stories can help give nuance to what is acknowledged as 'better' and help question what is good for who, when, where, and why. Doing qualitative research is a privilege that comes with some responsibility—a responsibility to scrutinize these stories and hopefully promote a society where humans can become who they wish to be, free of repression and discrimination.

Concluding Remarks

This chapter is based on a study that deals with the strategic, political, and civil processes of rationalization that *already* take place *around* and *in* planning theory and practice. It is based on the acknowledgement that language constitutes, shapes, and sometimes determines our perceptions of reality (Denzin 2001; Sandercock 1999; Sandercock 2003; Freudendal-Pedersen 2009; Flyvbjerg 1998). Using storytelling *as method* can help us be clearer about the rationalizations that we, as researchers and practitioners, produce and reproduce, and to be clearer about the context being investigated. *As representation*, storytelling can give voice, nuance, and atonement, and also

168   *Emmy Laura Perez Fjalland*

be a tool for negotiations in complex networked urban contexts. The power of stories lies in their ability to actualize the nuances of our acknowledged norms and realities and therefore holds the potential to enhance social imagination and ideas for other realities and orders. I still think I long to find out how to be able to combine representation, mobilities, and imagination, and to make them more vital in their fixed approach.

Notes

1. A concept based on Malene Freudendal-Pedersen's (2014) and Ulli Zeitler's (2008) introduction of 'response-ability' in ethical considerations on mobility and planning. Zeitler argues that "proper responses depend on our ability to respond, our 'response-ability'" (Freudendal-Pedersen 2014).
2. Drawing on classic sociological and geographical work with 'alienation,' and specifically Melvin Seeman's article 'On the Meaning of Alienation' (1959). Alienation seems to include isolation, powerlessness, meaninglessness, and self-estrangement, and seems to be highly connected to global and political structures.

References

Adichie, Chimamanda Ngozi. 2009. "The Danger of a Single Story." TED Global: TED Global.

Amin, Ash and Nigel Thrift. 2002. *Cities: Reimagining the Urban*. Cambridge: Polity Press.

Berney, Rachel Eloise. 2008. *The Pedagogical City: How Bogotá, Colombia, Is Reshaping the Role of Public Space*. Berkeley: University of California.

Caballero, Maria Cristina. 2007. "Academic Turns City into a Social Experiment— Mayor Mockus of Bogotá and His Spectaculy Applied Theory." *Harvard Gazette.*

Denzin, Norman. 2001. "The Reflexsive Interview and a Performative Social Science." *Qualitative Research* 1 (1): 23–46.

Fairclough, Norman, Bob Jessop and Andrew Sayer. 2002. "Critical Realism and Semiosis." *Journal of Critical Realism* 5: 1–26.

Flyvbjerg, Bent. 1998. *Rationality and Power: Democracy in Practice* (1st ed.). London and Chicago: University of Chicago Press.

Freudendal-Pedersen, Malene. 2009. *Mobility in Daily Life: Between Freedom and Unfreedom*. Vol. 2012. Farnham: Ashgate Publishing, Ltd.

Graham, Steve and Simon Marvin. 2001. *Splintering Urbanism: Networked Infrastructures, Technological Mobilities and the Urban Condition*. New York: Routhledge.

Hartmann-Petersen, Katrine. 2009. *I medgang og modgang: Fleksibilitet og flygtighed i buschaufførers mobile liv*. Roskilde: Roskilde University.

Harvey, David. 2000. *Spaces of Hope*. Berkeley: University of California Press.

Ingold, Tim. 2007. *Lines: A Brief History*. Oxon and New York: Routledge.

Leth, Kristian and Eske Willerslev. 2016. *Historien Om Det Hele: Fortællinger Om Magi Og Videnskab*. Copenhagen: People's Press.

Malene Freudendal-Pedersen. 2014. "Ethics and Responsiblities." In *The Routledge Handbook of Mobilities*, edited by Peter Adey, David Bissell, Kevin Hannam, Peter Merriman and Mimi Sheller, 143–153. London: Routledge.

Massey, Doreen. 1994. "A Global Sense of Place." In *Space, Place, and Gender*, 146–156. Cambridge: Polity Press.

Mockus, Antanas. 2002. "CO-EXISTENCE as Harmonization of Law, Morality and Culture." *Prospects* 32 (1): 1991–1993x.

Peñalosa, Enrique. 2007. "Politics, Power, Cities." In *The Endless City*, edited by Richard Burdett and Deyan Sudjic, 307–319. London: Phaidon.

Pink, Sarah. 2006. *Doing Visual Ethographies* (2nd ed.). London: Sage.

Sandercock, Leonie. 1999. "Expanding the 'Language' of Planning: A Meditation on Planning Education for the Twenty-first Century." *European Planning Studies* 7 (5): 533–544. doi:10.1080/09654319908720535

Sandercock, Leonie. 2003. "Out of the Closet: The Importance of Stories and Storytelling in Planning Practice." *Planning Theory & Practice* 4 (1): 11–28. doi:10.1080/1464935032000057209

Sandercock, Leonie. 2004. "Towards a Planning Imagination for the 21st Century." *Journal of the American Planning Association* 70 (2): 133–142. doi:10.1080/01944360408976368

Sayer, Andrew. 2011. *Why Things Matter to People: Social Science, Values and Ethical Life*. New York: Cambridge University Press.

Seeman, Melvin. 1959. "On the Meaning of Alienation." *American Sociological Review* 24 (6): 783–791.

Sheller, Mimi. 2004. "Automotive Emotions: Feeling the Car." *Theory, Culture & Society* 21 (4–5): 221–242.

Sheller, Mimi. 2014. "The New Mobilities Paradigm for a Live Sociology." *Current Sociology Review* 62 (6): 789–811. doi:10.1177/0011392114533211

Sheller, Mimi and John Urry. 2006. "The New Mobilities Paradigm." *Environment and Planning A* 38 (2): 207–226. PION LTD.

Silva, Alicia Eugenia. 2009. *Bogotá, de La Construcción Al Deterioro 1997–2007*. Bogotá: Editorial Universidad del Rosario.

Simonsen, Kirsten. 2007. "Practice, Spatiality and Embodied Emotions: An Outline of a Geography of Practice." *Human Affairs* 17 (2): 168–181.

Van Maanen, John. 1988. *Tales of the Field: On Writing Ethnography* (2nd ed.). Chicago and London: University of Chicago Press.

Vannini, Phillip. 2012. *Ferry Tales: Mobility, Place, and Time on Canada's West Coast* (Innovative Ethnographies). New York: Routledge.

Zeitler, Ullrich. 2008. "The Ontology of Mobility, Morality and Transport Planning." In *The Ethics of Mobilities: Rethinking Place, Exclusion, Freedom and Environment*, edited by Sigurd Bergmann and Tore Sager, 233–240. Farnham: Ashgate Publishing Limited.

30 Are Emerging Mobility Practices Changing Our Urban Spaces?

A Close Look at the Italian Case[1]

Bruna Vendemmia

This chapter gives a close look at some stories of highly mobile people in Italy. The profiles presented later in the chapter are part of wider research (Vendemmia 2015) which focused on emerging forms of mobility, in particular the ones that suggest the rise of a process of 'reversibilization' (Kaufmann 2002, 24) of mobility practices, such as: long-distance commuting, shuttling, and overnighting.

Starting from the observation of highly mobile people, this research focuses attention on the analysis of mobility as a system consisting of many differing 'mobilities,' "including corporal travels, physical movements of objects, imaginative, virtual and communicative travels" (Urry 2007, 47). In spite of being an architect and urban planner, in order to catch this complexity and to understand at what extent emerging forms of mobility are transforming contemporary urban environments, I decided to adopt the actor point of view, instead of looking at the physical network of infrastructure and mobility spaces. This approach goes beyond a definition of 'mobility spaces' as "places where mobility flows interconnect" (Bertolini and Dijst 2003, 28); rather it allows the inclusion in the observation of all the spaces that support a mobile lifestyle crossing different typologies and spatial scales: from the territory to the house, the office, and the train seat.

Furthermore, using the actor point of view allows exploitation of the ability of the individual to perceive "unexpected information and to enable unplanned encounters" (Levy 1994, 49–50),[2] thus giving back a rich, sensitive, and multifaceted description of mobility, and avoiding the consideration of mobility spaces as designated.

Adopting this approach also drove me to test a more dynamic method of research that allows me to catch some processes otherwise invisible. Some of the cases introduced later on in this chapter, as for example Beatrice, highlight the difficulty of statistical data to detect the effects of these forms of mobility on the use and organization of space. Indeed, as it will be better explained in next section, Beatrice is a resident in Asti, officially rents an apartment in Turin, but spends five days a week in Milan where she neither rents nor owns a house. As she is not commuting, she is not even included in the official statistics of workers that enter Milan by train every day, even though she intensely uses the city and its services. Although her

Emerging Mobility Practices   171

experience of mobility is relevant, she is completely invisible to traditional mobile methods and misrepresents statistical data.

The research method includes: traveling alongside highly mobile people, giving semi-structured interviews, and drawing interactive maps. Those tools allow me to investigate: the type of services used in different spatial contexts; the geography of personal relationships; the different profiles of inhabited places; and lastly, the strategies elaborated by the interviewees to deal with this extended space and their consequences on spatial configurations. In the remainder of the chapter I will analyze two case studies: Valentina and Beatrice. The whole case study, however, was composed of 11 highly mobile people, selected using the snowball technique. The small number of participants selected meant that I could afford to explore the rich details of their activities. The evidence contained in their interviews has been useful in characterizing the reasons behind their mobility, showing that being mobile is not always a matter of choice. All the information collected has contributed to the construction of short life stories of highly mobile people.

Life Stories of Mobility: The Case of Valentina and Beatrice

Valentina was born in Pavia, and is a long-distance commuter between Milan and Turin; however, Milan is not only her place of work. She was living in Milan for 20 years and she decided to move to Turin with her husband when she started a family. This city could offer her better opportunities of finding child care, mainly due to the support of parents or families, a more affordable house market, and the possibility of a more comfortable urban environment. At the same time Valentina has an open-ended contract and could not find the same job conditions in Turin, nor could she work in the same sector. Thus she is struggling with her career and professional opportunities, on one hand, and family life, on the other.

Beatrice also used to commute every day between Turin and Milan before she decided to rent a small apartment in Milan and become a shuttle. In the case of Beatrice it was the specificity of her jobs that makes her being first a commuter, then a shuttle. She works in fashion, the company she works for is based in Veneto though Milan is the place where clients come to see the merchandise, and thus it is in Milan that she needs to be. Turin is the city where her partner is living. When asking about the boundaries of her space Beatrice says: "I could say that my city is Turin, because my beloved one is there. But the rest, cinemas, theaters, exhibitions, are in Milan." Additionally, she is officially resident in Asti, the city where her parents live and where she goes from time to time to visit them and for administrative duties.

The Spaces of Highly Mobile People

The information collected thanks to Valentina's and Beatrice's short mobility life stories have been turned into maps (see Figure 30.1 and Figure 30.2). The

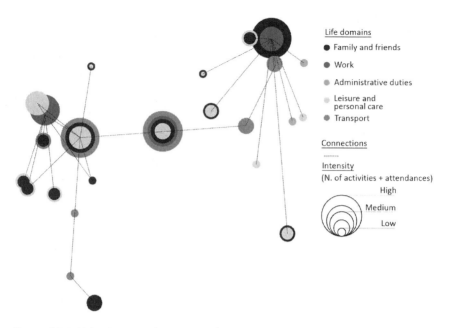

Figure 30.1 Valentina's synthetic map of activities, places, and intensities
Source: Bruna Vendemmia.

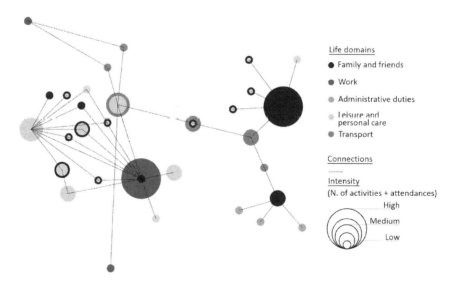

Figure 30.2 Beatrice's synthetic map of activities, places, and intensities
Source: Bruna Vendemmia.

maps are made of dots, of different shades of grey and dimensions, and lines. The dots are the places used by the interviewees in their everyday mobility, while the lines are the connections between these different places and activities. The types of activities are represented in different shades of grey, while the intensity of uses[3] defines the dimension of the dots. The larger the number and size of the dots, the more attractive the place for the interviewee.

The maps revealed the importance of all the spaces that support a mobile lifestyle, not only traditional spaces of mobility. Furthermore, traditional mobility spaces assume more complex meanings. For Valentina, for example, the railways station is a preferred meeting place. She says: "I don't care about the place. I love spending time with my friends. So the station can be a nice place to meet people." Due to her mobile lifestyle, she declares that what she values more is time, she doesn't care about spatial characteristics as long as she has more time to spend with significant others. What makes the railway station a central place in Valentina's life is that it allows a better organization of time. For the same reason she profits of the time spent on the train coach, which is a significant amount of time. When I traveled along with her on the train, her computer was open on the table and she was doing some work. Valentina explained to me that she had not been able to work at home the evening before, and so she had to catch up before arriving at office. Train coach can be an office as well as a veritable public space on wheels where one meets friends. Kesselring defines those spaces "connectivity spaces" (Kesselring 2006, 277): places for "interaction and contact" where one experiences the movement. Definitely mobility spaces can be also places for "dwelltime" (Sheller and Urry 2006, 220).

Moreover, at least twice a week Valentina uses her house as an office. Instead, for Beatrice the office is a second home. She said that the office is not only her place of work, but a more complex space where she can spend most of her time, feeling comfortable and at ease. This overlapping of home and working spaces, even though fragmented, does generate micro transformations of urban environment, making housing and offices more flexible; it proves a process of "reorganization or even dismantling of the functional division of urban space into basic functions of housing, work, leisure time, and mobility between them" (Di Marino and Lapintie 2014) and confirms the hypothesis suggested by François Ascher (1995, 39) that the rise of information and communication technologies promoted a comeback to residential spaces; those last are now often used also as place for work or leisure. Monday-to-Friday renting is also contributing to this transformation. Beatrice is renting a secondary house used only from Monday to Friday; aside from influencing the real estate market, this phenomenon creates a turnover of high- and low-intensity urban places.

Concluding Remarks

As shown in the stories of Valentina and Beatrice, understanding mobility in its complexity and simultaneity proved difficult when only using transport

174 *Bruna Vendemmia*

data as they are often based on static references and remain within administrative boundaries of space and population. Such data do not always correspond to the actual conditions of mobile people; furthermore it fails to highlight the spatial dynamics created by mobility itself. At the same time, analyzing mobility through the observation of transport spaces does not allow highlighting all the systems of spaces and services required to support a mobile life.

The methodology used in this research demonstrates that more mobile methods could facilitate an understanding of different spatial implications, and could offer better insights into the different spaces involved in highly mobile people's everyday lives.

Notes

1. This article is part of PhD research: Vendemmia, Bruna. 2015. 'What Spaces for Highly Mobile People? Analyzing Emerging Practices of Mobility in Italy.' PhD diss. Politecnico di Milano.
2. Original text in French and translated by the author.
3. The intensity has been calculated as the sum of the number of activities made in a place and its attendance.

References

Ascher, François. 1995. *Métapolis ou l'avenir des villes*. Paris: Odile Jacob.
Bertolini, Luca and Martin Dijst. 2003. "Mobility Environments and Network Cities." *Journal of Urban Design* 8 (1): 27–43.
Di Marino, Mina and Kimmo Lapintie. 2014. "New Spaces for Work in the Public Realm." Paper presented at Aesop Annual Conference From Control to Coevolution, Utrecht and Delft, Netherlands, July 9–12.
Kaufmann, Vincent. 2002. *Re-Thinking Mobility*. Aldershot: Ashgate.
Kesselring, Sven. 2006. "Pioneering Mobilities: New Patterns of Movement and Motility in a Mobile World." *Environment and Planning A* 38 (2): 269–279.
Lévy, Jacques. 1994. *L'espace Légitime*. Paris: Presses de la fondation nationale des sciences politiques.
Sheller, Mimi and John Urry. 2006. "The New Mobilities Paradigm." *Environment and Planning A* 38: 207–226.
Urry, John. 2007. *Mobilities*. Cambridge: Polity Press.
Vendemmia, Bruna. 2015. "What Spaces for Highly Mobile People? Analyzing Emerging Practices of Mobility in Italy." PhD diss., Politecnico di Milano.

31 (In)Consequential Planning Practices

The Political Pitfall of Mobility Policymaking in Lisbon's Metropolitan Area

João Mourato, Sofia Santos, Daniela Ferreira, and Renato Miguel Carmo

The analysis of the impact of mobility in the (re)production of spatial inequalities has only been marginally addressed. There is a paradoxical absence of space and mobility in studies of social inequality (Kaufmann et al. 2004; Ohnmacht et al. 2009; Manderscheid 2009) and a striking lack of attention to social inequality in studies, strategies, and public policy involving territory and mobility (Martens 2006; Preston 2009). This gap laid the opportunity for our research project, *Localways*.[1] This research project developed from a core assumption: Despite the global reach of the 2007-onwards economic and financial crisis, there is a still unmapped, extremely heterogeneous landscape of local impacts and adjustment strategies.

To this effect, *Localways* is a socioeconomic, institutional, and political snapshot, taken through the lenses of metropolitan mobility, of the impacts of the aforementioned crisis and the subsequent adjustment dynamics of citizens, communities, and the State. *Localways*' territorial focus zeroes in on Lisbon's Metropolitan Area (LMA), home of nearly a third of Portugal's population, a widely heterogeneous area socioeconomically, which sits at the forefront of a two-decades-long territorial administration decentralization process. The final image is one of complexity where multiple processes of transitional adaptation, more or less voluntary, more or less consequent, overlap. This diversity mirrors the often radically distinct capacities and resources that different actors have. In retrospect, *Localways* exposes some of these intricate symbiotic relationships at play. In particular, it highlights the extent to which State *(in)action*, despite its underlying purpose of mitigation of the societal impact of the economic and financial crisis, becomes itself one of its key exponentiation factors.

Mapping Citizen Mobility Behaviors and Practices in Times of Crisis

In Portugal, over a period of 20 years, the percentage of the population using cars tripled (21% in 1991 to 62% in 2011).[2] In Lisbon's Metropolitan

176 *João Mourato et al.*

Area, in 2011, the car was the main mean of transportation for 54% of the people working or studying. In our view, to fully understand the mobility-policies-driven production of socioeconomic (in)equality, it is of paramount importance to know who is more dependent of the public transport network, how dependent, and why? Via 1500 questionnaires a consistent image surfaced. The use of public transport is stronger in students and low-income workers, especially women, due to the lack of alternatives and lower cost. However, despite a recent downward trend in car use, it was nevertheless discernible that people depending on public transport are, in general, in a clear disadvantage. In effect, they spend more time in daily travels, and cost-wise, there is a significant proportion of people that spend more than one-fifth of the national minimum wage per month in public transport fares/monthly tickets. Having outlined how intertwined mobility and inequality were, the *Localways'* focus fell on the policy responses in place and how the latter addressed this issue.

Mobility Policymaking in Lisbon's Metropolitan Area

In Portugal, the democratization and generalization of car use is a 40-plus-year-old, highly politicized process that to a large extent mirrors the country's socioeconomic development and modernization. This is a fundamental fact in order to understand contemporary Portuguese mobility patterns. The political concept of national progress, and to a large extent of European integration, was fueled by a largely unopposed preference of public investment in road networks instead of public transport services (Costa 2007; Pereira and Silva 2008; Nunes 2011; Padeiro 2012). Accessibility was a key political theme all throughout the last two decades of the twentieth century in Portugal. Mobility, mobility policies, and their implications, on the other hand, were until recently relegated to a more backstage position.

In Lisbon's Metropolitan Area, with its 18 municipalities, the accessibility paradigm as a development driver was also undisputed. Furthermore, the regional road and public transport network evolved hindered by a biased focus on Lisbon municipality (Nunes 2011; Padeiro 2012), leaving the region with an unbalanced pattern of accessibilities. Mobility-wise, if we look into regional (metropolitan level) and local policies (municipalities) and guiding documents we can understand that fighting inequality—social or spatial—has not been a priority for public policy, starting by the insufficiency of available information and the absence of structural action. To breakdown the reasons underpinning such structural (in)action we must delve into the politics that underpin it.

The Political Pitfall of Mobility Policymaking

To begin with, there is no metropolitan government per se. In turn, we identified a dysfunctional multi-level network governance system, where

(In)Consequential Planning Practices   177

the central government lapsed as a regulator, failing to effectively manage private-sector transport providers. Furthermore, metropolitan and municipal authorities had too little to say about how public transport provision is ran in their territories (i.e. price-setting, route-definition, etc.). Overall, several structural problems persist between the scope of action and the actual scope of intervention of the different institutions in charge of the several aspects of the metropolitan mobility system.

These problems rendered the designed network governance model useless. For example, as far as the network's institutional design is concerned, a key actor in theory would be the supra-municipal Lisbon's metropolitan authority. However, the latter is non-directly elected and holds no relevant allocated budget or tax-raising capacity. Thus, its network-steering intervention is rendered largely ineffective. To make matters worse, a specifically created metropolitan transport authority, although formally existent, suffers from similar fragilities. Its real capacity to monitor and engage with key stakeholders in the public transport network system and to develop metropolitan-wide mobility strategies is extremely limited. It therefore comes as no surprise that previous and present mobility planning practices are largely inconsequential, mainly due to the absence of political capital to secure its implementation (Weir 2006).

Nevertheless, deeply entrenched in this fragmented policy landscape (Wagenaar 2007) we identified a myriad of different political and policy responses in the face of this institutional and policy void. If some municipalities have developed their own municipal and even inter-municipal mobility and transport strategies, some others simply have not. However, this scenario at the metropolitan level does not translate homogenously at the local level. In fact, what we witnessed is quite the opposite. In practical terms the absence of a metropolitan authority proper hampers the possibility of all municipalities to respond with equal adequacy to its citizens' mobility needs, thus undermining, for example, the metropolitan territorial cohesion.

Concluding Remarks

In sum, much has been discussed on how institutions are vehicles of the production and reproduction of socioeconomic inequality (Albiston 2009; Offe 2001) and how different institutional arrangements tend to produce different political outcomes, and the institutional design of democratic government is what most closely affects its performance (March and Olsen 1984). In this sense, *Localways* researched the impacts of not one but several crises, even though it focused on one crisis, namely one deeply rooted in the political and institutional culture underpinning Lisbon's metropolitan territorial governance. A crisis deeply rooted in a series of critical issues, from internal power unbalances, lack of clear leadership, unsuitable institutional design, unfitting legal and policy frameworks, institutional path dependency, etc.

178 João Mourato et al.

However, this status quo is soon to be challenged. In 2015, new legislation was brought to the fore to reinforce decentralization and supra-municipal governance autonomy, and to close the gap between citizen and political decision-maker at the metropolitan level. As its impacts are yet unknown, Lisbon's Metropolitan Area remains sitting on the fence of decentralization, embodying a clear deficit of effective supra-municipal coordination and the public tackling of prevailing inequalities.

Notes

1. The project *Localways: Mobilities, Inequalities and Citizenship* is financed by the Portuguese Foundation for Science and Technology (PTDC/ATP-EUR/5023/2012).
2. Statistics Portugal—INE, 2001 and 2011 Censuses.

References

Albiston, Catherine. 2009. "Institutional Inequality." *Wisconsin Law Review* 5: 1093–1165.

Costa, Nuno. 2007. "Mobilidade e Transporte em Áreas Urbanas. O caso da Área Metropolitana de Lisboa." PhD diss., Universidade de Lisboa.

Kaufmann, Vincent, Manfred Bergman and Dominique Joye. 2004. "Motility: Mobility as Capital." *International Journal of Urban and Regional Research* 28 (4): 745–756.

Manderscheid, Katharina. 2009. "Unequal Mobilities." In *Mobilities and Inequality*, edited by Timo Ohnmacht, Hanja Maksim and Manfred Max Bergman, 27–50. Aldershot: Ashgate.

March, James G. and Johan P. Olsen. 1984. "The New Institutionalism: Organizational Factors in Political Life." *The American Political Science Review* 78 (3): 734–749.

Martens, Karel. 2006. "Basing Transport Planning on Principles of Social Justice." *Berkeley Planning Journal* 19: 1–17.

Nunes, Joao P.S. 2011. *Florestas de Cimento Armado. Os Grandes Conjuntos Residenciais e a Constituição da Metrópole de Lisboa (1955–2005)*. Lisboa: Calouste Gulbenkian Foundation and Fundação para a Ciência e Tecnologia.

Offe, Claus. 2001. "Institutional Design." In *Encyclopedia of Democratic Thought*, edited by Paul Barry Clarke and Joe Foweraker, 363–368. London: Routledge.

Ohnmacht, Timo, Hanja Maksim and Manfred M. Bergman, eds. 2009. *Mobilities and Inequality*. Cornwall: Ashgate.

Padeiro, Miguel. 2012. "Conciliar os transportes e o ordenamento urbano: avanços recentes e aplicabilidade em áreas metropolitanas portuguesas." *Cidades, Comunidades e Territórios* 25: 1–20.

Pereira, Margarida and Fernando Silva. 2008. "Modelos de Ordenamento em confronto na área metropolitana de Lisboa: cidade alargada ou recentragem metropolitana?" *Cadernos Metrópole* 20: 107–123.

Preston, John. 2009. "Epilogue: Transport Policy and Social Exclusion—Some Reflections." *Transport Policy* 16: 140–142.

Wagenaar, Hendrik. 2007. "Interpretation and Intention in Policy Analysis." In *Handbook of Public Policy Analysis: Theory, Politics, and Methods*, edited by Frank Fisher, Gerald Miller and Mara Sidney, 429–441. New York: CRC Press.

Weir, Margaret. 2006. "When Does Politics Create Policy? The Organizational Politics of Change." In *Rethinking Political Institutions*, edited by Ian Shapiro, Stephen Skowronek and Daniel Galvin, 171–186. New York: New York University Press.

32 Motility Meets Viscosity in Rural to Urban Flows

Catherine Doherty

To understand urban spaces, we need to understand their contrast to rural spaces, and the relations, forces, and conditions behind mobilities that (re) produce these differences. While non-urban communities are often imagined as stable communities with little mobility, their viability relies on the mobility of professionals. Motility has proved a useful variable in mobility theory. A companion concept of viscosity can explain how contextual conditions facilitate or hinder a motile agent's accomplishment of mobility. This chapter demonstrates how a combination of motility and viscosity together better account for mobility with an interview narrative from a professional seeking to move his family from rural to urban space to further the children's educational opportunities. The analysis highlights the risks and fixities produced in the interaction between motility and viscosity. In this way, urban magnetism is shown to work through market forces that link rural and urban communities in an increasingly competitive network.

Coming to Mobility

My first projects concerned with international higher education students revealed how the social 'stuff' of institutional defaults can create problems for mobile projects. This led me to Urry's 'agenda of mobility' (2000, 2) and the mobilities paradigm, in particular its attention to "issues of movement, of too little movement or too much" (Sheller and Urry 2006, 208). As a sociologist my work is also deeply informed by the distinction between private troubles and public issues (Mills 1959). Meshing these two orientations, I conducted parallel research projects with contrasting populations of families with school-aged children—one group experiencing private troubles from too much movement (the hyper-mobile families of military members), the other experiencing too little movement and thus creating a social issue.

This second project[1] addressed the public issue around attracting qualified professionals for human services in rural and remote communities (Doherty, Patton, and Shield 2015), a familiar public issue in many other national settings. We treated professional credentials and their recognition as a 'mobility system' (Urry 2007, 12), that is, as social infrastructure that sponsors mobility. Urry (2000, 5) also offered a useful distinction between *'gardening and gamekeeping'* metaphors which helped us to understand how some localities must work to attract and retain professionals that cannot be produced in situ.

Issues of mobility thus necessarily implicate the relationship between localities. Massey's (1993) concept of a socially constructed, progressive sense of place helped capture this relational perspective. From Harvey (1993) we further understood this relation to be competitive. Our research demonstrated how this public issue stemmed from professional families' private solutions informing very selective mobility that protected educational opportunities for their children. This group's *'spatial autonomy'* and their choice of *'optimal environments'* (Weiss 2005, 714) in the deep educational markets of urban centers thus contributed to the social disadvantage in non-urban communities.

Thinking More Generally

So what has this got to do with networked mobilities? To understand the affordances of urban spaces, we need to understand their contrast to rural spaces, and the relations, forces, and conditions behind mobilities that intensify such differences in processes of urbanization. Rural communities are often imagined as stable communities involving little mobility. However, this idyll masks the necessary but problematic churn of professionals such as doctors, nurses, and teachers passing through with their families.

There is a normative ethic of families resisting relocation to protect continuity in their children's education (Holdsworth 2013). For this reason, household relocations with school-aged children are telling moments that reveal much about families and social conditions governing their mobility. Family relocations are infrequent, high-stakes mobility events that bring many assumptions operating in families to the surface for re-assessment. In addition, the mobility of families through school communities also brings to the empirical surface the static defaults built into everyday institutional routines which complicate mobile projects. Social practices within institutions thus contribute to spatial fixities and act as a deterrent to the mobility imperative.

Mobility scholars are understandably drawn to empirical sites of accelerating and intensifying mobilities, but there is an equal responsibility for the mobility turn to account for practices and forces cultivating immobility. To conceptualize the complicating institutional 'stuff' my participants described, I developed a concept of institutional 'viscosity' (Doherty 2015), being a structural variable to describe the degree to which an institution's practices enable or constrain mobility projects. In this sense, some institutional settings are considered more 'viscous' than others, making movement through their processes more difficult. This concept allows an analytic distinction between the different contributions from the structural conditioning of the social context and from more agentive 'motility' (Kaufmann, Viry, and Widmer 2010). Any realization of mobility will be the outcome of the interaction between these two variables.

Regarding the viscosity of educational settings, my research showed how the spread of neoliberal policies cultivating school choice under market logics is creating more viscous conditions for family mobility. Under these policies, parents, in particular the professional middle class, have embraced their right to choice. This logic elevates school choice to a strategic exercise of making comparative readings of various options. Together these trends of marketization and more reflexive strategies make the professional parent and the minimal market available in rural and remote towns an unlikely or unstable combination: The small town 'here' cannot compete with the spread of choice 'there.'

Connell (2013, 105) argues that "to create a market you have to restrict the service in some way. . . . What you sell, then, is a privilege—something that other people cannot get." In this process, certain schools gain reputations that increase demand for their services beyond their capacity. Education research talks of the 'magnet' school which draws enrollments away from its competitors. At this stage, such schools adopt practices such as selective screening, waiting lists, booking fees, and catchment zones. Researchers in different nations have documented the common strategy of family relocations into the desired school's catchment zone (e.g. Butler and van Zanten 2007). Though such studies foreground the initial family move, I would argue that these market practices inherently reward immobility, that is, families limit mobility in order to stay put over time and in place to guarantee access to the rationed commodity. Moving creates risks of not being able to relocate into a catchment of choice, or going to the bottom of the waiting list.

We could also think of 'magnet' towns. The density of urban communities, with multiple choices within reach of daily commuting, allows schools to differentiate and compete for different market niches, while the isolated school in the small rural town must service all comers, without the capacity to support differentiation (Doherty, Rissman, and Browning 2013). In these polarized market conditions, an ethic of school choice feeds urban magnetism, making families less willing to risk moving into or out of thinner markets. The following complicated narrative offers an example of how urban magnetism works on professional families. The data comes from an interview study with 32 professionals with school-aged children working in rural and remote communities in Queensland. Each professional was asked to recount the narratives around their families' sequence of moves, and how career and educational considerations were reconciled (see Doherty, Patton, and Shield 2015). This narrative also exemplifies the interaction between structural viscosity and agentive motility in the family's reflexive strategy to achieve an optimal 're-placing' of family life across the institutional fronts affecting family members.

A Sticky Situation

A male police officer in a rural town with a partner and three children—two attending primary school and one approaching high school—explained his plan to apply for a promotion 'back' at the Gold Coast, a large urban center close to metropolitan Brisbane "because it's more long-term there." The family were preparing for that possibility:

> What we're doing is we're picking our school first, okay, because what's most important to us is getting the kids' education. . . . If I get Gold Coast, we'll move to Gold Coast. . . . If I get Brisbane, we'll live at [Gold Coast suburb] . . . and I'll commute every day.

However, approaches to their schools of choice to place three children in different year levels encountered similar responses: "They said, 'Yeah, no worries. We'll put you on the waiting list with the other 50 people we've got on our waiting list. We can't guarantee you a spot.'" The most certainty the family could negotiate was booking into a school that could place the younger two in appropriate years, but place the older child only if the child repeated a year level:

> What we're saying to [the child] is if, if, if—if I get promoted, if we move, if you go to this school, you know, this is what happens . . . I'm not going to find out anything 'til September. If we then start ringing around it's going to be too late.

The tangled series of ifs and buts illustrates the intense work of reflexive strategy undertaken in the hope of, and prior to, winning a position in the urban conurbation. It also illustrates the high viscosity that can build in competitive educational markets, with waiting lists, booking fees, and entry conditions that privilege immobile families who remain in place over time. If the urban market practices weren't so viscous, this motile family's mobility would be much easier to achieve.

Concluding Remarks

The social institutions through which we live our lives will offer variable degrees of resistance to mobility. Just like the variable of traffic density, the 'stuff' of institutional practices moderates mobilities, allowing us to move more or less freely, thus contributing to flows and fixities. A companion concept of viscosity can theoretically account for the degree to which contextual conditions facilitate or hinder a motile agent's accomplishment of mobility. With a dual focus on both agency and structure, empirical studies can give a more comprehensive analysis of the conditions contributing to the rate, absence, or ease of mobility. Methodologically, mobility studies need

184   *Catherine Doherty*

to account for friction, inertia, and resistance as much as the kinetic energies behind mobility: "It is not a question of privileging a 'mobile subjectivity' but rather of tracking the power of discourses and practices of mobility in creating both movement and stasis" (Sheller and Urry 2006, 211).

Note

1. This project was funded by the Australian Research Council.

References

Butler, Tim and Agnes van Zanten. 2007. "School Choice: A European Perspective." *Journal of Education Policy* 22 (1): 1–5.
Connell, Raewyn. 2013. "The Neoliberal Cascade and Education: An Essay on the Market Agenda and Its Consequences." *Critical Studies in Education* 54 (2): 99–112.
Doherty, Catherine. 2015. "Agentive Motility and Structural Viscosity: Australian Families Relocating in Educational Markets." *Mobilities* 10 (2): 249–266.
Doherty, Catherine, Wendy Patton and Paul Shield. 2015. *Family Mobility: Reconciling Career Opportunities and Educational Strategy.* London: Routledge.
Doherty, Catherine, Barbara Rissman and Browyn Browning. 2013. "Educational Markets in Space: Gamekeeping Professionals Across Australian Communities." *Journal of Education Policy* 28 (1): 121–152.
Harvey, David. 1993. "From Space to Place and Back Again: Reflections on the Condition of Postmodernity." In *Mapping the Futures: Local Cultures, Global Change*, edited by Jon Bird, Barry Curtis, Tim Putman, George Robertson and Lisa Tickner, 3–29. London: Routledge.
Holdsworth, Clare. 2013. *Family and Intimate Mobilities.* Houndmills, Basingstoke: Palgrave Macmillan.
Kaufmann, Vincent, Gil Viry and Eric Widmer. 2010. "Motility." In *Mobile Living Across Europe II*, edited by Norbert Schneider and Beate Collet, 95–111. Opladen and Farmington Hills: Barbara Budrich Publishers.
Massey, Doreen. 1993. "Power-Geometry and a Progressive Sense of Place." In *Mapping the Futures: Local Cultures, Global Change*, edited by Jon Bird, Barry Curtis, Tim Putman, George Robertson and Lisa Tickner, 59–69. London and New York: Routledge.
Mills, Charles Wright. 1959. *The Sociological Imagination.* Oxford: Oxford University Press.
Sheller, Mimi and John Urry. 2006. "The New Mobilities Paradigm." *Environment and Planning A* 38: 207–226.
Urry, John. 2000. *Sociology Beyond Societies: Mobilities for the Twenty-First Century.* London: Routledge.
Urry, John. 2007. *Mobilities.* Cambridge: Polity Press.
Weiss, Anja. 2005. "The Transnationalization of Social Inequality: Conceptualizing Social Positions on a World Scale." *Current Sociology* 53 (4): 707–728.

33 Routes and Roots
Studying Place Relations in Multilocal Lifeworlds

Robert Nadler

In 2011, Jan Wilhelm Duyvendak published his monograph *The Politics of Home* in which he studied the sense of belonging of chronically mobile people. When I saw this book, I was very interested in the notion of belonging and rootedness in places. Although the field of mobility studies was a major reference for me, I had the impression this field of research focused strongly on mobility while missing the focus on the other side of that coin, which is immobility and rootedness. If mobility scholars speak about rootedness, it is often referred to as an outdated phenomenon superseded by an increasing uprootedness or homelessness (Braidotti 1994; Morley and Robins 1995; Rapport and Dawson 1998). However, I did not find satisfying conceptualizations regarding potential new ways of constructing a sense of belonging in the context of mobile lifestyles.

Based on my own empirical research, I want to introduce the notion of 'plug&play places' as a heuristic concept that enables an understanding of place relations in a mobile world. In this chapter, I will first sum up the theoretical debates around place relations as an interplay of localization and movement. I will then report on my own empirical findings from 25 biographical interviews with highly mobile and multilocal creative knowledge workers. Finally, I will sketch out the idea of 'plug&play places.'

The Interplay of Localization and Movement in a Mobile World

As mentioned above, mobility scholars often overlook immobility and localization when studying phenomena of increased mobility. Duyvendak (2011), however, picked up both sides of this coin. He used the terms 'roots' and 'routes' to describe the home-making practices of mobile people. I think that this pair of words describes quite well the new relations to places that people develop in a mobile world. From a theoretical perspective, the duality of 'settling' and 'being on the move' is also dealt with in the field of multilocality studies (Weichhart 2015). Multilocality studies developed as a research agenda during the late 2000s in German-speaking social sciences. According to Johanna Rolshoven (2006), multilocality is a phenomenon characterized

186   Robert Nadler

by the *vita activa*, the everyday life spread across different places. Austrian geographer Peter Weichhart (2015) adds that multilocality studies take a look at those specific practices that can be found in-between everyday circular mobility (e.g. commuting) and migration. Here, first approaches were made to explain the *rootedness* of highly mobile people by adding a pronounced focus on practices of home making and settling to the attention on traveling practices that are common in mobility studies.

As a geographer, I am interested in the social production of spaces and places. This includes the question of how people actually relate to places. I had read about the standardization of places and spaces, which is caused by globalization and increasing mobility. In 1995, Marc Augé wrote about the 'non-places,' which lacked a place-specific history and identity but are functional and provide orientation for mobile people. Duyvendak (2011) described 'generic places' that allow for homely feelings independently of one's geographic location. Then George Ritzer (2010) wrote about 'McDonaldization,' which involves places becoming efficient, calculable, predictable, and controllable. Bringing these two strands of research—multilocality and standardization of places—together, I assumed that multilocal people would be the prototype users of standardized places and services, and that the availability of such standardized places would be essential for rootedness in a mobile world.

Having a background in the study of creative industries (cf. Lange et al. 2009), I decided to look at the social practices of multilocal creative knowledge workers, using a combination of interviews and mental mapping techniques (for detailed information see Nadler 2014). I wanted to find out how they orientate themselves in new places and how they appropriate them, how they add these new places to the geography of their individual lifeworld. As such, I intended to address the interplay of mobility and immobility in their own lives. And, of course, I wanted to know if they used standardized places.

Place Relations of Multilocal Creative Knowledge Workers

Astonishingly, this was rarely the case in the everyday life practices of my 25 biographical case studies. I found that they develop individual strategies to organize their multilocal lives in an efficient way, but these strategies seldom included the use of standardized places—in the way they are being marketed. My interview partners orientate themselves in, and appropriate new places through practices such as walking around, doing sports, or loosing oneself voluntarily. They seek the specificity of places and want to profit from the functional complementarity of places. They do not look for a prefigured, anonymous, easy-to-use option, but they actively expose themselves to difference and diversity as well as local cultures and habits, and they try to find their place in it, or vice versa to fit a new place into their own lifeworld.

My interview partners organize their dwellings on the basis of sharing apartments and 'couch surfing' in order to economize, but also to get in touch with local people, and to avoid the cultural sterility of standardized places. They compare and adapt to place-specific cultures and develop a polyperspectivity—as one of my interviewees termed it—which helps to get along in the multilocal lifeworld, and which can also become an asset in the creative knowledge labor markets. My interview partners built up an every-day life character in their places, on the basis of an ubiquitous provision of small objects (e.g. clothes, CDs, toiletry) which is tailored to their individual needs. They do not adapt to objectively standardized places, if this adaptation process does not fit their own preferences.

An interesting aspect of the multilocality of my interview partners is that they indeed have a certain regularity to their travel routes. This means that they become used to handling their trips on these routes: Routes become 'routines.' As an outcome of this routinized traveling, my interview partners describe certain moments of travel and time spent in transit spaces (such as train stations and airports) as having a character of being in 'familiar places' (cf. Stock 2009). If traveling often on the same routes, travel itself is not so much perceived as travel anymore, it is not perceived as the transgression of a space that lies between two places, rather travel itself becomes perceived as a place. In this place, which could also be a place in motion, a train, or an airplane, everyday life takes 'place.' It is not anything particular anymore to travel on such routes; it is an ordinary activity in their everyday lives.

Plug&playability as an Outcome of Subjective Standardization of Place Relations

The way my interview partners attach to places, I think, has obvious anal-ogies to the plug&play functionality of a computer system. 'Plug&play' is a technological term that refers to the immediate usability of individual devices in a given system. If you put a USB key into your computer system, you extend the functionality of the system. But as it is a plug&playable device, you do not need to re-configure it after an initial configuration. Still you can detach it, liberating resources for other devices.

In a similar way, the interviewed multilocal people add places to their own everyday lifeworld. Places are adjusted in an initial configuration—through orientation, appropriation, and translation—and they are then 'plug&playable' in a flexible way. In moments of physical presence a place is metaphorically plugged into the lifeworld and it can be played accord-ing to its utility. Upon departure, and with the beginning of absence, the place is detached in a way that it does not consume the resources (like time, money, objects, emotional attachment, or cognitive capacities) of the mul-tilocal person.

Considering these practices of relating to places as constructions of 'plug&play places' allows for an understanding of the subjectivity of the

188 *Robert Nadler*

standardization of places, which complements scientific findings about the objective standardization of places (cf. Nadler 2014, 2016). Imagining place relations in multilocal lifeworlds as the subjective construction of plug&play attachments helps to grasp the interplay of mobility and immobility and to understand how new forms of flexible rootedness emerge in the frame of networked urban mobilities.

References

Augé, Marc. 1995. *Non-places: An Introduction to an Anthropology of Supermo-dernity.* London and New York: Verso.

Braidotti, Rosi. 1994. *Nomadic Subjects: Embodiment and Sexual Difference in Contemporary Feminist Theory* (2nd ed.). New York: Columbia University Press.

Duyvendak, Jan Willem. 2011. *The Politics of Home: Belonging and Nostalgia in Western Europe and the United States.* Basingstoke and New York: Palgrave MacMillan.

Lange, Bastian, Joachim Burdack, Robert Nadler, Katja Manz, Juliane Schröder, Kornelia Ehrlich and Christian Rost. 2009. *Leipzig: A Destination for Transnational Migrants in Creative and Knowledge-Intensive Industries? The View of Transnational Migrants.* Amsterdam: AMIDSt, University of Amsterdam. http://acre.socsci.uva.nl/results/documents/wp7.6leipzig_FINAL.pdf. accessed May 29, 2017.

Morley, David and Kevin Robins. 1995. *Spaces of Identity: Global Media, Electronic Landscapes and Cultural Boundaries.* London: Routledge.

Nadler, Robert. 2014. *Plug&Play Places: Lifeworlds of Multilocal Creative Knowledge Workers.* Berlin/Warsaw: De Gruyter Open. www.degruyter.com/viewbook toc/product/447763; accessed May 29, 2017.

Nadler, Robert. 2016. "Plug & Play Places: Subjective Standardization of Places in Multilocal Lifeworlds." In *Understanding Mobilities for Designing Contemporary Cities,* edited by Paola Pucci and Matteo Colleoni, 109–128. Berlin: Springer.

Rapport, Nigel and Andrew Dawson. 1998. *Migrants of Identity: Perceptions of Home in a World of Movement.* Oxford: Berg.

Ritzer, George. 2010. "An Introduction to McDonaldization." In *McDonaldization: The Reader* (3rd ed.), edited by George Ritzer, 3–24. Thousand Oaks: Pine Forge Press.

Rolshoven, Johanna. 2006. "Woanders daheim: Kulturwissenschaftliche Ansätze zur multilokalen Lebensweise in der Spätmoderne." *Zeitschrift für Volkskunde* 102 (2): 179–194.

Stock, Mathis. 2009. "Polytopisches Wohnen—ein phänomenologisch-prozessori-entierter Zugang." *Informationen zur Raumentwicklung* 1/2: 107–116.

Weichhart, Peter. 2015. "Residential Multi-Locality: In Search of Theoretical Frameworks." *Tijdschrift voor economische en sociale geografie* 106 (4): 378–391.

Index

Note: Page numbers in *italics* indicate a figure and page numbers in **bold** indicate a table.

Acuña, Esteban C. 5
aero-automobility 120, 122
aeromobility 119–122, 140
Airbnb 6, 94–97; aesthetics and atmosphere 96–97; digital aesthetic regimes and tourist experience 95; sensory uncanny 94–95; unpacking 'sharing' and illusions of authenticity 95–96
airports 119, 120, 121, 187; O'Hare International 120, 121, 122
air transportation 7, 119
Albertsen, Niels 15
alienation 167, 168n2
alternative: commute 152–153, 155; discourses 7, 150; future cities 92; lifestyles 131; social logics 76; transportation 124; urban mobilities 7, 124, 150, 153; ways of moving 140
Andersen, Hans Christian: *The Little Mermaid* 59, 62
Ascher, François 173
atmospheres 4, 13, 15, 16–17, 22, 43, 65, 75; aesthetics 96–97
Augé, Marc 186
automobility 7, 85, 119, 121, 150; aero- 120, 122

Bauman, Zygmund 33, 36, 112–113
'being away' 48, 49, 50, 84
'being back' 48, 49, 50
'being on one's way' 48, 49
belonging 6, 66, 67, 104, 108, 124, 185; mobile 83–86
Bennetsen, Nina Moesby 7

Bialski, Paula 6
Bissell, David 39
Böhme, Gernot 15
borderlands of urban mobility 73–76
boundaries 5, 49, 50, 51, 55, 59, 171, 174
Brown, Katrina 101
buses, rhythms, and communities 32–36; community on the bus 34–35; connecting the dots within the bus 35–36; fluidity 33; rhythms in the bus 33–34
business travelers 5, 48, 50
bus stop design 5, 27–30, *28*, *30*, 68, 70; armatures in relation to lived moment 28–29; waiting time 29

Carmo, Renato 8
Cidell, Julie 7
Ciolfi, Luigina 107
'code-alongs' 6, 89
Code for Boston 88
Code for Ireland 88
coding 6, 65, 88–93, *90*, 97, 121; 'code-alongs,' coding, and soundscape 89–91; coded spaces to spaces of coding 88–89; spaces of coding 89, 92, 93
Coding Grace 89
Collins, Randall 40, 107, 108
communities and collaborations 5–6
Connell, Raewyn 182
Copenhagen cycling **113**, 113–115, *115–116*, 129–133, 154;

190 *Index*

competencies 131–132; ethnicity 131; materials 130–131; meanings 131; staging from below 129–130
'Copenhagen left' 132, *132*
Cosmobilities Network 2, 61, 63n3, 139, 140
Couchsurfing.org 95
Cox, Peter 6, 139; *Cycling Cultures* 101
creative knowledge workers 8, 185, 186–187
Creswell, Tim 129
cycle BOOM study 141–142
Cycle Super Highways 152–153, 154, *155*
cycling 6–7, 101–104, 153; comparing and learning from each other in the Netherlands and Denmark 135–138; Copenhagen **113**, 113–115, *115–116*, 129–133, 154 (*see also* Copenhagen cycling); 'Cycling Futures' session at Cosmobilities conference 140; do's and don'ts 7, 135; emotions 106–109 (*see also* emotional geographies on cycling infrastructure); findings 103–104, 137–138; future 135–138; methodological concerns 102–103; promotion 150; research methods 101–102; social sciences 136–137; social practice 7, 135; spatial problems 112–117; Stockholm **113**, 113–115, *115–116*; *Understanding Walking and Cycling* (*UWAC*) study 140–141; velomobility 112–117, 139–142
Cycling and Society Research Group 139
Cycling and Society Symposia 139–140

D'Andrea, Anthony 107
Danish Broadcasting Corporation 32
Degen, Monica 129
Denzin, Norman 3, 165
Després, Michel 5–6
digital aesthetic regimes and tourist experience 95
digitalization 5, 19, 129
digital mobility 5, 59–63, 152; *parcours* project and method 59–62
directed waiting 19, 22, *22*; dislocating the wait and diffusion in activities 23; increased time sensibility and new dependencies 23; lack of (creative) interstices 24; reinforcing

the otherness of waiting 22–23; speculations and ambiguities 22–24
disruption 21, 40, 78–81, 97; definitions **79**; meaning and experiences 79–81; methodology 78–79
Doherty, Catherine 8
Doucet, Andrea 103
Doughty, Karolina 6
Duyvendak, Jan Wilhelm: *The Politics of Home* 185, 186
dwelling 2, 129, 187
Dziekan, Katrin 23

Ehn, Billy 40, 77n3
embodied mobilities 17, 81, 163–164
emotional geographies on cycling infrastructure 106–109; everyday practice 107–108; into the trees: emotions, community, and everyday practice 107–108; methodological approach 106–107; seeing both the woods and the trees 108–109
everyday life 5, 6, 8, 19, 24, 32, 33, 35, 36, 38, 39, 41, 73, 74, 76, 79, 81, 83, 84, 86, 91, 112, 113, 125, 152, 153, 154, 163, 174, 186, 187
everyday mobility 78, 80, 81, 86, 173
everyday movement 84, 113, 147
Eyjafjallajökull 119

Fallov, Mia Arp 6, 83
Fernald, Anne 44
Ferreira, Daniela 8
Fischer, Frank 148
Fjalland, Emmy Laura Perez 7–8
fluidity and solidity 6, 86
Freudendal-Pedersen, Malene 39, 168n1
functional health 29, 30
Funk, Oskar 7

Geographical Information System 83
Graham, Stephen 80
Gray, Breda 107

Hans Böckler Foundation 51n1
Hartmann-Petersen, Katrine 5
highly mobile people 8, 84, 170–174, 185, 186; life stories 171; spaces 171–173
Hobro Train Station 13–17, *14*; arrival of train 16–17; DING-DING-DONG 15–16

Index

home-stays 6, 94
Horn, Eva 97
Horton, Dave: *Cycling and Society* 139
hospitality networks 6, 94, 95
hub-and-spoke network 120, 121
humans-as-mobile 4, 64
Hunecke, Marcel 7
hybrid long-distance travel 119–120

ICT (information and communication technologies) 7, 123–127
information and communication technologies *see* ICT
Ingold, Tim 75, 76, 103, 165
Ingress 5, 59, 60, 61, 62
interaction rituals 107, 108
Interdisciplinary Research Group on Suburbs 69

Jensen, Hanne Louise 5
Jensen, Ole B. 4, 39, 40, 129
Jones, Peter 129
Jones, Tim 7
Jørgensen, Anja 6, 83

Kellermann, Robin 4–5
Kjærulff, Aslak Aamot 5
Knies, Karl 97
Knoxville Area Transit 27
Knudsen, Lisbeth B. 83
Koglin, Till 6
Konrad, Kathrin 125
Kottenhoff, Karl 23

Lanng, Ditte Bendix 4
Larsen, Jonas 7, 107, 130
Latham, Alan 129
Laurier, Eric 38
Lenting, Henk 7
Lin, Weiqiang 122
Lissandrello, Enza 7
Little Mermaid, The 5, 59; *see also* OP: *The Little Mermaid*
local belonging 6, 83, 84, 85
Localways 175–176, 177
Löfgren, Orvar 15, 40, 77n3

Magelund, Julie Overgaard 7
magnetism 65, 180; schools 182; towns 182
Manderscheid, Katharina 107, 109
mapping 86; citizen mobility behaviors and practices in times of crisis 175–176

Marcus, George E. 53–54
Massey, Doreen 84, 181
Mauthner, Natasha S. 103
McDonaldization 186
Mead, George Herbert 24
meshwork 5, 76; Ingoldian 75; viscosity 64, 65–67
Miciukiewics, Konrad 147
micro-mobilities 2, 6, 76
Mobile Acquaintances 40, 41
mobile belonging 83–86
Mobile Friends 5, 38, 41
Mobile Others 39, 41
mobile technologies 6, 59, 68–69, 71, 72n2, 123, 126; statistical and cartographic study of users and their lifestyles 69–70
Mobile Withs 40, 41
mobilities design 4, 13–17, 129; Hobro Train Station 13–17
mobilities turn 2, 4, 7, 8, 136–137, 139, 140, 141, 142, 148
Mobility in the Working World 51n1
mobility management 156
mobility patterns 5, 7, 48, 50, 124, 126, 158, 159, 160, 176
Mockus, Antanas 164
modal split 113, *113*, 117n1, 125
modes and emotions 6–7
moorings 20–21, 140
Morgan, Njogu 6
Mourato, João 8
moving and pausing 4–5
Murray, Lesley 6
mutuality 6, 106, 108, 109

Nadler, Robert 8
networked urban mobilities 1–8; practices, flows, methods 2–3; reflecting on experiences with mobilities research practice 3
Networked Urban Mobilities conference 2, 4, 60, 67, 139, 140
new mobilities paradigm 2, 73, 148, 152, 153
Nies, Sarah 5
noise 40, 85

O'Hare International Airport 120, 121, 122
OP: *The Little Mermaid* 61, 69–62
Oxford Brookes University, School of the Built Environment 140

192 *Index*

parcours project and Parkour Method 5, 59–62
'parked students' 6, 69, 70
Parkour Method 5
participant observation 27, 55, 73, 103
pathways 64, 66, 67
Peñalosa, Enrique 164
Perng, Sung-Yueh 6
Petrova, Lilyana 5
physical activity 27, 167
physical mobility 123, 124, 125, 126, 127
'plug&play places' 8, 185, 187–188
plurality 33, 141
policymaking 7, 8, 147–150, 167; Lisbon's metropolitan area 175–178; local and mobility realities 149; mobilities in policymaking and mobilities of policy 148–149
public spaces 68, 70, 97, 102, 112, 115, 116, 173
public transportation 19–20, 21, 22, 23, 27, 45, 89, 115, 124, 125, 126, 127, 131, 138, 176, 177

qualitative methodologies 3, 32, 68, 83, 86, 121, 139, 140, 154, 167
quantitative methodologies 6, 69, 83, 112, 116, 117, 139, 140

Rasmussen, Jon Dag 6
real time information systems (RTIS) 5, 19, 21–24
Research Council UK Energy Programme 78
rhythms 5, 32–36, 83
Ritzer, George 186
Road Radio 43–46; *The Family Tank* 44–45; four themes; four radio shows 44–45; *Motor City, Animal Farm* 45; *Nature, Future and Death* 45; *Not Just 'From A to B'* 45; on-the-road production 44; why it is made 43
Roller, Katrin 5
Romani trans-Atlantic im/mobilities 5, 52–55; im/mobile ethnography 54–55; research process and challenges 53–54
rootedness 8, 185–188; interplay of localization and movement in mobile world 185–186; place relation of multilocal creative knowledge workers 186–187; 'plug&play places' 8, 185, 187–188
Rose, Gillian 129

Rosen, Paul 106; *Cycling and Society* 139
Roskilde University, Urban Bicycle Mobilities project 130
routes and roots 185–188
RTIS *see* real time information systems
rural to urban flows 180–184; coming to mobility 180–181; thinking more generally 181–182

Saldanha, Arun: *Psychedelic White* 65
Santos, Sofia 8
Seeman, Melvin: 'On the Meaning of Alienation' 168n2
Sennett, Richard: *Flesh and Stone* 158, 159
sensory uncanny 94–95
September 11 (2001) 119
shared spaces 158–161; dominant discourses 160–161; governance and regulation 160–161; prioritization of mobilities 160; use 160
Sheller, Mimi 1, 45; *Mobile Technologies of the City* 71; 'The New Mobilities Paradigm' 2, 71, 165
short-term rental websites 6, 94, 95
sites and strategies 7–8
Skinner, Dave: *Cycling and Society* 139
small-scale mobilities 73, 75
social cracks 38, 39, 40, 41
social infrastructures 73, 180
'sociology of mobilities' 148
sound-making 91–92
spaces of coding 89, 92, 93
spatial-temporal structures 48–49, 51
Spinney, Justin 101, 129
Spinoza 63
spoke travelers 120–121
Stanford Institute, Center for Infant Studies 44
'stepchild of mobility' 23, 24
storytelling 8, 163, 164, 166, 167
'strong regime' 7, 129
Super Cycle Highways 7
surfing workers 6, 69, 70–71
sustainability 152–156; alternative commute 152–153; future 154–155; Greater Copenhagen Area 154; theoretical and methodological approach 153–154
Svejstrup, Kaare 5

tales 166–167
third places 6, 68, 69, 70, 71, 72n2
Thrift, Nigel 80, 102

Index   193

train commuting 38–43; findings 39–41; inspiration and fieldwork 38–39
train stations 68, 155, 187; *see also* Hobro Train Station
transformations 5, 19, 59, 60, 61, 62, 149, 167, 173
travels, typing, and tales 163–168; embodied mobilities 163–164; tales 166–167; travels 163–164; typing 164–166; 'Waking Up in Bogotá' 165–166; writing mobilities 164–166
Tschoerner, Chelsea 7, 148
typing 164–166

UK Engineering and Physical Sciences Research Council: *Understanding Walking and Cycling (UWAC)* study 140–141
U.Move 2.0 123–127; digital age and physical mobility 123–124; empirical findings 125–125; ICT and mobility 124; survey approach 124–125
unconventional elderly city people 73–76; flows 74–76; overture 73–74
Understanding Walking and Cycling (UWAC) study 140–141
University of Edinburgh 38
University of Illinois at Urbana-Champaign 120
University of Wisconsin at Madison 120
University of Wisconsin at Oshkosh 120
Urban Bicycle Mobilities project 130
Urry, John 1, 45, 149; 'agenda of mobility' 180; '*gardening and gamekeeping*' 181; *Mobile*

Technologies of the City 71; 'The New Mobilities Paradigm' 2, 71, 165
US Department of Transportation 120

Vannini, Phillip 76, 165
velomobility 112–117, 139–142; combining with mobilities research 139–140; excavations of contemporary experiences with movement and design 140–142
Vendemmia, Bruna 8
Victoria, Anne 5, 29
Vigar, Geoff 147
viscosities: meshwork 5, 8, 64–67; motility 180–184
visualizations 8, 89
Vogl, Gerlinde 5

Wagner, Lauren 5
waiting: directed 19, 22, 23, 24; objects of research 20–21; public transport 4, 13, 15, 16–17, 19–25, 27, 29, 68, 107, 131; real time information systems (RTIS) 5, 19, 21–24; social 40
waiting lists 182, 183
'Waking Up in Bogotá' 165–166
Weichhart, Peter 186
Wind, Simon 4
Wittowsky, Dirk 7, 125
Wood, Peter R. H. 129
working context 48–51; analytical scheme for studying spatial-temporal structures 48–49; commuters and business travelers 49–50
writing mobilities 164–166

Yanow, Dvora 149

Zeitler, Ulli 168n1